Teen Chick Lit

Genreflecting Advisory Series

Diana Tixier Herald, Series Editor

The Real Story: A Guide to Nonfiction Reading Interests
Sarah Statz Cords; Edited by Robert Burgin

Read the High Country: A Guide to Western Books and Films
John Mort

Graphic Novels: A Genre Guide to Comic Books, Manga, and More
Michael Pawuk

Genrefied Classics: A Guide to Reading Interests in Classic Literature
Tina Frolund

Encountering Enchantment: A Guide to Speculative Fiction for Teens
Susan Fichtelberg

Fluent in Fantasy: The Next Generation
Diana Tixier Herald and Bonnie Kunzel

Gay, Lesbian, Bisexual, and Transgendered Literature: A Genre Guide
Ellen Bosman and John Bradford; Edited by Robert B. Ridinger

Reality Rules!: A Guide to Teen Nonfiction Reading Interests
Elizabeth Fraser

Historical Fiction II: A Guide to the Genre
Sarah L. Johnson

Hooked on Horror III
Anthony J. Fonseca and June Michele Pulliam

Caught Up in Crime: A Reader's Guide to Crime Fiction and Nonfiction
Gary Warren Niebuhr

Latino Literature: A Guide to Reading Interests
Edited by Sara E. Martinez

Teen Chick Lit

A Guide to Reading Interests

Christine Meloni

Genreflecting Advisory Series
Diana Tixier Herald, Series Editor

Libraries Unlimited
An Imprint of ABC-CLIO, LLC

A B C 🛆 C L I O

Santa Barbara, California • Denver, Colorado • Oxford, England

Library of Congress Cataloging-in-Publication Data
Meloni, Christine F.
  Teen chick lit : a guide to reading interests / Christine Meloni.
     p. cm. — (Genreflecting advisory series)
  Includes bibliographical references and index.
  ISBN 978-1-59158-756-9 (acid-free paper) 1. Young adult fiction, American—
Bibliography. 2. Young adult fiction, American—Stories, plots, etc. 3. Chick lit—
Bibliography. 4. Teenage girls—Books and reading—United States. I. Title.
Z1232.M45   2010
[PS374.Y57]
011.62—dc22   2009045691

14 13 12 11 10   1 2 3 4 5

This book is also available on the World Wide Web as an eBook.
Visit www.abc-clio.com for details.

ABC-CLIO, LLC
130 Cremona Drive, P.O. Box 1911
Santa Barbara, California 93116-1911

This book is printed on acid-free paper ∞
Manufactured in the United States of America

*For my three boys, Ryan, Nico, and Miles,
and all my girls at John W. Dodd Middle School*

Contents

Introduction

I have a lot to say on the topics of guys, makeup, and shopping. Trust me.
—Tammy Swoish, *Hot Scots, Castles, and Kilts*

For young teen girls, reading has become hot again. With their appealing covers, witty heroines, and humorous plots, teen chick lit books are bringing girls out of the malls and into local libraries and bookstores in search of the next must-have title. Like the Sweet Valley High series that was so popular in the 1980s, the recent chick lit books are especially popular with the middle-school and junior-high set who enjoy reading about the adventures and misadventures of girls in high school, while teenage girls in high school are embracing books about young women starting a glamorous career and juggling the dating scene. Collectively, teen chick lit titles are a very lucrative market and often have the biggest displays in the chain bookstores.

When Helen Fielding's *Bridget Jones* crossed the pond in 1998, chick lit became one of the most popular genres for women in their twenties and thirties, and now the time has come for their younger sisters. Publishers have known for years that many adolescent girls are avid readers. They have now seized the opportunity to flood this previously untapped market with a fresh and exciting genre that teenage girls can spend their babysitting money on. So far the results have been astounding: tween and teen girls are devouring the new books, and the latest release in a series like The Clique or Sisterhood of the Traveling Pants often spends weeks on the *New York Times* best-seller list.

With the push from publication departments, teen chick lit displays have moved from young adult and children's departments to the front of the of big chain bookstores. Teens are plowing through the genre as quickly as publishers can get the books on the shelves, and still they clamor for more. Likewise, the demand for teen chick lit books in the library is strong. At the present time librarians and the teens they are serving are discovering new chick lit titles through professional journals, word of mouth, fashion magazines, and the Internet. Because chick lit is a relatively new genre, there are very few reference books that include chick lit titles, and there are no other readers' advisory guides specific to the genre.

Teen Chick Lit: A Guide to Reading Interests is intended to assist public librarians and school media specialists with collection development and provide ways to promote this popular collection. As teen chick lit continues to attract avid and reluctant readers alike, this guide will aid public and school librarians with readers' advisory and reference questions. For example, librarians can use this guide when asked questions like, "I just read Meg Cabot's *All American Girl.* Can you recommend another title?" and "In the A-list series, which book should I read after *Girls on Film*?"

This guide is intended for school media specialists; public librarians in children's, young adult, and adult departments; graduate students; parents; and—most important —fans of teen chick lit.

Definition

What exactly is teen chick lit? Simply put, the books are upbeat, entertaining, beach-type reads centering on young, female characters. These fun books could be about boys, friendship, family, fitting in, or vacations, but they almost always have some form of self-discovery and an uplifting ending.

What makes the teen chick lit genre so popular is that girls have found a way to escape into a fantasy world in which they see themselves and their friends as the characters. The reader may not be a socialite or work in New York City like the heroine, but she does share the ups and downs of growing up and wanting to fit in. Although these are not the issue-driven types of novels that are considered for the Newbery and Michael L. Printz Awards, they are often traditional coming-of-age stories that girls can readily identify with. Even though the characters' ages vary from middle school to adults in their twenties, they all go through challenging obstacles while still making the reader laugh and, in turn, make the reader want to pick up another book with a fluorescent pink cover.

Teens can tell a chick lit book by the cover: they stand out on the shelf, saying, "Pick me up, read me, and you won't regret it!" The eye-catching cover designs fall into two distinct categories that illustrate what type of chick lit the books are. The original *Princess Diaries* cover, with a sparkling tiara in front of a cotton-candy backdrop, typifies the trend for the funny, traditional chick lit novels. The title appears in a glittery font on a cover that could be the final project from a junior-high art class. Most chick lit covers show whimsical cartoons of pretty girls, clothes, or accessories (think shoes, handbags, lipstick cases) against backdrops in bright colors such as hot pink and turquoise. In fact, the ubiquitous pink covers have led to the coining of the term "pink lit" for teen chick lit titles. If a reader is more interested in reading about the scandalous lives of being a nanny or an heiress, she will gravitate to covers that are more suggestive, with photographs of beautiful models.

Although first romance is regularly a major ingredient of these stories, chick lit varies from traditional romance novels. Only a few titles are about very deep love, and just because a book has romance in it does not make it chick lit; the key is a personal, often self-deprecating humor. Frequently, teen chick lit is about falling for someone, and the reader is allowed to tag along as the new couple has their first, somewhat awkward date and kiss. With the overwhelming majority of chick lit about heterosexual love, lighthearted novels about homosexual dating are few. However, it is important to have a few of the best titles in the stacks for those readers as well.

In the 1980s young girls could be found reading the immensely popular Babysitters Club series by Ann M. Martin and the Sweet Valley High series, created by Francine Pascal. As commercial success for those books and others like them began to fad away by the turn of the century, a door was left open for something new. What came next would be the beginning of a new genre for teen girls, inspired by the success of the television series *Sex and the City*, Regency romance novels, as well as romantic comedies written for exclusively for women in their twenties and thirties.

The history of teen chick lit is not difficult to trace. It all began in 2000 with the hilarious British teen Georgia Nicholson in *The Confessions of Georgia Nicholson* by Louise Rennison. Like those of her adult contemporary, Bridget Jones, Georgia's diary entries are full of laugh-out-loud episodes about obsessing over her looks (specifically her nose) and over boys (specifically the hunky rocker Robbie). Here is a sample entry: "7:00 p.m. In my room in front of the mirror. Practicing smiling without making my nose spread. It's impossible. I must never smile again." The series has been translated into several languages, and each book includes Georgia's Glossary so that her American and other friends can learn exactly what British slang words like "stroppy" and "lurker" mean. Among the plethora of books about witty teens, Rennison's diarist is by far the funniest.

Proving that not all teen chick lit is strictly fluff, the following fall a pair of magic pants pushed the trend into the mainstream. In <u>The Sisterhood of the Traveling Pants</u> series, author Ann Brashares created characters who deal successfully with complex issues like sex, cancer, and death, without weighing the novels down. In the sisterhood, four teenage friends discover that a pair of old jeans is magical because, despite their different body shapes, the jeans look fantastic on all four of them. Understanding how special the pants are, the girls vow to follow rules about the pants, including passing them on to each other during the summer and never washing them. In the sequels, the foursome grows a little closer to finding out who they really are.

In 2002 *Gossip Girl* author Cecily von Ziegesar introduced readers to a new type of teen chick lit that later became known as "gossip lit." Although gossip lit books may have similar themes to traditional chick lit (such as dating, family, and growing up), they are exclusively about wealthy, beautiful girls who live in exciting places, wear trendy clothes, and date hot guys.

After the success of these three series, new chick lit titles were quickly published at the beginning of the twenty-first century. Now, more than five years later, teen chick lit encompasses almost all genres, including fantasies and mysteries. Today teen chick lit heroines come in all shapes and sizes. The heroine may be a teen witch who needs a date to the prom, a varsity cheerleader who also is an undercover government operative trained in hand-to-hand combat, or one of three pretty British East Indian sisters who decide to marry off their meddling aunt. Now even inspirational teen chick lit titles are being published that would be a nice addition for Christian school libraries.

For high-school students, these chick lit novels are a diversion from their hectic lifestyles and the pressure to do well in school and get into a good college. For tweens, chick lit is a way of looking forward to when they too will have hectic lifestyles, boyfriends, and pressure to get into college.

Scope and Purpose

The purpose of this easy-to-use readers' advisory guide is to identify, organize, and describe current chick lit that appeals to tweens and teen readers. As more teen chick lit floods the already saturated market, the once common themes of dating and humor are crossing over to other genres like mystery and paranormal romance. Since readers who enjoy the subgenre of traditional romantic comedies may not like reading about the secret lives of young starlets, this guide categorizes and describes more than 500 titles in the following subgenres to help readers find the books they want to read.

- **Traditional Chick Lit**—The most common form of chick lit, including romantic comedies, dating dilemmas, first love, break-ups and hook-ups, friendship, and celebrations such as proms and sweet-sixteen parties. Christian chick lit is also located in this chapter.

- **Gossip Lit**—The novels that reveal the secrets of beautiful people, whether they're models, socialites, heiresses, superstars, boarding school students, magazine editors, or the people who work for them.

- **International Relations**—Those novels that focus on young girls who live outside the United States. Also included are stories about world travelers whose vacations lead to romance and self-discovery.

- **Magical Maidens**—Books with a spotlight on lighthearted tales that involve paranormal romance, spells, magical objects, bewitching cheerleaders, witches, vampires, and the undead.

- **Mystery Solvers**—Books about ordinary young women who divide their time between schoolwork and solving mysteries, as well as those who are undercover secret agents and international spies.

- **Lad Lit**—Funny books about dating and fitting in, written from the male point of view. These lighthearted books will be of interest to female readers who want to know what boys think about dating and kissing. Many of the novels in this section have the same breezy comical style of the novels found in the traditional teen chick lit chapter.

- **Lesbian and Gay Relationships**—Fun books about self-discovery, dating, and sexual identity. This chapter will appeal to homosexual readers looking for light novels that they can identity with as well as heterosexual readers looking for something different.

Even though the number of new teen chick lit titles with Hispanic American, Asian American, and African American characters being published each season increases, the majority of novels are primarily about Caucasian girls. If literature should be a mirror as well as a window, then girls from every background and nationality should be able to read escapist novels that they can imagine themselves in. In this guide, books are given a multicultural subject tag to help librarians servicing a diverse population.

Selection Criteria

The selected titles included are primarily teen chick lit books published in the English language from 2002 to 2009; however, a few earlier titles still in print are included. The titles were selected from a variety of sources, including professional journals, *Books in Print*, Library of Congress, Nassau County Library System's Online Catalog, *New York Times Book Review*, Children's Literature Comprehensive Database, online booksellers and libraries, catalogs, browsing retail chains such as Borders and Barnes and Noble, and the requests by my students at John W. Dodd Middle School in Freeport, New York.

Titles were selected based on the content, recommended age, and overall quality. Books must have been written specifically for tweens and teens in middle, junior, or high school. Some adult books that are appropriate for high school juniors and seniors have also been included.

Organization and Features

The annotations are arranged alphabetically by author name and book title for stand-alone titles. Series books and sequels are arranged first alphabetically by the author, then the books in the series are listed in chronological order. This includes prequels that may be published after the original series is complete. The purpose is to allow readers to enjoy the events in the order they occurred, not as they were originally published. For series that have no definite titles, a working title has been used for convenience and is enclosed in brackets, for example, [The Girl's Guide to Witchcraft].

Each entry in the bibliography includes the author name, book title, publisher, publication date, and ISBN. When more than one edition was available, the ISBN and publication information represent the hardcover edition. If only the paperback edition is in print, the ISBN listed represents the paperback edition. Each book or series has a suggested grade range, obtained from catalogs, book jackets, publisher suggestions, and the author's assessment. Age recommendations have also been determined with the guidance of reviews in professional journals such as *School Library Journal*, *Voice of Youth Advocates*, *Booklist*, *Library Media Center*, *Publishers Weekly*, and *Horn Book*.

The grade levels used in this guide are indicated using the following boldface letters at the end of the bibliographic information:

M middle school, grades 6–8

J junior high school, grades 7–9

S senior high school, grades 9–12

A adult books for grades 11 and up

Beginning with an introduction, each succeeding chapter starts with a brief synopsis about the subgenre, then includes a selection of titles found in that section, followed by an annotated bibliography subdivided into thematic sections. A few subject terms (called keywords) are identified for each title. Books that include sexual acts have a *sexual content* subject term, whereas books in which the main character is thinking about sexual acts or starting a sexual relationship have the subject keyword *sexuality*.

Book Awards and Booklists

Several chick lit novels have been recognized by the Young Adult Library Service Association (YALSA), an arm of the American Library Association that advocates and promotes service to young adults. Books that have received awards have a 🏆 symbol at the beginning of the entry; the specific award and the year the title was on the list appear at the end of the annotation, following the keywords. These are the awards included:

BBYA   **Best Books for Young Adult:** An annual list of the significant adult and young adult books.

Printz   **Michael L. Printz Award:** Since 2000 YALSA has presented an annual award to one winner and up to four honor books for the best young adult book published from the previous year.

Quick Picks   **Quick Picks for Reluctant Readers:** A annual list that identities titles for recreational reading that will appeal to young adults who are reluctant readers.

Controversies

Although chick lit has had vocal supporters from the beginning, the instant success of the genre has not come without some backlash from critics, librarians, parents, and educators. *New York Times* columnist Maureen Dowd, in her 2007 op-ed piece "Heels Over Hemingway," complained that chick lit has taken over the bookstores, and after reading a few titles, she declared, "They're all chick and no lit." Of course, some educators and librarians would prefer for young women to focus on reading more serious-minded novels as well as the classics—and let's be honest, there are some really bad chick lit books with stereotypical characters and weak plots. However, there are also real gems out there that include insightful observations on the human psyche while entertaining the reader. Longtime chick lit editor Farrin Jacobs wrote in her 2005 *Publishers Weekly* article, "Go, Girls: Chick Lit Can Be Lit": "Commercial women's fiction has always gotten a bad rap from those on the literary-minded side of publishing." Although at times it feels that chick lit has gotten a bad rap, there still are many out there who staunchly believe in the importance of escapist literature in this post-9/11 world, in which there is so much uncertainty about the future.

Gossip Girl, A-List, and The Clique, as well as their spin-offs, are by far the best-selling teen chick lit series. They are also the front-runners for criticism. In fact, the Gossip Girl series ranked number 30 on the American Library Association's top 100 banned/challenged books for 2000–2007. In 2006 author Naomi Wolf pointed out in a two-page *New York Times* spread that these novels are filled with self-centered, materialistic girls who have no positive paternal influence and are obsessed with status and casual sex. Wolf further commented that the novels, filled with brand-name products, reflect a greater concern about the current consumer culture: "Seventh grade girls have Palm Pilots, red Coach clutches, Visas and cellphones in Prada messenger bags. Success and failure are entirely signaled by material possessions—specifically, by brands" (Wolf 2006).

Although some consider chick lit fluff, librarians cannot deny that it is one of the fastest growing genres of the twenty-first century. As evidence of the permanence of the genre, in 2002 the Library of Congress began to classify titles as chick lit in the subject-heading field.

Promoting Your Collection

Once a library has a great collection of teen chick lit titles, the first step to make sure the students or public library patrons know about them is to create a few attractive pamphlets (probably in pink) for the library. Don't forget to post the lists on the library Web site and let teens make further recommendations. The last chapter in this guide is a compilation of annotated bibliographies intended for this purpose.

The next step is to think about designing a display. Bookstores have had tremendous success displaying teen chick lit titles, visible as soon as the customer walks into the department. The key is showing the covers of as many books as possible. The cover is what attracts young readers—so let them see it! If space is not an issue in your library, consider shelving the collection in a few endcaps, or set aside a few shelves at the end of the fiction collection, just as libraries already do for mysteries. One public library I visited designated a paperback spinning rack for teen chick lit series books in the young adult department and devoted four endcaps in its adult fiction department to chick lit books. In my middle-school library, I have a three-foot bulletin board display with pictures of popular characters taken from various catalogs. Under the bulletin board are rotating titles and teen chick lit books like the <u>Princess Diaries</u>, <u>Students Across the Seven Seas</u>, and <u>The Clique</u> series housed together to make sure readers find browsing effortless. This display is great for my avid readers to see which books are new or just returned. It also helps students who are unsure what they should select. If there is not enough room in your facility for a permanent space, periodically create displays and watch your circulation figures go up.

Consider hosting a girls-only book discussion group once a month, or just occasionally select a teen chick lit title for your next book club meeting. Devoted readers of the genre already enjoy discussing the novels in an informal setting, and a book club provides an opportunity for like-minded people to meet and share books that they really connect with and are inspired by. Before the book club meeting concludes, leave time for members to share recent books they enjoyed reading. Included in the appendix is a list of serious teen chick lit books with depth that would be perfect for a book discussion group.

Booktalks are another excellent way to advertise your chick lit collection. Booktalks may be short, promotional presentations conducted formally in the school media center or informally in the public library. Tech-savvy librarians are also creating podcasts on their Web sites as a new way to promote books. If time allows, ideally the booktalker would select at least one teen chick lit title from each chapter in this guide, so all interests would be reflected. Also, keep in mind that you will have both avid and reluctant readers in the class (audience), so select humorous, short titles along with longer ones.

Remember that it is always easier for librarians to influence younger teens. Around tenth grade, older teens are starting to drift away from young adult literature to reading solely adult books. To ensure that you hang on to chick lit readers as they get older, purchase adult books about glamorous young women who are looking for the dream guy to go along with their dream job in a metropolitan city.

One way to find out what your students or patrons are interested in reading is by starting a teen advisory board. Traditionally, the members of the board look through catalogs, read reviews, and provide monthly feedback on titles they want to see in the library. The members may also write their reviews for the library Web site or newsletter. A perk to being a member of the advisory board is that teens can really shape the library collection and have the first crack at the new books!

References

Dowd, Maureen. 2007. "Heels Over Hemingway." *New York Times*, February 10.

Jacobs, Farrin. 2005. "Go Girls: Chick Lit Can Also Be Lit." *Publishers Weekly*, June 16.

Padgett, Tania. 2006. "Page Burners: Sex and the Teenage Girl." *Newsday*, April 4.

Winerip, Michael. 2008. "In Novels, for Girls, Fashion Trumps Romance." *New York Times*, July, 13.

Wolf, Naomi. 2006. "Wild Things." *New York Times*, March 12.

Chapter 1

Traditional Chick Lit

Can I explain the weirdness that is my life right now?
—Catherine Clark, *Rocky Road Trip*

Like their adult contemporaries, traditional chick lit novels for teens come in a variety of styles and forms. Some are light and breezy romantic comedies, while others are deep and meaningful stories of friendship and loss. The issues written about in teen magazines, such as self-esteem, friendship, dating, clothes, school, and embarrassing moments, are often the themes found in novels written for today's tween and teen readers. Whatever the theme, traditional chick lit is lighthearted stories written for and about young women that have a personal, confidential tone.

In general, traditional teen chick lit novels are upbeat, humorous stories that feature girls whom teens can relate to—girls who attend public schools, like to shop at the mall, and have a small group of close friends. Frequently, the friendly main character is a junior high or high school student who is flawed but attractive; she may be the tallest girl, flat chested (or too curvy), but somehow manages to attract the right boy. Like the readers, the characters may struggle to fit in at school and are embarrassed by their families.

Through catchy writings, the chatty heroine shares her most embarrassing moments and deepest thoughts in her diary, journal, or blog. In some of these novels, the typical girl next door is thrust into the spotlight; for example, Jamie becomes a famous author virtually overnight when her journal is accidentally submitted to her English teacher, in *How My Private, Personal Journal Became a Bestseller* by Julia DeVillers.

These amusing, lighthearted books commonly tell the story of first romance, including all the awkward details. At times the reader knows before the heroine whom she should be with. It is the reader who is rooting for the girl to realize that the boy of her dreams is right under her nose. Like football fans shouting at the TV screen, readers are shouting, "No, you don't love Jack! Ryan is the guy for you! Kiss him! Kiss him!" Other teen chick lit novels follow the framework established by author Judy Blume and are about first sexual experiences, with a more mature tone. Unlike the heroine who experiences her first kiss, these young couples share a deep first love in which they commit to each other not only emotionally, but sexually as well.

Chick lit author Meg Cabot has written many successful books, including *All-American Girl*, *Teen Idol*, *Size 12 Is Not Fat*, and *Queen of Babble*. However, her main claim to fame is how she tapped into the secret desire most girls have to be a princess. At the beginning of *The Princess Diaries*, Mia Thermopolis is a typical teenager living in New York City with her artist mother. She is a vegetarian who wears combat boots and is failing algebra. When Mia's mom starts dating her math teacher, she thinks nothing could get worse. But when Mia discovers that she is the heir to the throne of Genovia and her full name is Princess Amelia Mignonette Grimaldi Thermopolis Renaldo, her life turns upside down. Mia has to go everywhere with a bodyguard and take princess lessons with her strict grandmother. With fourteen sequels, teens can't get enough of this reluctant princess in training. Meg Cabot's characters live the life that teenage girls daydream about, whether taking a movie star to the spring formal or discovering they are royalty. But her success lies in the fact that her heroines are so normal, readers can relate to them.

Many girls look forward to that special night when they can dress up and dance the night away. So it is no wonder that sweet-sixteen parties, high school junior and senior proms, and *quinceañeras* are the subject of several teen chick lit books. The preparations leading up to the big night can be stressful and inevitably involve hilarity and mix-ups, but always produce a magical outcome. In the romantic comedy *Prom Crashers* by Erin Downing, Emily sneaks into all the neighboring high school proms with her best friends to find her dream guy.

These coming-of-age parties can also lead to important life lessons. Like the teens showcased on MTV's *My Super Sweet Sixteen*, Kate Brian's Teagan is a self-centered, vain young lady who expects her dad to host the most fabulous party; after a freak accident, she learns the consequences of living in a materialistic world. In *Cuba 15* by Nancy Osa, Violet Paz feels she knows little about her family's Cuban history, so she is initially reluctant to agree to her grandmother's suggestion for her to have a *quinceañera*, the Hispanic celebration of a girl's fifteenth birthday. Yet while planning the traditional party, Violet learns more about her Cuban culture and herself.

Since accepting one's role in a family is a big part of being a teenager, in many traditional chick lit novels dating and romance take a backseat, and the focus is on family and sisterhood. In *Cubanita* by Gaby Triana, Isabel Diaz's number one requirement for selecting a college is that it be far away from Miami, Florida, and her Cuban American family. After her high school graduation, Isabel thinks she will just coast through the next two months and then be free of her crazy family. However, when her mom is diagnosed with breast cancer, Isabel quickly learns just how important her family really is. On the other hand, Murphy, Leeda, and Birdie from Jodi Lynn Anderson's <u>Peaches</u> trilogy discover that sometimes your friends are more your real family than your blood relatives.

Traditional chick lit novels feature clumsy and sweet girls who possess the qualities you would want in a best friend, such as compassion and honesty. For readers, the characters become like close friends, and teens can often be found in the library gossiping about what happened in each book.

Chapter Organization

This chapter organizes selected titles that fall within the traditional teen chick lit subgenre. Many of the books are about crushes, dating, and friendship, including the titles located in the self-acceptance and family ties sections.

Self-Acceptance/Self-Discovery

These are coming-of-age stories about a teenage girl who realizes what kind of person she wants to become. After making some mistakes, the heroine learns the valuable life lesson that although she may not be perfect, it is best not to deny who she is. Over time the protagonist gains confidence, moves closer to what she wants to become, and may even discover what she is really good at.

Alegria, Malin.

Sofi Mendoza's Guide to Getting Lost in Mexico. Simon & Schuster Books for Young Readers, 2007. ISBN 9780689878114. **S**

During the Memorial Day weekend, seventeen-year-old Sofie Mendoza sneaks across the border with her friends to attend a house party in Mexico. After the wild party Sofie is denied reentry into California because her documents are false, and she is temporarily forced to live with her Aunt Luisa in Tijuana, while her immigrant parents try to find a legal way to bring Sofie back.

Keywords: crushes; family; Hispanic American

Banks, Piper.

Geek High. NAL Jam, 2007. ISBN 9780451222251. **J S**

After fifteen-year-old math genius Miranda Bloom is forced to plan the Notting Hill Independent School for the Gifted's Snowflake Gala, she has to find a date because her stepsister is going with her crush.

Keywords: crushes; dances; school; self-acceptance; sisters

Geek Abroad. NAL Jam Books, 2008. ISBN 9780451223937. **J S**

After Miranda says good-bye to her new boyfriend Dex and goes to visit her mother in London, she guiltily spends time with a cute British boy. Upon her return Miranda discovers her friends are fighting, and her family forgets her sixteenth birthday.

Keywords: dating; family; friendship; school

Barnholdt, Lauren.

The Secret Identity of Devon Delaney. Aladdin Mix, 2007. ISBN 978-1416935032. **M J**

On her summer vacation at her grandmother's house, seventh-grader Devon Delaney told her new friend, Lexi Cortland, that she was super popular and was dating Jared Bentley, the hottest boy in school. When Lexi unexpectedly relocates to Devon's school, Devon attempts to keep her lies a secret by hanging out with the popular crowd.

Keywords: crushes; dating; friendship

Boggess, Eileen.

[Mia]. M J

The following titles, although not formally a series, deal with the same protagonist, and are listed in chronological order.

Mia the Meek. Bancroft Press, 2006. ISBN 9781890862466.

At the start of her freshman year at Saint Hilary's Catholic High School, Mia Fullerton is determined to shed her former geeky image by being more outgoing. When Mia wins the election for class president, her crush, Jakes, asks her out.

Keywords: dating; family; friendship; humor; school

Mia the Melodramatic. Bancroft Press, 2008. ISBN 9781890862565.

During the summer before her sophomore year of high school, Mia's plans to work on the crew at Little Tyke's Theatre lead her to discover that she prefers to be on the stage, not behind it.

Keywords: acting; break-ups; dating; friendship; humor; school

Cabot, Meg.

The Princess Diaries. J S

Avid diary writer Mia Thermopolis is a geeky, vegetarian, high school freshman living in New York City with her artist mother when she finds out that her father is really the Prince of Genovia, a small principality near the south of France. As the heir to the throne, Mia has to take princess lessons with her grandmother while still being a typical high school student with friends, a serious crush, and ineptitude in math.

Keywords: diary; family; friendship; humor

🎗 *Princess Diaries Volume I.* HarperCollins, 2000. ISBN 9780060292102.

After learning she is really a princess, Mia has to go everywhere with a bodyguard and take princess lessons with her strict grandmother.

Keywords: crushes; movie tie-in; school
Awards: BBYA 2001

🎗 *Princess in the Spotlight, Volume II.* HarperCollins, p2001, c2001. ISBN 9780060294656.

During her first national interview, Mia admits that she is not popular and that her mom is pregnant with her algebra teacher's baby while hopeful that her secret admirer is her best friend brother Michael.

Keywords: crushes; school
Awards: Quick Picks 2003

🎗 *Princess in Love, Volume III.* HarperCollins, 2002. ISBN 9780060294670.

Now that Mia is dating her biology partner, Kenny, she tries to find a nice way to break up with him and confess her feelings for Lilly's brother Michael.

Keywords: dating; school

Awards: Quick Picks 2003

Princess in Waiting, Volume IV. HarperCollins, 2003. ISBN 9780060096076.

Mia has to spend the first month as Michael Moscovitz's girlfriend in Genovia, attending parliament sessions and formal dinners with dignitaries. When Mia finally returns to New York, she looks forward to her first official date with Michael and tries to figure out what her special talent is.

Keywords: dating

Project Princess, Volume IV and a Half. HarperTrophy, 2003. ISBN 978-0060571313.

Mia and her best friends from Gifted and Talented decide to spend spring break building a home for Housing for the Hopeful in West Virginia. Mia soon realizes that she will spend more time holding up plywood and sleeping on the floor than kissing Michael.

Keywords: dating

Princess in Pink, Volume V. HarperTeen, p2008, c2004. ISBN 9780061543630.

Mia laments that her one true love, Michael, thinks going to the prom is lame. With a little help from her Grandmére, Mia comes up with a plan to have Michael's band, Skinner Box, play at the prom. In addition to dressing up and slow dancing, it is truly a night to remember, because Mia's half-brother Rocky is born.

Keywords: dating; prom

Princess in Training, Volume VI. HarperCollins, p2005. ISBN 9780060096144.

Mia doesn't know which is worse, running for student counsel president against her archnemesis Lana Weinberger, or having the important sex talk with her boyfriend, Michael.

Keywords: dating; school

The Princess Present, Volume VI and a Half. HarperCollins, p2004. ISBN 9780060754334.

This year Michael and Lilly are joining Mia in Genovia for Christmas, and Mia still cannot think of the perfect present for Michael.

Keywords: dating

Party Princess, Volume VII. HarperCollins, 2006. ISBN 9780060724542.

As class president, Mia has to raise $5,000 dollars for graduation after she spent all the funds on recycling containers. As if that weren't bad enough, Michael is going to have a party with all his college friends. Nervous that Michael will learn she is not a party girl, Mia overcompensates at his party by doing a sexy dance, but she redeems herself as the lead in her grandmother's original musical.

Keywords: acting; dating; school

Sweet Sixteen Princess, Volume VII and a ½. HarperTeen, 2006. ISBN 9780060847166.

> After her disastrous birthday party last year, Mia's worst fears almost come true when she thinks that her Grandmére has arranged for MTV to film a special, *My Super ROYAL Sweet Sixteen*, in Genovia. After squashing the MTV plans, Mia is amazed to find that her family and friends have organized a magical surprise party at the rink in Rockefeller Center.

Keywords: dating

Valentine Princess, Volume VII and ¾ths. HarperCollins, 2006. ISBN 9780060847180.

> Sixteen-year-old Mia reads in her old diary how she was not sure how to celebrate Valentine's Day with her new boyfriend Michael because, like his sister Lilly, Michael does not believe in the holiday.

Keywords: dating

Princess on the Brink, Volume VIII. HarperCollins, 2007. ISBN 9780060724566.

> At the start of her junior year, Mia is already feeling pressure from her classes and the student council election, when Michael announces that is moving to Japan for a year. Mia considers losing her virginity as a way to keep Michael in New York.

Keywords: break-ups; dating; school; sexuality

Princess Mia, Volume IX. HarperTeen, 2008. ISBN 9780060724610.

> Heartbroken over her break-up with Michael and devastated by Lilly's "I hate Mia Thermopolis Web site," Mia is forced to see a therapist, who encourages Mia to do something scary, even if that includes going out with J. P., befriending Lana Weinberger, and sharing the secret documents of a seventeenth-century Genovian princess at a large gala.

Keywords: break-ups; dating; school

Forever Princess, Volume X. HarperTeen, 2009. ISBN 9780061232923.

> In the finale of The Princess Diaries series, Mia slowly confesses all her secrets as her elaborate eighteenth birthday party and her high school graduation approach, including that she got into every college she applied to, wrote a romance novel that is going to be published, and is still a virgin; the biggest secret she reveals is that she is still in love with Michael Moscovitz.

Keywords: break-ups; dating; school

Clark, Catherine.

Wish You Were Here. **HarperTeen, 2008. ISBN 9780060559830.** **J** **S**

> During a two-week bus tour to America's Heartland with her newly separated mom's family, sixteen-year-old Ariel writes postcards to her kind of boyfriend Dylan, flirts with a cute boy, runs with her grandfather, and is able to deal with her gambling father.

Keywords: divorce; family; road trip; travel

Cohn, Rachel.

[Cyd Charisse]. S

Chronicles Cyd Charisse, an uncontainable sixteen-year-old, as she gets kicked out of school, falls deeply in love, and becomes an independent, eighteen-year-old woman living in New York City.

🎗 *Gingerbread.* Simon & Schuster Books for Young Readers, 2002. ISBN 9780689843372.

Sixteen-year-old Cyd Charisse returns to her San Francisco home still clutching her childhood rag doll, Gingerbread, after secretly having an abortion and being expelled from her exclusive boarding school. When Cyd continues to hang out with her new surfer boyfriend, Shrimp, and breaks her curfew, her mom and stepdad send Cyd to live with her estranged biological father in New York City for the summer.

Keywords: abortion; break-ups; dating; family

Awards: BBYA 2003; Quick Picks 2003

Shrimp. Simon & Schuster Books for Young Readers, 2005. ISBN 978-0689866128.

After spending the summer in Manhattan with her dad's family, a more mature but still feisty Cyd returns home to San Francisco to finish her senior year of high school, reunite with her ex-boyfriend Shrimp, make her first female friends, and rebuild her relationship with her mom and stepdad.

Keywords: family; friendship; school

Cupcake. Simon & Schuster Books for Young Readers, 2007. ISBN 978-1416912170.

After graduating from high school and turning down Shrimp's marriage proposal, eighteen-year-old Cyd Charisse moves back to New York City to live with her gay stepbrother Danny, planning to attend culinary school. But she ends up breaking her leg and longing for Shrimp. When Cyd starts to get her new life in order, Shrimp shows up and wants to get back together.

Keywords: dating; family; gay; sexual content

Cook, Eileen.

What Would Emma Do? Simon Pulse, 2009. ISBN 9781416974321.

In the small religious town of Wheaton, Indiana, Emma Proctor's senior year at a Christian high school is one of questions and change as she hopes to win a full track scholarship to Northwestern University, kisses her best friend's boyfriend, and must decide to share a secret she witnessed.

Keywords: friendship; kissing; religion

Czech, Jan M.

Grace Happens. **Speak, 2007, c2005. ISBN 9780142407523.** **J**

> As the daughter of a famous actress, fifteen-year-old Grace Meredith wants two things: to live a normal life and to discover who her father is. During a summer spent on Martha's Vineyard, Grace's wishes come true.
>
> **Keywords:** family

Day, Karen.

No Cream Puffs. **Wendy Lamb Books, 2008. ISBN 9780375937750.** **M** **J**

> In the summer of 1980 twelve-year-old Madison joins her Michigan town's boy's baseball league. As the first girl to play on the league, Madison faces some obstacles while she pitches her team to the championships and develops a crush on a teammate.
>
> **Keywords:** crushes; family; friendship; sports

de la Cruz, Melissa.

Fresh Off the Boat. **HarperTrophy, p2006, c2005. ISBN 9780060545420.** **J** **S**

> After immigrating to San Francisco from the Philippines, Vicenza is trying to fit in at her exclusive all-girls' school, where she is on a scholarship. When Vicenza e-mails her friends back home, she lies about how horrible her new life is. Only when she stops denying her new life do her new peers accept her.
>
> **Keywords:** crushes; family; friendship; Hispanic American; moving; school

Echols, Jennifer.

Major Crush. **Simon Pulse, 2006. ISBN 9781416918301.** **J** **S**

> Sixteen-year-old Virginia Sauter is excited and proud to be her high school band's first-ever female drum major, until she realizes that she has to share the title with her secret crush, Drew.
>
> **Keywords:** marching bands; romantic comedy

Harper, Charise Mericle.

Flashcards of My Life. **Little, Brown, 2006. ISBN 9780316756211.** **M** **J**

> For five weeks junior high school student Emily uses the "Flashcards of My Life" set that she received as a surprise birthday present from her Aunt Chester as a way to describe her relationships with her family and friends and work through her problems.
>
> **Keywords:** crushes; family; first kiss; friendship; school

Hughes, Mark Peter.

I Am the Wallpaper. **Delacorte Press, 2005. ISBN 9780385902656.** **M** **J**

> Now that her beautiful sister is married, thirteen-year-old Floey Packer keeps her vow to break out of her shell and get a boyfriend during her summer vacation, even when her annoying younger cousins post her diary and an embarrassing photo on the Internet.
>
> **Keywords:** body image; diary; family; friendship

Kantor, Melissa.

Confessions of a Not It Girl. Hyperion, 2004. ISBN 9780786818372. **J** **S**
Instead of finishing her college applications, high school senior Jan Miller fantasizes about her newest crush, Josh; wishes she were more like her stylish best friend, Rebecca Larkin; and avoids her former crush, Tom.

Keywords: college applications; crushes; friendship; kissing

Lamba, Marie.

What I Meant . . . Random House, 2007. ISBN 9780375840913. **M** **J**
Before her spying aunt from India moved in, fifteen-year-old Sangeet Jumnal's only concern was convincing her strict Sikh dad that she should date. In addition to making up with her best friend, Gina, Sangeet now has to try to get her parents to trust her again after she is caught sneaking out to date her crush, Josh.

Keywords: crushes; dating; East Indian American; family; friendship; religion

Littman, Sarah Darer.

Confessions of a Closet Catholic. Dutton, 2005. ISBN 9780525473657. **M** **J**
After her family laughs at her idea to go kosher like their grandmother, eleven-year-old Justine Silver continues to explore her spirituality and decides to become a Catholic like her best friend, Mary Catherine McAllister.

Keywords: family; friendship; religion

Lockhart, E.

[Ruby Oliver]. **J** **S**
The following titles, although not formally a series, deal with the same protagonist and are listed in chronological order.

The Boyfriend List: (15 Guys, 11 Shrink Appointments, 4 Ceramic Frogs and Me, Ruby Oliver). Delacorte Press, 2005. ISBN 9780385732062.
Fifteen-year-old Ruby Oliver starts having panic attacks after her boyfriend, Jackson Clarke, begins dating her best friend, Kim Yamamoto. For her mental health, Dr. Z., Ruby's new shrink, asks Ruby to write a list of every boy that she ever liked, kissed, or dated.

Keywords: break-ups; dating; friendship; humor

🌸 *The Boy Book: (A Study of Habits and Behaviors, Plus Techniques for Taming Them).* Delacorte Press, 2006. ISBN 9780385732086.
Now a junior at Tate Prep, Ruby Oliver laments the loss of her former friends and ex-boyfriend, Jackson, as she re-reads their boy book. Her only salvation comes from her internship at the zoo and her new friend, Noel DuBoise.

Keywords: friendship; humor; internships

Awards: Quick Picks 2006

The Treasure Map of Boys: Noel, Jackson, Finn, Hutch, Gideon—and Me, Ruby Oliver. Delacorte BFYR, 2009. ISBN 9780385734264.

> Still suffering from occasional panic attacks, sixteen-year-old Ruby continues her therapy as a way to cope with her new crush, friends, running the school bake sale, and her mother.
>
> **Keywords:** crushes; family; humor; school

Mackler, Carolyn.

[Mara and V]. J S

> The following titles, although not formally a series, deal with the same characters and are listed in chronological order.

> 🏆 *Vegan Virgin Valentine.* Candlewick Press, 2006. ISBN 9780763621551.
>
> > Mara has been working nonstop to beat her ex-boyfriend for the position of class valediction, and with all her advanced placement classes, she barely has time to socialize. Unexpectedly Mara falls madly in love with Dan and decides to decline a summer program at Johns Hopkins so she can spend more time with him.
> >
> > **Keywords:** dating; family; love; graduation; school
> >
> > **Awards:** Quick Picks 2005

> 🏆 *Guyaholic.* Candlewick Press, 2007. ISBN 9780763625375.
>
> > After being let down by her mom again, V discovers a lot about herself during her drive from New York to California after graduating from high school, including how to let herself love. (Mara from *Vegan Virgin Valentine* is V's aunt.)
> >
> > **Keywords:** dating; family; sexual content
> >
> > **Awards:** Quick Picks 2008

McKayhan, Monica.

Indigo. S

> In Atlanta, Indigo Summer and her best friend Jade are feeling the pressures and joys of high school. Popular Indigo discovers she is in love with her next door neighbor Marcus, is on the school dance squad, and is close with her family, while her best friend Jade struggles to accept her parents' divorce.
>
> **Keywords:** African American; dating

> 🏆 *Indigo Summer.* Kimani Tru, 2007. ISBN 9780373830756.
>
> > After her best friend moves away, Marcus Carter moves next door to fifteen-year-old Indigo Summer and immediately falls for her. Unfortunately for Marcus, Indigo makes the dance squad and starts dating Quincy Rawlins, an older football player.
> >
> > **Keywords:** dating; family; friendship; school
> > **Awards:** Quick Picks 2008

Trouble Follows. Kimani Tru, 2007. ISBN 9780373830879.

> After making trouble in New Jersey, Indigo's best friend Jade moves back to Atlanta with a plan of getting her parents back together. She ends up being sexually abused by her teacher. Meanwhile Indigo is throwing up after meals to stay thin for the dance squad, and her perfect boyfriend, Marcus, is arrested for a crime he did not commit.

> **Keywords:** body image; divorce; family; friendship; moving; school

The Pact. Kimani Tru, 2008. ISBN 9780373830930.

> Indigo convinces her boyfriend Marcus that they should make a pact to temporarily break up for the summer because he will be in Texas with his mom and she will be in Chicago visiting her family. Despite her Nana's warnings, Indigo spends time with her independent seventeen-year-old cousin, then call Marcus when she is in serious trouble.

> **Keywords:** break-ups; family; pregnancy; sexual content

Jaded. Kimani Tru, 2008. ISBN 9780373830992.

> As Jade's relationship with Terrence becomes more serious, Terrence hides the fact that he is supporting his younger brother and sister while his drug-addicted mother disappears for weeks at a time. Meanwhile Jade has to accept that her father is going to get married to his girlfriend, Veronica.

> **Keywords:** college, dances, family, friendship

Deal with It. Kimani Tru, 2009. ISBN 9780373831418.

> Although she has a great boyfriend and is popular, Indigo becomes jealous when her best friend Jade is asked to become captain of the school dance team, and Tameka scores higher on the SATs.

> **Keywords:** friendship; jealousy; school

Mills, Claudia.

Makeovers by Marcia. **Farrar, Straus & Giroux, 2005. ISBN 9780374346546.** M J

> When one of the prettiest and most popular eighth-graders at West Creek Middle School, Marcia Faitak, is assigned to volunteer at a nursing home for her community service project, she discovers the value of inner beauty while painting the residents' nails.

> **Keywords:** community service; crushes; family; school

Morris, Taylor.

Class Favorite. **Aladdin Mix, 2007. ISBN 9781416935988.** M J

> On Valentine's Day eighth-grader Sara Thurman is completely humiliated and embarrassed when her mother sends flowers to Bowie Junior High congratulating Sara on getting her period. Meanwhile, new girl Kirstie helps Sara come up with a plan to get Jason Anderson's attention after Sara gets in a big fight with her best friend, Arelne.

> **Keywords:** crushes; divorce; friendship; humor; kissing; puberty; school

Myracle, Lauren.

[Winnie Perry]. **M** **J**

A lot can change in a year. In each novel, Winnie Perry provides a month-by-month account of her life as she moves from a kid to a tween who has new friends and a boyfriend.

Keywords: family; friendship

Eleven. Dutton Children's Books, 2004. ISBN 9780525471653.

After Winnie Perry turns eleven, she slowly drifts away from her longtime best friend, Amanda, and becomes better friends with Dinah, a girl Winnie previously thought was strange.

Keywords: school

Twelve. Dutton, 2007. ISBN 978052547786.

Winnie experiences many changes after turning twelve, including starting junior high, having her ears pierced, getting her first period, and going bra shopping with her mom.

Keywords: puberty; school

Thirteen. Dutton, 2008. ISBN 9780525478966.

Winnie Perry's thirteenth year is one of many firsts, including first boyfriend, first kiss, first makeover at the mall, first boy-girl party, first break-up, and more seriously, the first time she is faced with childhood illness.

Keywords: break-ups; kissing; school

Noel, Alyson.

Faking 19. St. Martin's Griffin, 2005. ISBN 9780312336332. **S**

As her grades dramatically slip and her estranged father refuses to pay for college, seventeen-year-old Alex escapes on the weekends with her best friend M to the hippest clubs in Los Angeles, where they convince Connor and Trevor that they are nineteen.

Keywords: family; friendship; school; sexual content

Papademetriou, Lisa.

How to Be a Girly Girl in Just Ten Days. Scholastic, 2007. ISBN 9780439890588. **M**

Tomboy Nicolette "Nick" Spicer has never been interested in shopping and makeup, until she bumps into Ben, the new boy at James Garfield Middle School. When it appears that Ben is more interested in a girly girl on her basketball team, Nick decides to get a makeover for an upcoming party.

Keywords: crushes; friendship; sports

Rosten. Carrie.

Chloe Leiberman (Sometimes Wong). Delacorte, 2005. ISBN 9780385732482. **J** **S**

High school senior Chloe Leiberman-Wong has to break the news to her high-achieving parents that the only school she applied to was The Central Saint Martins Fashion Design School in London.

Keywords: Asian American; college applications; family; fashion

Rupp, Rebecca.

Sarah Simpson's Rules for Living. Candlewick Press, 2008. ISBN 978-0763632205. **M**

One year after her father moved to California and remarried, twelve-year-old Sarah Simpson fills a journal with lists and rules about her crazy life, which includes her parents and their significant others as well as her part in the school play.

Keywords: acting; diary; divorce; family

Schorr, Melissa.

Goy Crazy. Hyperion, 2006. ISBN 9780786838523. **S**

During her sophomore year of high school, Rachel Lowenstein tries to fit in with the popular crowd, struggles with her Jewish faith, and convinces her parents that she is dating her Jewish neighbor Matthew Wallen, while secretly dating Luke Christiansen, a blonde-haired, blue-eyed basketball player.

Keywords: dating; family; humor; religion; school

Scott, Elizabeth.

Stealing Heaven. HarperTeen, 2008. ISBN 9780061122804. **J S**

Eighteen-year-old Danielle has grown up moving from town to town with her professional thief mother. Then they move to Heaven, a small New England beachfront town where Danielle gets her first best friend, her first boyfriend, and a chance to settle down.

Keywords: dating; death; family; friendship; moving

Scott, Kieran.

Geek Magnet: A Novel in Five Acts. Putnam, 2008. ISBN 9780399247606. **S**

As the first high school junior to be stage manager of the school musical, realizing her father is an alcoholic, and avoiding a group of unsavory admirers, KJ Miller has a lot on her mind. When KJ takes the advice of the musical's lead, Tama Gold, KJ temporally loses the geeks and alienates her real friends.

Keywords: body image; family; first kiss; friendship; school

Steele, J. M.

The Market. Hyperion, 2008. ISBN 9781423100133. **S**

A month before graduation, Millbank High School senior Kate Winthrop changes her 71 out of 140 ranking on the Millbank Social Stock Market to Blue Chip Status by creating a six point business plan that includes a major makeover. Once Kate becomes popular and is dating the school hottie, Will Bochnowski, she gives up her old friends as well as a chance for a lasting relationship with her coworker, Jack Clayton.

Keywords: cliques; crushes; dating; family; friendship; school

Urban, Linda.

A Crooked Kind of Perfect. Harcourt, 2007. ISBN 9780152060077. **M**

Ten-year-old Zoe Elias dreams of being a piano-playing prodigy who performs at Carnegie Hall like her idol, Vladimir Horowitz. Instead, every afternoon Zoe practices on the Perfectone D-60, an electric organ, while her semireclusive dad bakes with her friend Wheeler Diggs.

Keywords: crushes; family; friendship; humor; school

Vega, Denise.

Click Here: (to Find Out How I Survived Seventh Grade). Little, Brown, p2006, c2005. ISBN 9780316985598. **M J**

At the start of middle school Erin Swift reveals in her private weblog her anxiety about fitting in, her best friend Jilly, her crush Mark, and her hatred of popular Serena. When her weblog is accidentally published on the school's online newspaper, Erin learns to speak up for herself.

Keywords: blogs; crushes; friendship; school

Body Image

In this section some main characters already are proud of their bodies; however, many of the protagonists are embarrassed and uncomfortable that they look different from the accepted beauty standard. Eventually they learn to feel comfortable in their own skin and embrace what makes them unique.

Baratz-Logsted, Lauren.

Me, in Between. Aladdin Mix, 2008. ISBN 9781416950684. **M J**

For the last two years, twelve-year-old Lacey Underhill has endured taunts and teasing by her classmates at Wainscot Academy in Connecticut because she has large breasts. When her developed body attracts the attention of sixteen-year-old Chad Wilcox, Lacey lies to her grandmother and goes on a date with Chad. Then she realizes that her heart belongs to Sam Samuel, her childhood friend, who recently moved back to town.

Keywords: dating; family; friendship; kissing; puberty; school

Dionne, Erin.

Models Don't Eat Chocolate Cookies. Books for Young Readers, 2009. ISBN 9780803734357. **M J**

When her meddling aunt signs her up for the Miss Husky Peach Pageant for larger girls, thirteen-year-old Celeste Harris goes on a diet and starts exercising so she will be ineligible for the contest.

Keywords: family; friendship; modeling; school

Edwards, Jo.

Go Figure. Simon Pulse, 2007. ISBN 9781416924920. **S**

High school senior Ryan Burke tries to complete her personal goals of the week (suggested by her psychiatrist) and stop obsessing about her weight even though her rock star ex-boyfriend's new hit song is about her, her best friend returns home skinny after secretly going to fat camp, and she is developing a major crush on her next door neighbor, Josh.

Keywords: crushes; dating; family; friendship; kissing

Franklin, Emily.

At Face Value. Flux, 2008. ISBN 9780738713076. **J S**

In this modern version of the Cyrano de Bergerac story, high school senior Cyrie Bergerac is the talented editor of the school newspaper, counting the days until she can turn eighteen and get a nose job. When Cyrie discovers that her secret crush, Eddie Roxanninoff, is interested in her best friend Leyla, Cyrie writes e-mails to Eddie for Leyla.

Keywords: crushes; humor; school

Hogan, Mary.

Pretty Face. HarperTeen, 2008. ISBN 9780060841119. **S**

The summer before her senior year, binge-eater Hayley leaves behind her skinny best friend Jackie in Santa Monica, California, to stay with her mother's former college roommate in Umbria, Italy, determined to loose a few pounds; she develops an improved self-image after she meets Enzo.

Keywords: dating; self-acceptance

Kizer, Amber.

Gert Garibaldi's Rants and Raves: One Butt Cheek at a Time. Delacorte Press, 2007. ISBN 9780385904391. **S**

Brainy high school sophomore Gertrude "Gert" Doyle Garibaldi transforms from a self-pitying loner after her gay best friend Adam gets a boyfriend, to super-self-assured after her sex education teacher assigns them to examine their bodies intimately.

Keywords: gay; humor; school; self-acceptance; sexuality

Mackler, Carolyn.

🎖 *The Earth, My Butt and Other Big Round Things.* Candlewick, 2005. ISBN 9780763619589. **J S**

As a way to cope with her skinny, attractive Manhattan family, fifteen-year-old Virginia Shreves hides her junk food, follows a fat girl code of conduct, and secretly hooks up with Froggy Welsh the Fourth. Then she discovers some dark secrets that change how she feels about her perfect family and herself.

Keywords: dating; family; friendship; kissing; school; self-acceptance

Awards: BBYA 2004, Printz Honor 2004

Medina, Nico.

Fat Hoochie Prom Queen. **Simon Pulse, 2008. ISBN 9781416936039.** **S**

Madge Diaz, a well-liked high school senior, bets popular Bridget Benson that she will become this year's prom queen. As the prom gets closer the campaign schemes get ugly, especially when Bridget suggests that Madge is too fat to wear the crown.

Keywords: dating; friendship; gay; Hispanic American; prom; school

Mo'Nique.

Beacon Hills High. **Amistad, 2008. ISBN 9780061121067.** **J** **S**

After getting into Millwood High with her three best friends, thirteen-year-old Eboni Michelle Imes is nervous to start over in Los Angeles, where big girls don't exactly fit in. However, Eboni quickly makes new friends at her prestigious school and even runs for student council president against one of the most popular girls in her class.

Keywords: African American; crushes; family; friendship; moving; school; spirituality

Na, An.

The Fold. **Putnam, 2008. ISBN 9780399242762.** **J** **S**

During the summer before her senior year of high school, Joyce Kim's Aunt Gomo offers to pay for eyelid surgery to make Joyce look more American, and perhaps as attractive as her older sister Helen.

Keywords: Asian American; crushes; family; friendship; lesbian; school; work

Paley, Sasha.

Huge. **Simon & Schuster, 2007. ISBN 9781416935179.** **J** **S**

While April Adams plans to lose a lot of weight at a weight-loss spa, her room-mate Wilhelmia Hopkins plans to punish her parents by gaining weight. During the summer the unlikely pair become close and even win the Wellness Canyon Olympics.

Keywords: camp; dating; friendship; self-acceptance

Rayburn, Tricia.

[Maggie Bean]. **M** **J**

The following titles, although not formally a series, deal with the same protagonist and are listed in chronological order.

The Melting of Maggie Bean. **Aladdin Mix, 2007. ISBN 9781416933489.**

Straight-A student Maggie Bean has been using chocolate as a way to cope with her out-of-work dad and stressed-out mom. Then she has a chance to fulfill her childhood dream of becoming a water wing. When two seventh-grade spots open up on the prestigious synchronized swim team Maggie has only four weeks to practice her routine with her best friend and lose some weight.

Keywords: family; friendship; sports

Maggie Bean Stays Afloat. Aladdin Mix, 2008. ISBN 9781416933472.

Now in great shape after months of swimming practice and avoiding chocolate, Maggie is enjoying new-found attention from the a popular crowd at Camp Sound View, where she is a junior swim instructor. However, Maggie remembers too late who her real friends are.

Keywords: camp; crushes; family; friendship; school; work

Salter, Sydney.

My Big Nose: And Other Natural Disasters. Graphia, 2009. ISBN 9780152066437. **S**

In the summer before her senior year of high school, seventeen-year-old Jory Michaels takes a job delivering wedding cakes as a way to save up money for a nose job.

Keywords: dating; family; friendship; self-acceptance; work

Sarkar, Dona.

Shrink to Fit. Kimani TRU, 2008. ISBN 9780373830954. **J** **S**

Pressured by her model mother, Sonoma High School basketball star Leah Manderville thinks dieting and taking diet pills will solve all her problems.

Keywords: African American; crushes; family; modeling; sports

Supplee, Suzanne.

Artichoke's Heart. Dutton Books, 2008. ISBN 9780525479024. **J** **S**

As her sixteenth birthday gets closer, overweight binge-eater Rosemary Goode is sick of being an outcast at school and being mocked at her mother's beauty salon. After she goes on a strict diet, Rosemary starts to reconnect with her mother, makes new friends, and gets her first boyfriend.

Keywords: dating; family; school

Vaught, Susan.

Big Fat Manifesto. Bloomsbury, 2008. ISBN 9781599902067. **S**

To win a journalism scholarship for college, high school senior Jamie Carcaterra writes "The Fat Girl Manifesto," a weekly column in the school newspaper that addresses stereotyping, humiliations, and fears about her boyfriend Burke's recent weight loss surgery. (The paperback title is *My Big Fat Manifesto.*)

Keywords: break-ups; crushes; dating; friendship; school

Weiner, Jennifer.

Good in Bed. **Washington Square Press, 2002. ISBN 9780743418171.** **A**

Twenty-eight-year-old reporter Candace Shapiro is publicly humiliated by the article "Loving a Larger Woman," penned by her ex-boyfriend, Bruce Guberman.

Keywords: dating; family; humor; work

Family Ties

In these stories families can frustrate, annoy, and embarrass the teenage girl, but they also can teach her where she comes from and how special she really is.

Bowers, Laura.

Beauty Shop for Rent—: Fully Equipped, Inquire Within. **Harcourt, 2007. ISBN 9780152057640.** **J S**

Left by her mother four years earlier, fourteen-year-old Abbey Garner grew up listening to stories of heartache from the clients at her great-grandmother Granny Po's salon. Then Granny Po retires, and glamorous Gena transforms the shop and Abbey's view of the world.

Keywords: self-acceptance

Caletti, Deb.

Honey, Baby, Sweetheart. **Simon & Schuster Books for Young Readers, 2004. ISBN 9780689867651.** **S**

Quiet sixteen-year-old Ruby McQueen agrees to go with her librarian mother, Ann, to a weekly book club for retirees as a way to break away from her relationship with motorcycle-riding bad boy Travis Becker. When they learn that book club member Lillian is the long-lost lover of the author they are reading, Ruby and Ann "kidnap" Lillian from a nursing home and take her on a road trip to reunite the lovers.

Keywords: dating; road trip; romance

The Queen of Everything. **Simon Pulse, p2008, c2002. ISBN 9781416957812.** **S**

On a small island in the Puget Sound, seventeen-year-old Jordan Mackenzie is disturbed as her divorced father begins an obsessive relationship with their married neighbor, Gayle D'Angelo. When her father with is sent to jail for Gayle's husband's murder, Jordan runs away with her bad boy boyfriend, Kal Kramer, until she realizes that she has to move back in with her bohemian mother.

Keywords: affairs; dating; murder; sexual content

Caseley, Judith.

The Kissing Diary. **Farrar, Straus & Giroux, 2007. ISBN 9780374363468.** **M J**

Twelve-year-old Rosie Goldglitt starts writing in the diary her dad gave her about her feelings about her newly divorced mom dating, her sick grandfather, being bullied by popular Mary Katz, and her desire to be kissed by her crush, Robbie Romano.

Keywords: crushes; diary; divorce; friendship; school

Greenwald, Lisa.

My Life in Pink & Green. **Amulet Books, 2009. ISBN 9780810983526.** Ⓜ Ⓙ
In a small Connecticut town, twelve-year-old Lucy Desberg combines her interests in makeup and the environment to create an eco-spa, in the hope of saving the family pharmacy from foreclosure.

Keywords: crushes; friendship

Johnson, Maureen.

🏵 *Suite Scarlett.* **Point, 2008. ISBN 9780439899277.** Ⓙ Ⓢ
Fifteen-year-old Scarlett Martin is responsible for taking care of Mrs. Amy Amberson, the flamboyant former actress who is a guest at Hopewell, her parents' historic but nearly bankrupt hotel in Manhattan. She is also pursuing a relationship with her brother's co-star.

Keywords: humor; kissing; work

Awards: BBYA 2009

Komaiko, Leah.

Malibu Carmie. **Random House Children's Books, 2007, c2005. ISBN 9780440420149.** Ⓜ Ⓙ
Thirteen-year-old Carmie dreams of a life more exciting than her boring one in Van Nuys, California, with her hard-working mom, Elaine, who suffers from chronic fatigue syndrome. On a trip to Malibu Beach with her best friend Jenny, Carmie discovers that her mom was a top surfer and that her old surfer boyfriend Moondoggie still lives close by.

Keywords: crushes; divorce; surfing

Norris, Shana.

Something to Blog About. **Amulet Books, 2008. ISBN 9780810994744.** Ⓜ Ⓙ Ⓢ
Things go from bad to worse for tenth-grader Libby Fawcett when she accidentally sets her hair on fire in front of her crush, her mom announces that she is dating her archenemy Angel Rivera's dad, and Angel posts Libby's secret blog for all of Yeardy High to read.

Keywords: blogs; crushes; school

Paratore, Coleen.

The Wedding Planner's Daughter. Ⓜ Ⓙ
Willafred "Willa" Havisham is a romantic lover of books who is very close to her mother, a wedding planner who gets remarried and pregnant during the series.

The Wedding Planner's Daughter. Simon & Schuster Books for Young Readers, 2005. ISBN 9780689873409.

> When twelve-year-old Willa Havisham moves to Bramble, Cape Cod, she finds her first real best friend, spends time with her Nana, and plots to get her serious-minded mother Stella remarried so she will have a father.

> **Keywords:** friendship; humor; weddings

The Cupid Chronicles. Simon & Schuster Books for Young Readers, 2006. ISBN 9781416908678.

> Book lover Willa puts aside her feelings for Joseph Francis Kennelly to focus on saving the local library by having a fancy Valentine dance.

> **Keywords:** crushes; dances; family; friendship; humor

Willa by Heart. Simon & Schuster Books for Young Readers, 2008. ISBN 978-1416940760.

> Willa looks forward to the beginning of summer dating JFK, until Mariel moves to Cape Cod and lands the lead role in *Our Town* opposite Willa's boyfriend, she has to help plan two weddings at Bramblebriar Inn, and her mother announces that Willa will soon have a new sibling.

> **Keywords:** dating; jealously; pregnancy

Sones, Sonya.

🎖 *One of Those Hideous Books Where the Mother Dies*. **Simon & Schuster Books for Young Readers, 2004. ISBN 9780689858208.** **J** **S**

> After her mother's death fifteen-year-old Ruby Milliken has to leave behind her friends and boyfriend to move in with her estranged movie star father in California.

> **Keywords:** death; gay; novels in verse

> **Awards:** BBYA 2005

Tigelaar, Liz.

Pretty Tough Series.   **J** **S**

> Stories of strong, athletic teen girls, affiliated with the www.prettytough.com, a Web site designed to inspire, motivate, and address the needs of all girls who participate in sports.

> **Keywords:** sports

Pretty Tough. Razorbill, 2007. ISBN 9781595141125.

> In alternating voices, California sisters Charlie and Krista Brown share how they have to forget their intense sibling rivalry and learn how to work together when social outcast Charlie joins the soccer team where popular high school senior Krista is already the star player.

> **Keywords:** dating; friendship; school; sisters

Playing with Boys. Razorbill, 2008. ISBN 9781595141132.

> Following the death of her mother, fifteen-year-old Lucy Malone moves from Ohio to Malibu, California, and takes the school soccer coach's advice to join the varsity football team, despite her father's disproval.
>
> **Keywords:** crushes; school

Triana, Gaby.

Cubanita. **Harper Collins, 2005. 9780060560225.** **S**

> After her high school graduation, Isabel Diaz breaks up with her longtime Cuban boyfriend, starts dating an older boy from the day camp where she works, and learns to appreciate her crazy Cuban American family after her mother is diagnosed with breast cancer.
>
> **Keywords:** break-ups; college; dating; Hispanic American

Trueit, Trudi Strain.

Julep O'Toole. **M**

> Julep O'Toole often feels like an invisible girl at home because she has a perfect older sister and a mischief-making little brother, Cooper.

Julep O'Toole : Confessions of a Middle Child. Puffin Books, p2007, c2005. ISBN 9780142407981.

> > Eleven-year-old Julep is forced to trade rooms with Cooper because of his allergies. Perhaps Julep will no longer be invisible at school now that the most popular girl asked Julep to her Halloween party.
> >
> > **Keywords:** friendship; humor; parties; school

Julep O'Toole: Miss Independent. Dutton Children's Books, 2006. ISBN 9780525476375.

> > Lately sixth-grader Julep and her mother have been arguing a lot about cell phones, clothes, bra shopping, piano lessons, and Julep's growing independence.
> >
> > **Keywords:** friendship; puberty; school

Julep O'Toole: What I Really Want to Do Is Direct. Dutton Children's Books, 2007. ISBN 9780525477815.

> > To bring up her English grade, Julep tries out for her school's production of *The Princess and the Pea* to earn extra credit. After she bombs her audition, Julep is promoted from stage crew to assistant director and saves the show from being canceled.
> >
> > **Keywords:** friendship; humor; school

Vega, Denise.

Fact of Life #31. **Knopf, 2008. ISBN 9780375948190.** **S**

> In Colorado, sixteen-year-old Kat Flynn begins a secret relationship with her longtime crush Manny Cruz and works part-time with her midwife

mother, Alba. When the most popular girl at school shows up pregnant at the birth center and develops a bond with Alba, Kat becomes jealous.

Keywords: crushes; dating; jealousy; pregnancy; work

Sisters

The unique relationship between sisters is a complex one that consists of friendship, jealousy, arguments, and solidarity. Sisters in the following novels may grow apart but ultimately come back together again.

Abbott, Hailey.

The Bridesmaid. Delacorte Press, 2005. ISBN 9780385902496. **M** **J**

Fifteen-year-old Abby Beaumont's older sister Carol not only breaks their childhood pact never to marry, but turns into a bridezilla like the countless brides Abby grew up watching at the catering hall her parents manage. In addition to the wedding plans, Abby is torn between accepting a soccer scholarship in Italy or staying home to be with Noah, her first real boyfriend.

Keywords: dating; family; humor; sports; wedding

Carey, Anna.

The Sloane Sisters. HarperTeen, 2009. ISBN 9780061175763.

When their New York financier father marries a British model, ninth-grade queen bee at Ashton Prep Cate Sloane and her twelve-year-old, wanna-be model sister Andie have to quickly adjust to their new stepsisters, Stella and Lola Child.

Keywords: family; school

Friedman, Aimee.

The Year My Sister Got Lucky. Scholastic, 2008. ISBN 9780439922272. **J** **S**

When they were students of the Anna Pavola School of Ballet in New York, fourteen-year-old Katie Wilder felt close to her eighteen-year-old sister Michaela. But then the family relocates to Fir Lake, a rural town in the Adirondacks, where Michaela embraces her new life and becomes homecoming queen, while Katie feels homesick and betrayed.

Keywords: family; friendship; moving

Klam, Cheryl.

The Pretty One. Delacorte Press, 2008. ISBN 9780385903882. **J** **S**

Megan has always lived in the shadow of her attractive, slightly older sister Lucy, until Megan is injured in a car accident and requires major cosmetic surgery and dental work. When Megan returns to the high school of performing arts she receives attention usually reserved for Lucy, like starring in the school play and having cute boys flirt with her.

Keywords: acting; body image; family; school

Sarkar, Dona.

How to Salsa in a Sari. **Kimani TRU, 2008. ISBN 9780373830886.** **J** **S**

Sixteen-year-old Issa Mazumder, a proud African American and Hindu, is upset when her mother announces her engagement to spoiled Cat Morena's father. It is bad enough that Cat is a Latina princess who recently stole her boyfriend Adam, but she has also made it clear that she has little respect for Issa's heritage.

Keywords: African American; break-ups; dating; family; Hispanic American; wedding

Weiner, Jennifer.

In Her Shoes. **Atria Books, 2002. ISBN 9780743418195.** **A**

The rift between thirty-year-old attorney Rose Feller and her younger, flighty sister Maggie gets bigger when Maggie moves in with Rose, until their estranged grandmother contacts them.

Keywords: family; humor; movie tie-in; work

Friendship

Almost everyone knows that during adolescence friendship, especially between girls, is very important. In these teen chick lit stories friends are loyal confidantes who stand by your side, listen to your daily problems, and are a constant source of entertainment. Unfortunately, there are also stories about friends who have turned into frenemies when they have grown apart or competed for the same goal.

Allie, Debora.

The Meanest Girl. **Roaring Brook Press, 2005. ISBN 9781596430143.** **M**

At the start of sixth grade, popular Alyssa Fontana lives a perfect life; then Hayden Martin moves into town, her best friend Chelsea starts acting weird, and she discovers the truth about her dad.

Keywords: family; puberty; school

Anderson, Jodi Lynn.

Peaches. **S**

In Georgia, Murphy McGowen, Leeda Cawley-Smith, and Birdie Darlington start a lifelong friendship after working together one summer on the Darlington Peach Farm.

Keywords: dating; family; first love

Peaches. HarperCollins, 2005. ISBN 9780060733063.

In the summer before their senior year, three very different girls—uncontrollable Murphy, flawless Leeda, and shy Birdie—find love and an unlikely friendship when they come together at the Darlington Peach Farm in Georgia.

The Secrets of Peaches. HarperTempest, 2007. ISBN 9780060733087.

> Shortly after carving their initials in a magnolia tree to symbolize lasting friendship, Murphy, Leeda, and Birdie struggle to remain close as Leeda seeks her mother's approval, Birdie misses her boyfriend, and Murphy reluctantly plans to move to New York City.
>
> **Keywords:** work

Love and Peaches. HarperTeen, 2008. ISBN 9780060733117.

> In the concluding story about Murphy, Birdie, and Leeda, the girls return to Georgia after being away at college, only to discover that the peach farm will be sold. During that summer Birdie breaks her engagement, Leeda's large inheritance changes her destiny, and Murphy reconnects with her true love.
>
> **Keywords:** break-ups; college; work

Brashares, Ann.

Sisterhood of the Traveling Pants. J S

Right before their first summer apart in fifteen years, best friends Lena Kaligaris, Tibby Rollins, Bridget Vreeland, and Carmen Lowell discover that Carmine's thrift store jeans magically fit and flatter their different bodies.

Keywords: dating; family; Hispanic American

Sisterhood of the Traveling Pants. Delacorte, 2001. ISBN 9780385729338.

The girls create and vow to follow ten rules, which include rotating the jeans throughout the summer. Lena falls in love in Greece, Tibby works at Wallman's in Washington, DC, Bridget goes too far at her soccer camp, and Carmen deals with her father getting remarried.

Keywords: death; humor; movie tie-in; sexual content; vacation; weddings; work
Awards: BBYA 2002

The Second Summer of the Sisterhood. Delacorte, 2003. ISBN 9780385729345.

> During their second summer apart, best friends Bridget, Carmen, Lena, and Tibby continue to share the magic jeans, as Carmen's mom begins dating, Tibby is in a special filmmaking program at Williamstown College, Lena's Greek boyfriend Kostos shows up, and Bridget travels to Alabama to see her estranged maternal grandmother.
>
> **Keywords:** death; first love; movie tie-in

Girls in Pants: The Third Summer of the Sisterhood. Delacorte Press, 2005. ISBN 9780385729352.

> Prior to their final weekend together before heading off to different colleges, Bridget, Carmen, Lena, and Tibby have a summer filled with family and boyfriend drama: Carmen's mother is pregnant, Lena's strict parents refuse to pay for art school, Bridget is back at the Baja soccer camp with Eric, and Tibby's relationship with Brian gets complicated.
>
> **Keywords:** college; dating; family; first love; school; work

Forever in Blue: The Fourth Summer of the Sisterhood. Delacorte Press, 2007. ISBN 9780385729369.

> In the final installment, Lena and Tibby loose their virginity, Bridget dangerously flirts with a married professor during an archeological dig in Turkey, and Carmen surprisingly becomes the star actress at a Vermont Theater program. After being apart for almost a year, Bridget, Carmen, Lena, and Tibby come together to find the lost magical pants in Greece and realize the power of their friendship as they grow into young adults.
>
> **Keywords:** acting; break-ups; college; dating; family; first love; sexual content

Brian, Kate.

Fake Boyfriend. Simon & Schuster, 2007. ISBN 9781416913672. **J S**

> Lane Morris and Vivi Swayne enlist Vivi's younger brother, Marshall, to create a MySpace page for the perfect boy as a way to cheer up their best friend Isabelle Hunter, who caught her boyfriend cheating right before the prom.
>
> **Keywords:** dances; humor

The Virginity Club. Simon Pulse, 2005, c2004. ISBN 9781416903468. **S**

> Four Ardsmore High seniors—Eva Farrell, Mandy Walters, Kai Parker, and Debbie Patel—form the V Club, with hopes of winning the $160,000 Treemont scholarship, which requires students to exemplify purity of soul and body. (Formerly titled *The V Club.*)
>
> **Keywords:** blogs, dating, sexuality

Burnham, Niki.

Goddess Games. Simon & Schuster Books for Young Readers, 2007. ISBN 9781416927006. **S**

> Glamorous Seneca, athletic Drew, and local girl Claire at first can only see their differences, but eventually they become close friends while they room and work together at King's Crown, an upscale mountain resort in Colorado.
>
> **Keywords:** work

Cabot, Meg.

Pants on Fire. HarperTeen, 2007. ISBN 9780060880156. **J S**

> Photography buff Katie Ellison's constant lying catches up with her when her old friend Tommy Sullivan unexpectedly returns after being run out of town.
>
> **Keywords:** dating; kissing; humor; work

Calonita, Jen.

Sleepaway Girls. Little, Brown, 2009. ISBN 9780316017176. **J S**

> After her boyfriend starts dating her best friend, Samantha "Sam" becomes a counselor-in-training at Whispering Pines sleepaway camp, where she

learns how to stand up for herself, makes three best friends, and finds a great boyfriend.

Keywords: camp; crushes

Clairday, Robynn.

Confessions of a Boyfriend Stealer: A Blog. Delacorte Press, 2005. ISBN 9780385732420. **J S**

A sixteen-year-old aspiring documentary filmmaker and former member of the Terrible Threes explains in her online blog how she "stole" the boyfriends of shallow and spoiled best friends CJ and Tasha.

Keywords: blogs; dating; family; school

Craft, Liz, and Sarah Fain.

[Harper Waddle]. **S**

The following titles, although not formally a series, deal with the same characters and are listed in chronological order.

Bass Ackwards and Belly Up. Little, Brown, 2006. ISBN 9780316057936.

Instead of admitting that she was rejected by NYU, Harper Waddle announces that she will stay in Boulder, Colorado, to pursue her dream of writing a novel. She convinces her three best friends, Sophie Bushell, Becca Winsberg, and Kate Foster, to join the dream team and forget about college. Sophie moves to Hollywood to act, Becca becomes a ski coach at Middlebury College, and Kate defers attending Harvard to travel through Europe.

Keywords: acting; college; dating; family; romance; sexual content

Footfree and Fancyloose. Little, Brown, 2008. ISBN 9780316057950.

Halfway through their "Year of Dreams," Harper, Sophie, Becca, and Kate realize that although their plans have changed, they are closer to achieving their goals and finding real love.

Keywords: acting; college; dating; romance; sexual content; sisters

Dower, Laura.

The Boy Next Door. Scholastic, 2006. ISBN 9780439929295. **M**

In alternating chapters, next door neighbors Taryn and Jeff explain how their friendship changed once they started sixth grade.

Keywords: crushes; puberty; school

Elliot, Jamie.

Girls Dinner Club. HarperCollins, 2005. ISBN 9780060595401. **S**

Seventeen-year-old Junie Wong-Goldstein bonds with her two friends Celia and Danielle while they cook dinner together and share stories of their romantic and family problems.

Keywords: Asian American; dating; family; food; sexual content

Fredericks, Mariah.

The True Meaning of Cleavage. **Atheneum Books for Young Readers, 2003. ISBN 9780689850929.** **S**

High school freshman Jess struggles with her art class assignment and is worried that her beautiful best friend Sari is being used by David Cole, the most popular senior at Manhattan's Eldridge Alternative School.

Keywords: cliques; school

Friedman, Aimee.

Breaking Up. **Scholastic, 2007. ISBN 9781428707412.** **J** **S**

High school junior Chloe Sacks temporarily has a falling out with her three best friends when Chloe starts dating, Adam, a social outcast at the Georgia O'Keeffe School for the Arts.

Keywords: cliques; dating; graphic novel

Gabel, Claudia.

In or Out. **J** **S**

Former best friends spirited Marine Fitzpatrick and shy Nola James share their points of view about popularity, dating, and friendship.

Keywords: crushes; dating; school

In or Out. Scholastic, 2007. ISBN 9780439918534.

Best friends and high school freshmen Marine Fitzpatrick and Nola James's relationship is strained when confident Marine becomes friends with Lizette Levin, the leader of "The Majors" at Poughkeepsie Central. Although shy Nola makes new friends, she is hurt that Marine abandoned her.

Keywords: cliques

Loves Me, Loves Me Not. Point, 2007. ISBN 9780439918541.

After their very public fight about betrayal and loyalty, former best friends Nola and Marine try to move on. Marine focuses on her new boyfriend, Dane Harris, and securing her place in "The Majors" by winning the upcoming student council elections; Nola gets closer with her crush, Matthew Heatherly, who already has a serious girlfriend.

Keywords: cliques; kissing

Sweet and Vicious. Point, 2008. ISBN 9780439918565.

As Nola continues to get close with Matt and her brother's babysitter Ian, she also plots her revenge against Marine by arranging that Marine will bump into her ex-boyfriend, Weston Briggs. Meanwhile Marine has growing suspicions about her best friend Lizette and her boyfriend Dane, at the same time that she is secretly crushing on Lizette's boyfriend Sawyer.

Keywords: kissing

Friends Close, Enemies Closer. Point, 2008. ISBN 9780439918572.

As the homecoming dance approaches, the tables have turned. With several boys interested in her, it appears that Nola is in, while Marine has been kicked out of "The Majors" and dumped by Dane.

Keywords: break-ups; dances; family

Gehrman, Jody Elizabeth.

Confessions of a Triple Shot Betty. **Dial Books, 2008. ISBN 9780803732476.** ⓢ

In Sonoma, California, sixteen-year-old Geena thinks working at a drive-through coffee shop with her cousin Hero and best friend Amber will be a fun way to pass the time during the summer, but it becomes clear that Hero and Amber do not like each other. The girls eventually come together to seek revenge on John, a boy who is trying to ruin Hero's reputation. Inspired by William Shakespeare's *Much Ado about Nothing.*

Keywords: dating; humor; work

Goldschmidt, Judy.

Raisin Rodriguez. Ⓜ Ⓙ

After she moves to Philadelphia, seventh-grader Raisin Rodriguez keeps her best friends current on her daily drama through a private blog.

Keywords: Hispanic American

The Secret Blog of Raisin Rodriguez. Razorbill, 2005. ISBN 9781595140180.

After moving to Philadelphia, twelve-year-old Raisin Rodriguez keeps a private blog to keep in touch with her two best friends. When Raisin forgets to logout at Franklin Academy, her secrets about trying to fit in are revealed to the entire school.

Keywords: blogs; moving; puberty; school

Raisin Rodriguez and the Big-Time Smooch. Razorbill, 2005. ISBN 9781595141255.

In the secret blog Raisin shares with her best friends in California, she writes about her encounters with her crush, CJ Mullen, that lead up to her first real kiss.

Keywords: crushes; first kiss; puberty

Will the Real Raisin Rodriguez Please Stand Up? Razorbill, 2007. ISBN 978-1595140586.

Raisin reluctantly leaves behind her new boyfriend CJ to visit her father during Christmas break and discovers that her best friends Pia and Claudia have a new best friend.

Keywords: dating; puberty

Griffin, Adele.

My Almost Epic Summer. **Putnam, 2006. ISBN 9780399237843.** **J** **S**
While stuck babysitting all summer, fourteen-year-old Irene Morse meets and befriends the beautiful lifeguard Starla Molloy at Larkin's Pond in New Jersey. When Irene begins a romantic relationship with Starla's ex-boyfriend Drew Fuller Irene sees Starla's true colors.

Keywords: dating; work

Han, Jenny.

Shug. **Aladdin Mix, 2006. ISBN 9781416909422.** **M** **J**
Twelve-year-old Annemarie "Shug" Wilcox's seventh-grade year has a rough start because her parents are constantly fighting, her childhood friend and crush Mark asks another girl to the dance, and her best friend Elaine is obsessed with a new boyfriend. Shug feels totally alone until she is asked to tutor her former enemy, Jack, and discovers that they have a lot in common.

Keywords: crushes; family; school

Kimmel, Elizabeth Cody.

Spin the Bottle. **Dial Books for Young Readers, 2008. ISBN 9780803731912.**
M **J**
At the beginning of seventh grade, best friends Phoebe and Harper temporarily fight and go their separate ways after Phoebe lands a small part in the school musical, obsesses over her first crush, and tries to impress the older members of the drama club.

Keywords: acting; crushes; humor; school

Larson, Hope.

Chiggers. **Atheneum Books for Young Readers, 2008. ISBN 9781416935841.**
M **J**
After her older friend Rose moves on, bookish Abby struggles to fit in at her summer camp in North Carolina, until she befriends her new roommate Shasta and has her first kiss with her crush, Teal.

Keywords: camp; crushes; first kiss; graphic novel

Lenhard, Elizabeth.

Chicks with Sticks. **J** **S**
When high school juniors Scottie, Amanda, Tay, and Bella discover knitting at their local yarn store in Chicago, their lives become intertwined.

Keywords: knitting

Chicks with Sticks: (It's a Purl Thing). Dutton, 2005. ISBN 9780525476221.

> Scottie, Amanda, Tay, and Bella are four very different high school juniors who join a knitting class at KnitWit, a local yarn shop in Chicago, and bond as they share their stories.

> **Keywords:** school

Chicks with Sticks: (Knit Two Together). Dutton, 2006. ISBN 9780525477648.

> Scottie has never had a boyfriend before, so when she starts dating Beck, the new boy at school, she seeks advice from her more experienced friends Amanda, Tay, and Bella.

> **Keywords:** dating

Chicks with Sticks: (Knitwise). Dutton, 2007. ISBN 9780525478386.

> In between college applications and graduation, the knitters support each other as Scottie has mixed feelings about leaving high school, Amanda is forced to be a debutante, Tay's parents are getting a divorce, and Bella rebels from her new age family.

> **Keywords:** college applications; divorce; family; graduation

Lockhart, E., Sarah Mlynowski, and Lauren Myracle.

How to Be Bad. HarperTeen, 2008. ISBN 9780061284236. **S**

> In alternating chapters, high school seniors and Waffle House coworkers describe how they tried to leave behind their problems, such as Jesse's mom's breast cancer, by taking Jesse's old car and Mel's credit cards to surprise visit Vick's college freshman boyfriend in Miami. The three girls create a strong bond of friendship and discover their own strength during the road trip.

> **Keywords:** break-ups; dating; family; kissing; road trip; self-acceptance; work

McCoy, Mimi.

The Accidental Cheerleader. Scholastic, 2006. ISBN 9780439890564. **M**

> Shy Sophie and outgoing Kylie's close friendship is tested when both girls try out for the middle school cheerleading team and Sophie makes the squad, while Kylie has to wear the school mascot costume.

> **Keywords:** cheerleading; crushes; dances; school

The Babysitting Wars. Scholastic, 2007. ISBN 9780439929547. **M**

> Super-competitive Kaitlyn is the most requested babysitter in her neighborhood until Nola, a new seventh-grader, moves in on Kaitlyn's territory.

> **Keywords:** crushes; school; work

Myracle, Lauren.

The Fashion Disaster That Changed My Life. Dutton, 2005. ISBN 9780525472223. **M** **J**

> Allsion is thrilled and confused when the most popular girl in seventh grade, Rachael Delaney, invites Allison into her inner circle. Allison tries to stay close to

her old friends, Megan and Kathy, while she is hanging out with the popular kids, until she discovers how mean Rachael really can be.

Keywords: cliques; divorce; school

Ttyl. S

In an instant messaging format, best friends Maddie, Angela, and Zoe share their day-to-day experiences from tenth grade through their high school graduation.

🎗 *Ttyl.* Amulet Books, 2004. ISBN 9780810948211.

In the beginning of tenth grade longtime best friends Maddie, Angela and Zoe instant message after school about Maddie's new friendship with popular Jana, Zoe's relationship with her teacher and Angela's constant boyfriend drama.

Keywords: crushes; dating; religion; school
Awards: Quick Picks 2005

Ttfn. Amulet, 2006. ISBN 9780810959712.

After sixteen-year-old Angela moves from Atlanta to Northern California she continues to IM with her best friends Maddie and Zoe even after Zoe starts dating Angela's old crush and Maddie smokes marijuana to impress a boy.

Keywords: dating; moving; school

L8r, g8r. Amulet Books, 2007. ISBN 9780810912663.

Throughout their senior year of high school best friends Angela, Maddie, and Zoe share instant messages about parents, boyfriends, college choices, sex, and the prom.

Keywords: college; dating; family; prom; school; sexual content

Noel, Alyson.

Kiss and Blog. St. Martin's Griffin, 2007. ISBN 9780312355098. J S

After best friends Winter and Sloane make a pact that sophomore year will be the year they get noticed, Sloan becomes a cheerleader, but Winter is left behind. Winter gets back at her former best friend by writing an anonymous blog revealing Sloane's secrets.

Keywords: blogs; cheerleading; cliques; crushes; divorce; school

Papademetriou, Lisa.

Sixth-Grade Glommers, Norks, and Me. Hyperion Books, 2005. ISBN 978-0786851690. M

Sixth-grader Allie Kimball's plans of being on the Grover Cleveland Middle School soccer team with her best friend Tamara Thompson change when Tamara joins the cheerleading squad with Renee Anderson. Allie is confused and upset until she makes some new friends.

Keywords: school; sports

[Accidentally. . .] Ⓜ

When Amy Flowers earns a full scholarship to the super-exclusive Allington Academy, she looks forward to making new friends, but first she has to be accepted by Fiona, who runs The League.

Keywords: humor; school

Accidentally Fabulous. Scholastic, 2008. ISBN 9780545046671.

Seventh-grader Amy Flowers is determined to get in with the popular clique at her new school, even if that means listening to snobby Fiona.

Keywords: cliques; family

Accidentally Famous. Scholastic, 2008, ISBN 9780545055819.

Newcomer Amy Flowers's passion for fashion gets her noticed by the other students at Allington Academy, but at the risk of letting down her friends on the Academic Challenge team.

Keywords: family; fashion

Accidentally Fooled. Scholastic, 2009. ISBN 9780545055826.

When Amy has to work with popular Fiona and Preston on their seventh-grade service project teaching health to first graders, Amy questions why Fiona is acting so friendly.

Keywords: community service; friendship

Pollack, Jenny.

Klepto. **Viking, 2006. ISBN 9780670060610.** Ⓙ Ⓢ

In 1981 fourteen-year-old Julie Prodsky becomes best friends with one of the most fashionable freshmen at the High School of Performing Arts in New York City, Julie Braverman. Together Julie P and Julie B shoplift clothes from boutiques and department stores, until Julie P begins to feel remorse.

Keywords: crushes; family; friendship

Preble, Laura.

The Queen Geeks. Ⓙ Ⓢ

During their four years at Green Pines High School in California, self-proclaimed geeks Shelby, Becca, Amber, and Elisa become the heart of the queen geek social club.

Keywords: humor; school

The Queen Geek Social Club. Berkley Jam Books, 2006. ISBN 9780425211649.

During their freshman year at Green Pines High School, smart Shelby Chappelle teams up with eccentric Becca Gallagher to form the queen geek social club to empower and hang out with other girls like themselves.

Keywords: cliques; crushes; dances; kissing

Queen Geeks in Love. Berkley Jam, 2007. ISBN 9780425217177.

> Although Shelby likes Fletcher, she is freaking out about having a real boyfriend. Meanwhile, Becca is crushing on artistic Jon and has big plans for the queen geek social club that include winning a Web site contest and hosting a GeekFest talent show.

> **Keywords:** crushes; dating

Prom Queen Geeks. Berkley Jam, 2008. ISBN 9780425223383.

> When Becca decides to host an alternative prom, Shelby has to choose which prom she should attend with her boyfriend.

> **Keywords:** dating; prom

Rallison, Janette.

Life, Love and the Pursuit of Free Throws. Walker, 2004. ISBN 9780802789273. **M** **J**

> At the start of their freshman year in high school, childhood best friends Cami and Josie compete for Ethan Lancaster's attention and on the basketball court, where they both want to be named MVP.

> **Keywords:** crushes; school; sports

Sandoval, Lynda.

Who's Your Daddy? Simon Pulse, 2004. ISBN 9780689864407. **J** **S**

> Sixteen-year-olds Caressa, Lila, and Meryl are perpetually dateless due to their fathers' intimidating jobs. As the junior prom approaches, the three friends conduct a Celtic ritual to discover their true loves.

> **Keywords:** dating; family; prom

Schaefer, Laura.

The Teashop Girls. Simon & Schuster Books for Young Readers, 2008. ISBN 9781416967934. **M** **J**

> Thirteen-year-old Annie Green is thrilled to get a job as a barista at her grandmother's old-fashioned teashop with cute Jonathan, until she discovers that the Steeping Leaf may close. Annie enlists her best friends Gemma and Zoe, the original teashop girls, to come up with a plan to save the shop.

> **Keywords:** crushes; family; work

Scott, Kieran.

Non-Blonde Cheerleader. **J** **S**

> When high school cheerleader Annisa Gobrowski moves to Florida, she learns how to be an equal member of the squad and remain true to herself.

> **Keywords:** cheerleading; humor; school

I Was a Non-Blonde Cheerleader. Putnam, 2005. ISBN 9780399242793.

As a daughter of a professor, Annisa Gobrowski has moved with her family six times. She is taken aback when she transfers from New Jersey to Florida, where every student is a shade of blonde. As an obvious outsider, this brunette has to make friends and learn how to win a state cheerleading competition with a team that resents her presence.

Keywords: moving

Brunettes Strike Back. Putnam, 2006. ISBN 9780399244933.

As her team prepares to compete in the Nationals against her former New Jersey squad, sixteen-year-old Annisa feels pressured to dye her hair blonde for uniformity.

Keywords: crushes

A Non-Blonde Cheerleader in Love. G.P. Putnam's Sons, 2007. ISBN 9780399244940.

Annisa is initially thrilled when her boyfriend Daniel quits the wrestling team and joins the newly coed cheerleading squad, but she quickly finds herself in the middle of a battle of the sexes as the cheerleaders adjust to the change.

Keywords: dating; romantic comedy

Sedita, Francesco.

Miss Popularity. **Scholastic, 2007. ISBN 9780439888141.** **M**

Popular Cassie Knight has to leave her cute summer dresses and her best friends in Texas when her family relocates to Maine. As the newest sixth-grader at Oak Grove Prep School, Cassie is not accepted until she organizes a charity fashion show.

Keywords: fashion; school

Serros, Michele.

[Evie Gomez]. **S**

The following titles, although not formally a series, deal with the same characters and are listed in chronological order.

Honey Blonde Chica. Simon Pulse, 2006. ISBN 9781416915911.

Ever since her former best friend, Dee Dee, came back from Mexico as a glamour girl, fifteen-year-old Evie Gomez is torn between her old easygoing Flojo crew and the fashionable Sangro clique.

Keywords: cliques; dating; Hispanic American

Scandalosa! Simon Pulse, 2007. ISBN 9781416915935.

Instead of looking forward to her upcoming extravagant sixteenth birthday party Evie is preoccupied because her surfer boyfriend Alex is acting distant, her best friend Raquel is drinking, her other best friend Dee Dee may move back to Mexico, and she has to do volunteer work to get her grades up.

Keywords: dating; family; Hispanic American; sweet-sixteen party

Tuttle, Cameron.

Paisley Hanover Acts Out. Dial Books, 2008. ISBN 9780803733442. **J**

After being switched from yearbook to drama class, with the unpopular students, Pleasant Hill High sophomore Paisley Hanover starts writing a column in the school newspaper under the pseudonym "Miss UnPleasant," about her views on how the popular crowd act; soon being unpopular is the way to be. Includes *Paisley Notebook*, filled with drawings, notes, and quizzes.

Keywords: cliques; school

Vail, Rachel.

Lucky. HarperTeen, 2008. ISBN 978006089045. **J S**

Pretty and wealthy Phoebe Avery and her four best friends are planning an elaborate eighth-grade graduation party when Phoebe's mom is fired, and Phoebe realizes how truly lucky she is to have wonderful friends and a new boyfriend.

Keywords: crushes; family; parties

Withrow, Sarah.

What Gloria Wants. Groundwood Books, 2005. ISBN 9780888996282. **J S**

Gloria has always followed her best friend's Shawna's lead until Gloria starts to date Marc, the hottest boy in ninth grade, despite her friend's warnings.

Keywords: dating; first love

Ziegler, Jennifer.

How Not to Be Popular. Delacorte Press, 2008. ISBN 9780385734653. **J S**

When seventeen-year-old Sugar Magnolia "Maggie" Dempsey moves to Austin, Texas, she decides to follow "operation avoid friends" but ends up being nominated for homecoming queen.

Keywords: dating; family; humor; moving; school

Zindel, Lizabeth.

The Secret Rites of Social Butterflies. Viking, 2008. ISBN 9780670062171. **J S**

High school senior Maggie Wishnicks moves to New York City with her newly separated mother and is invited to join the Revelers, the most popular clique at Berkley Prep, who write down the secrets of their classmates and teachers on the Wall during their weekly ritual. When the Wall is discovered, Maggie could lose her social status and her new boyfriend, Connor.

Keywords: cliques; dating; divorce; family; kissing; moving; school

Coming-of-Age Celebrations

This section features novels about the special occasions that teenage girls look forward to and prepare for with their familird and friends for weeks, including sweet-sixteen parties, proms, *quinceañeras*, and bat mitzvahs.

Anderson, Laurie Halse.

Prom. Viking, 2005. ISBN 9780670059744. **J S**

Eighteen-year-old Ashley Hannigan discovers that sometimes it is just better to let the boy go, when she unexpectedly goes to the prom, dumps her loser boyfriend, and has a great time.

Keywords: family; friendship; humor; prom

Brian, Kate.

Sweet 16. Simon & Schuster, 2006. ISBN 9781416900320. **J S**

At her ultra-fabulous sweet-sixteen party, self-centered Teagan Phillips has a ghostly encounter that shows her what is truly important.

Keywords: family; friendship; sweet-sixteen party

Downing, Erin.

Prom Crashers. Simon Pulse, 2007. ISBN 9781416935599. **J S**

After high school senior Emily Bronson loses Ethan's telephone number, she convinces her cousin Charlie and his two best friends to crash every upcoming prom to find her mystery man.

Keywords: dating; friendship; gay; kissing; prom; romantic comedy; work

Karasyov, Carrie, and Jill Kargman.

Bittersweet Sixteen. HarperCollins, 2006. ISBN 9780060778460. **J S**

Lauren Finnegan feels like a third wheel when her best friend and the most popular girl at school, Whitney Blake, decides to join forces with Sophie Mitchum and have a joint, super extravagant sweet-sixteen party.

Keywords: friendship; sweet-sixteen party

Nelson, Blake.

Prom Anonymous. Speak, 2006. ISBN 9780142407455. **S**

After attending the Evergreen high school prom last year with her boyfriend Mike, Laura Truman convinces her oldest friends Julia "Jace" Torres and Chloe Truman that they will all go together. The only problem is finding a dating for artsy Chloe.

Keywords: break-ups; dating; friendship; humor; prom

Osa, Nancy.

🏅 *Cuba 15.* **Delacorte Press, 2003. ISBN 9780385900867.** **M** **J** **S**

Despite growing up in a family that pumps with Cuban pride, Violet Paz agrees to have a *quinceañera*, as long as she can change certain parts of the traditional ceremony.

Keywords: family; first love; Hispanic American; humor; *quinceañera*

Awards: BBYA 2004

Ponti, Jamie.

Prama. **Simon Pulse, 2008. ISBN 9781416961000.** **J** **S**

As six people, including the head of the prom committee, the sexy foreign exchange student, the prom queen, and their dates get ready for the prom, the night turns out to be romantic for some and revealing to others.

Keywords: break-ups; dating; friendship; humor; kissing; lesbian; prom

Rosenbloom, Fiona.

[Stacy and Lydia]. **M** **J**

The following titles, although not formally a series, deal with the same characters and are listed in chronological order.

You Are So Not Invited to My Bat Mitzvah! Hyperion Paperbacks, 2007, c2005. ISBN 9780786838912.

As her bat mitzvah party gets closer, seventh-grader Stacy Adelaide Friedman is worried about her Torah reading, her dress, and how to get her crush, Andy Goldfarb, to kiss her. When Stacy catches her best friend Lydia kissing Andy, she "uninvites" Lydia to the celebration.

Keywords: crushes; friendship; humor; kissing; religion

We Are So Crashing Your Bar Mitzvah! Hyperion, 2007. ISBN 9780786838905.

Determined to get into the most popular clique at school, the chicas, like their friend Kelly, eighth-graders Stacy and her best friend Lydia decide to crash an exclusive bar mitzvah party.

Keywords: cliques; crushes; friendship; humor; school

Williams, Kathryn.

The Debutante. **Hyperion, 2008. ISBN 9781423100454.** **S**

When high school senior Annie MacRae relocates from Connecticut to her dad's childhood town of Beaufort, Alabama, she reluctantly listens to her grandmother and prepares to make her social debut at the Magnolia Ball.

Keywords: family; moving; school

First Love

The chick lit novels in this section are not stories of puppy love; rather, they are about a young girl's first deep romantic experience.

Cabot, Meg.

[Samantha Madison]. J S

The following titles, although not formally a series, deal with the same protagonist and are listed in chronological order.

🎗 *All American Girl*. HarperTeen, p2008, c2002. ISBN 9780061479892.

> After saving the president of the United States from an attempted assassination attempt, artistic Samantha Madison is appointed the teen ambassador to the United Nations and starts dating the president's cute son, David.
>
> **Keywords:** dating; family; humor; school
>
> **Awards:** Quick Picks 2003

Ready or Not. HarperCollins, 2005. ISBN 9780060724504.

> After dating the president's son, David, for a year, Sam questions how far she is ready to go sexually when David invites her to Camp David for Thanksgiving vacation.
>
> **Keywords:** dating; family; humor; sexuality

Goldblatt, Stacey.

Stray. Delacorte Press, 2007. ISBN 9780385904483. J S

> Sixteen-year-old Natalie Kaplan has always listened to her strict veterinarian mother, until Carver Reed, a very cute recent high school graduate, moves into her house for the summer to intern at the dog hospital, and Natalie and Carver fall in love.
>
> **Keywords:** animals; dating; family; humor

McCafferty, Megan.

The Jessica Darling Series. S

Chronicles intelligent sassy Pineville, New Jersey, girl Jessica Darling as she grows from an observant teenager into a confused Columbia University student and postgraduate, who tries to find her way in the adult world living in New York City, all the while being connected in some way to her true love, Marcus Flutie.

Keywords: humor

🎗 *Sloppy Firsts*. Three Rivers Press, 2001. ISBN 9780609807903.

> The humorous diary entries of sixteen-year-old Jessica Darling after her best friend Hope moves away from Pineville, New Jersey. During her junior year Jess feels surrounded by shallow, materialistic classmates; is bored by her honors classes; writes honest editorials in the school paper; and begins a strange relationship with Marcus Flutie.
>
> **Keywords:** crushes; diary; family; friendship; school
>
> **Awards:** Quick Picks 2003

Second Helpings. Three Rivers Press, 2003. ISBN 9780609807910.

> During her senior year of high school, Jess takes Marcus Flutie's advice and starts dating his best friend and fellow brainiac, Len Levy, while secretly pin-

ing for Marcus and agonizing about her decision to attend Columbia University in New York City.

Keywords: college; dating; diary; family; friendship; prom; school; sexual content

Charmed Thirds. Crown, 2006. ISBN 9781400080427.

From her freshman summer interning for a magazine to the time she graduates from Columbia University, Jessica Darling has a few lovers, loses a few friends, works at a couple of lousy places, and moves out of her childhood home, all the while trying to get over her first love, Marcus.

Keywords: break-ups; college applications; dating; death; diary; family; friendship; sexual content; work

Fourth Comings. Crown Publishers, 2007. ISBN 9780307346506.

In early September, Jessica's plans to break up with Marcus because she does not want to be the girlfriend of a twenty-two-year-old college freshman are thrown for a loop when Marcus proposes. Unsure how to answer, Jessica returns to her tiny Park Slope sublet to deliberate, while working at a small magazine and babysitting her niece, Marin.

Keywords: dating; family; friendship; sexual content; work

Perfect Fifths. Crown Publishers, 2009. ISBN 9780307346520.

In the concluding volume of the series, Jessica bumps into Marcus at an airport as she is heading to her friend's Caribbean wedding. When Jessica misses her flight, she catches up with Marcus, whom she hasn't spoken to since she turned down his wedding proposal more than three years before.

Keywords: friendship; sexual content

Snadowsky, Daria.

Anatomy of a Boyfriend. **Delacorte Press, 2007. ISBN 9780385733205.** **S**

High school senior Dominique Baylor starts dating and subsequently falls in love with shy Wesley Gershwin, after they meet at a local football game. The inexperienced couple have their first sexual experiences together, including losing their virginity on prom night.

Keywords: college; dating; prom; sexual content

Sones, Sonya.

[Sophie and Robin]. **J** **S**

The following titles, although not formally a series, deal with the same characters and are listed in chronological order.

🏵 *What My Mother Doesn't Know.* Simon & Schuster Books for Young Readers, 2001. ISBN 9780689841149.

After her passion for kissing Dylan fizzles out, popular fourteen-year-old Sophie Stein realizes that Robin Murphy, the biggest dork in the ninth grade, is actually a sweet, talented artist, and during winter break when all her friends are away, Sophie and Robin quickly fall in love.

Keywords: dating; family; friendship kissing; novels in verse

Awards: BBYA 2002, Quick Picks 2002

🎗 *What My Girlfriend Doesn't Know.* Simon & Schuster Books for Young Readers, 2007. ISBN 9780689876028.

High school freshman Robin Murphy is distraught that his new girlfriend Sophie has become a social outcast because of him and only finds solace at the art class he is attending at Harvard College.

Keywords: college; dating; friendship; kissing; novels in verse

Awards: Quick Picks 2008

Break-ups and Hook-ups

Breaking up with your boyfriend can be devastating; in fact, the teen girls in the chick lit novels often feel that they may never recover from the loss. On the other hand, a prospective hook-up with a cute boy can really turn the heat up.

Barnholdt, Lauren.

Two*way Street. Simon Pulse, 2007. ISBN 9781416913184. **S**

In alternating chapters, recent exes Courtney and Jordan explain their feelings about the events leading up to and during their three-day road trip from their hometown in Florida to Boston University, including the real reason they broke up.

Keywords: break-ups; dating; family; friendship; road trip

Brian, Kate.

Megan Meade's Guide to the McGowan Boys. Simon & Schuster Books for Young Readers, 2005. ISBN 9781416900306. **S**

When army brat and only child Megan Meade refuses to relocate to South Korea with her military parents, they agree that Megan may spend her junior year of high school with the large McGowan family in Massachusetts. Megan quickly makes enemies with Doug, the oldest of the seven brothers; develops a huge crush on Evan McGowan, whose girlfriend Hailey becomes her chief rival on the soccer team; and in the end falls for the quiet brother, Flinn.

Keywords: Asperger's syndrome; crushes; family; sports

Clark, Catherine.

[Courtney Von Dragen Smith]. **J** **S**

The following titles, although not formally a series, deal with the same characters and are listed in chronological order.

Banana Splitsville. HarperTeen, p2008, c2000. ISBN 9780061367151.

After her college-bound boyfriend breaks up with her, Courtney Von Dragen Smith vows to spend her senior year boy free, become a vegan, and run for student council, while working at the Truth or Diary Café. (Originally titled *Truth or Dairy*.)

Keywords: dating; diary; family; friendship; romantic comedy; work

Rocky Road Trip. HarperTeen, p2008, c2001. ISBN 9780061367168.

At college, Courtney struggles with being a vegetarian in rural Wisconsin and maintaining a long-distance relationship with her boyfriend, Grant. (Originally titled *Wurst Case Scenario*.)

Keywords: break-ups; college; dating; diary; friendship; work

Davidson, Dana.

Played. **Jump at the Sun/Hyperion, 2005. ISBN 9780786836901.** S

To secure his place in an exclusive fraternity, Ian Striver, one of the biggest players at Cross High School, has three weeks to seduce Kylie Winship, a plain but sweet junior. After Ian wins the challenge, he confesses that he is really in love with Kylie.

Keywords: African American; dating; friendship; school; sexual content

Divine, L.

🏵 Drama High. S

Jayd Jackson is a sixteen-year-old, street savvy Compton native who is one of the few from the hood to be bused into South Bay High, a privileged white school known as Drama High. As a descendent of spiritual healers, Jayd is having more dreams that are prophesies of future events. Her grandmother Lynne Mae Williams, the neighborhood mystical healer, teaches Jayd about herbs, potions, and charms.

Keywords: African American; family; school
Awards: Quick Picks 2009

The Fight. Dafina Books for Young Readers, 2006. ISBN 9780758216335.

Despite her plans to start her junior year at South Bay High drama-free Jayd Jackson discovers that her former friend Misty is making trouble, her ex-boyfriend KJ is giving mixed messages, and KJ's new girlfriend Trecee is looking for a fight.

Keywords: break-ups; friendship

Second Chance. Dafina Books for Young Readers, 2006. ISBN 9780758216359.

Jayd ignores KJ's attempts to win her back and focuses on her budding relationship with Jeremy Weiner, a half-Jewish rich boy who is very popular at South Bay High.

Keywords: dating; friendship

Jayd's Legacy. Dafina Books for Young Readers, 2007. ISBN 9780758216373.

Race is on everyone's mind at Drama High as Jayd and Jeremy become an official couple, and Jayd's best friend Nellie is the first African American to be nominated for homecoming queen.

Keywords: dating; friendship

Frenemies. Dafina Books for Young Readers, 2008. ISBN 9780758225320.

> Jayd becomes confused about her relationship with Jeremy when her ex-boy-friend Rah kisses her; meanwhile Jeremy's ex-girlfriend Tania, who is pregnant, steals Nellie away from Jayd.

> **Keywords:** break-ups; dating; friendship; kissing

Lady J. Dafina Books/Kensington Publishing, 2008. ISBN 9780758225344.

> After her break-up with Jeremy, Jayd has her friends back together and lands the lead in the school play, but is having trouble at work and with her danger-ous older neighbor, Esmeralda.

> **Keywords:** acting; friendship

Courtin' Jayd. Dafina Books for Young Readers, 2008. ISBN 9780758225368.

> While Jayd questions what Rah's true intentions are, the drama is all about how Mickey is five weeks pregnant and decided to tell her boyfriend Nigel he is the father, although Mickey suspects another man, from the hood.

> **Keywords:** dating; friendship; pregnancy

Hustlin'. Dafina Books, 2009. ISBN 9780758231055.

> As the holiday season gets into full swing, Jayd is practicing for her lead in the school play, while her best friends Nellie and Mickey are constantly fight-ing about Mickey's pregnancy, and Rah's ex-girlfriend, Sandy, won't let him spend time with his young daughter.

> **Keywords:** acting; dating; friendship; pregnancy

Keep It Movin'. Dafina Books, 2009. ISBN 9780758231079.

> During Christmas vacation Jayd is worried about the piece of-junk car her fa-ther gave her, hair braiding, Rah's jealousy, and his fight for custody of his daughter Rahima. Then a real tragedy strikes.

> **Keywords:** dating; death; friendship; pregnancy

Ferraro, Tina.

Top Ten Uses for an Unworn Prom Dress. **Delacorte Press, 2006. ISBN 9780385903837.** **J** **S**

> Sophomore Nicolette Antonovich was devastated when Rascal dumped her right before the junior prom, so she comes up with ten possibilities for her perfect vin-tage dress, including wearing it to the homecoming dance with her best friend's older brother.

> **Keywords:** break-ups; dances; dating; friendship; humor

Freeman, Martha.

1,000 Reasons Never to Kiss a Boy. **Holiday House, 2007. ISBN 97808233420445.** **J** **S**

> Sixteen-year-old Jane swears off boys after she spies her first real boyfriend, Elliot Badgi, kissing another girl. She gets up to the forty-second reason never to kiss a boy when she meets that someone special who makes her forget the rules.

> **Keywords:** break-ups; dating; family; humor; kissing

Hoffmann, Kerry Cohen.

It's Not You, It's Me. Delacorte Press, 2009. ISBN 9780385736961. **J** **S**

Chronicles how sixteen-year-old Zoe goes from heartbreak and obsession to eventually moving on during the thirty-one days after she is dumped by her musician boyfriend, Henry.

Keywords: break-ups; dating; humor

Hogan, Mary.

Perfect Girl. HarperTempest, p2008, c2007. ISBN 9780060841102. **J** **S**

Ruthie Bayer goes behind her overprotective mother's back and enlists her glamorous Aunt Marty in a plot to woo her best friend and love, Perry Gould.

Keywords: crushes; dating; family; school

Kantor, Melissa.

The Breakup Bible. Hyperion, 2007. ISBN 9780786809622. **J** **S**

High school junior Jen Lewis is so devastated when her boyfriend breaks up with her for another girl on the school newspaper that she follows the commandments in Dr. Emerson's *Breakup Bible*.

Keywords: break-ups; dating; humor

Girlfriend Material. Disney/Hyperion Books, 2009. ISBN 9781423108498. **S**

When her parents informally separate, sixteen-year-old Kate spends her summer vacation with her mother, visiting wealthy friends in Cape Cod. There she gets a job teaching tennis and unexpectedly falls in love with Adam.

Keywords: dating; family; love; work

Kemp, Kristen.

The Dating Diaries. Push/Scholastic, 2004. ISBN 9780439622981. **J** **S**

After high school senior Katie James is dumped by her longtime boyfriend Paul, she gets a much-needed makeover and is determined to go on twelve dates in the six weeks before the senior prom.

Keywords: break-ups; dating; friendship; prom

Robar, Serena.

Giving up the V. Simon Pulse, 2009. ISBN 9781416975588. **S**

Since Spencer Davis is not sexually active, she has no plans to use the prescription for birth control pills she receives from her mom on her sixteenth birthday—until Benjamin Hopkins transfers to her school.

Keywords: dating; friendship; sexual content; sexuality

Ruby, Laura.

Good Girls. **HarperTempest, 2006. ISBN 9780060882242.** $\boxed{\text{S}}$

Sixteen-year-old honor student Audrey Porter's good girl reputation gets ruined when a photo of her performing oral sex on her crush, Luke DeSalvio, is passed around school. When her father sees the photo, Audrey has her first gynecological exam and evaluates her friends-with-benefits relationship with Luke.

Keywords: dating; family; prom; school; sexual content

Spooner, M.

Entr@pment: A High School Comedy in Chat. **Margaret K. McElderry Books, 2009. ISBN 9781416958895.** $\boxed{\text{J}}$ $\boxed{\text{S}}$

After high school junior Annie is dumped by her boyfriend, she convinces her friends Bliss and Tamra to assume false online identities to prove their boyfriends' fidelity. The novel is written in an instant messaging format.

Keywords: dating; friendship; humor

Van Draanen, Wendelin.

Confessions of a Serial Kisser. **Knopf, 2008. ISBN 9780375842481.** $\boxed{\text{S}}$

Not wanting to end up alone reading romance novels like her newly separated mother, high school junior Evangeline Logan goes on a quest to have a heart-stopping, life-changing kiss but ends up losing her best friend and getting a bad reputation.

Keywords: family; friendship; kissing

Wasserman, Robin.

<u>Seven Deadly Sins.</u> $\boxed{\text{S}}$

In small-town America, the seniors of Haven High are bored and looking for trouble. Ignored by their parents, they put most of their efforts into seducing each other. The seven-volume series reads like a soap opera in which the reader needs a chart to keep track of who is after whom. But it is not all fun and games when someone is killed in a car accident.

Keywords: crushes; friendship

Lust. Simon Pulse, 2005. ISBN 9780689877827.

All-American Adam and sweet Beth are so in love with each other that they are oblivious to their so-called friends' lusting after them and counting the days until they break up. At the just-for-seniors secret party that Harper organized, Adam's love is put to the test when newcomer Kaia sets her sights on him.

Keywords: dating; jealousy; school; sexual content

Envy. Simon Pulse, 2006. ISBN 9780689877834.

Despite their differences, Kane, Kaia, and Harper all join forces to break up Beth and Adam, whose relationship is already strained. Sexy Kaia also finds time to seduce her hot French teacher.

Keywords: break-ups; dating; school; sexual content

Pride. Simon Pulse, 2006. ISBN 9780689877841.

> Kane and Harper get what they want after they successfully break up Beth and Adam. Meanwhile, Miranda looks for love on a computer dating Web site, and to her surprise Kaia cannot stop thinking about the handsome pizza delivery boy who rescued her.

> **Keywords:** dating; school

Wrath. Simon Pulse, 2006. ISBN 9780689877858.

> While Harper tries to make amends, Beth and Miranda seek revenge by exposing their former friend's most embarrassing secrets to the entire school. Kaia could care less, because a lover is stalking her, and Miranda wonders what will happen after she fulfills her ultimate fantasy and hooks up with Kane.

> **Keywords:** dating; school

Sloth. Simon Pulse, 2006. ISBN 9781416907183.

> All the lies and deceptions are forgiven when Kaia tragically dies in a car accident and Harper is hospitalized. Miranda, Kane, and Adam try to reconnect with Harper, whose guilt over the accident has left her withdrawn; Reed and Beth find consolation in each other.

> **Keywords:** dating; death; school

Gluttony. Simon Pulse, 2007. ISBN 9781416907190.

> After trying to conceal their role in Kaia's death, Beth's, Harper's, and Kane's secrets are exposed when they join their classmates in Las Vegas and it is Adam, not Reed, who comes to Beth's rescue when she attempts suicide. Meanwhile, Kane is scared about starting a real relationship with Miranda.

> **Keywords:** dating; school

Greed. Simon Pulse, 2007. ISBN 9781416907206.

> Popular Harper wins the crown at the prom and eventually the heart of her only love, Adam. As graduation day approaches, there are unexpected break-ups, arrests, and sincere good-byes.

> **Keywords:** break-ups; dating; prom; school

Wells, Pamela.

[Sydney, Raven, Kelly, and Alexia]. **J** **S**

> The following titles, although not formally a series, deal with the same characters and are listed in chronological order.

The Heartbreakers. Point, 2007. ISBN 9780439026918.

> When high school juniors Sydney, Raven, and Kelly coincidentally are dumped by their boyfriends on the same night, they pledge to follow their single friend, Alexia's twenty-five rules of the break-up code to help them survive.

> **Keywords:** break-ups; dating; friendship; school

The Crushes. Point, 2008. ISBN 9780439026932.

> Best friends Alexia, Sydney, Raven, and Kelly trade their break-up code and vow to follow the forty-one rules of the crush code in the summer before their senior year, when their relationships are tested.

> **Keywords:** crushes; dating; friendship

Romantic Comedy

As in the movies, romantic comedies are sweet girl-meets-boy love stories with an amusing plot that almost always concludes with a happy ending.

Barkley, Brad, and Heather Hepler.

Dream Factory. **Dutton Books, 2007. ISBN 9780525478027. S**

> In alternating chapters, recent high school graduates Ella and Luke tell how they met and became friends, and try to answer the question, can two people really live happily ever after while working as costumed characters in Disney World?

> **Keywords:** family; work

Bergen, Lara.

Drama Queen. **Scholastic, 2007. ISBN 9780439929530. M**

> Best friends Charlie and Nicole try out for their junior high school's musical production of *Robin Hood* although sixth-graders rarely land a big role. Charlie is crushed by her small part, until she has to step in for the female lead opposite her crush on opening night.

> **Keywords:** acting; crushes; family; friendship

Bloss, Josie.

Band Geek Love. **Flux, 2008. ISBN 9780738713588. S**

> For the past three years Ellie Snow has been a devoted member of the school marching band. Now that she is a senior Ellie is thrilled to be the trumpet section leader, with a solo, until Connor, a new sophomore, joins the band and captures her heart.

> **Keywords:** crushes; friendship; marching bands; school

Burnham, Niki.

Scary Beautiful. **Simon Pulse, 2006. ISBN 9780689876196. J S**

> Beautiful Chloe Rand's perfect life changes at the start of her junior year when her boyfriend moves away, her girlfriends get jealous, and she falls for the class geek, Billy.

> **Keywords:** body image; break-ups; friendship; school

Cabot, Meg.

🏆 *The Boy Next Door.* Avon Trade, 2002. ISBN 9780060096199. **A**

Melissa (Mel) Fuller's boss at the *New York Journal* was already on her back about late assignments before her elderly neighbor, Mrs. Friedlander, is hospitalized, leaving behind an apartment full of pets. Despite the e-mails from the human relations department about her tardiness, Mel feels obligated to walk the Great Dane, Poco, every morning. When Mrs. F's attractive nephew Max decides to move in, he comes to Mel's rescue in more ways than one.

Keywords: dating; work
Awards: Quick Picks 2004

Every Boy's Got One. Avon Trade, 2005. ISBN 9780060096199. **A**

Jane is so thrilled to be the maid of honor at her best friend's secret wedding in Italy that she decides to write a travel log to remember all the details about her first trip abroad. Before Jane even steps on the plane, there is already a lot to write about, especially the best man, Cal Langdon, who infuriates Jane so much that she has no choice but to fall madly in love with him.

Keywords: friendship; wedding

Teen Idol. HarperCollins, 2004. ISBN 9780060096168. **J** **S**

Likable Jenny Greenley is assigned to keep the identity of teenage heartthrob Luke Stryker a secret, while he poses as a transfer student at Clayton High School to do research for a movie role.

Keywords: crushes; dating; friendship; school

Queen of Babble. **A**

With a big heart that matches her big mouth, twenty-two-year-old Lizzie Nichols's passion for vintage clothes has led to a degree in the history of fashion and a dream of owning her own wedding gown restoration store in New York City.

Keywords: family; fashion; friendship; humor; sexual content

Queen of Babble. William Morrow, 2006. ISBN 9780060851989.

After her graduation party, where she learns that she must complete a thesis before officially graduating with a degree in the history of fashion from the University of Michigan, Lizzie Nichols travels to London to stay with her new boyfriend, Andy, only to discover that Andy is a liar and a gambler. Then Lizzie joins her best friend Shari in France to help out at a friend's chateau, where Lizzie falls in love with the chateau owner's son, Jean-Luc (Luke).

Keywords: dating; wedding

Queen of Babble in the Big City. W. Morrow, 2007. ISBN 9780060852009.

Unbeknown to her Midwest parents, Lizzie Nichols moves into an upscale Fifth Avenue Apartment in New York City with her boyfriend Luke while looking for work in the wedding gown and vintage clothing industry. After landing a nonpaying position at a well-known French bridal gown restorer, Lizzie wonders if Luke is going to propose.

Keywords: lesbian; work

Queen of Babble Gets Hitched. William Morrow, 2008. ISBN 9780060852023.

Immediately after getting engaged to perfect Luke, Lizzie Nichols starts to have doubts, because she breaks out in hives whenever she thinks about the wedding and her stomach does flip-flops when she thinks about Luke's best friend, Chaz. While Luke is away in Paris, Chaz and Lizzie confess their feelings at her grandmother's funeral in Ann Arbor, Michigan.

Keywords: dating; death; lesbian; wedding; work

Center, Katherine.

The Bright Side of Disaster. Ballantine Books, p2008, c2007. ISBN 9780345497963. **A**

Jenny Harris unexpectedly becomes a single mother when her live-in rocker fiancé, Dean Murphy, walks out the night before her baby Maxie is born; he only returns after Jenny has fallen for her attractive single neighbor, John Gardener.

Keywords: break-ups; motherhood

Clark, Catherine.

Icing on the Lake. Avon Books, 2006. ISBN 9780060815349. **J S**

High school senior Kirsten spends a month in St. Paul, Minnesota, helping out her recently injured older sister Gretchen while hoping to keep her New Year's resolution to find a date for an upcoming ski trip with friends. Kirsten quickly finds two candidates, but unfortunately it turns out that Sean and Conor are brothers.

Keywords: dating; family

Maine Squeeze. Avon, 2004. ISBN 9780060567255. **S**

The summer before starting college, Colleen Templeton has her island home off the coast of Maine all to herself while her parents are in Europe. Colleen spends her summer vacation working at Bobb's Lobster Restaurant and trying to get close to Ben; then her ex-boyfriend Evan shows up.

Keywords: dating; work

Picture Perfect. HarperTeen, 2008. ISBN 9780061374975. **J S**

During her family beach vacation, seventeen-year-old Emily Matthias reunites with her old friends Spencer, Adam, and Heather; explores photography; and pursues a fling with the cute surfer next door.

Keywords: family; friendship; vacation

So Inn Love. HarperTeen, 2007. ISBN 9780061139048. **S**

Before starting college in the fall, Liza McKenzie hopes to get a tan, make friends, and find romance while working at The Tides Inn on the coast of Rhode Island.

She ends up being assigned to the housecleaning crew and snubbed by her old friends, and hanging out with the cute lifeguard Hayden only is private.

Keywords: dating; friendship; humor; work

Collins, Yvonne, and Sandy Rideout.

Girl v. Boy. **Hyperion, 2008. ISBN 9781423101574.** S

When Chicago sophomore Luisa Perez accepts her surprise offer to be the anonymous female columnist writing about Dunfield High's fund-raising competition, she tries to balance working at a diner, babysitting her niece, and dating while trying to uncover her male counterpart.

Keywords: dating; family; friendship; Hispanic American; school; work

Davis, Stephie.

Smart Boys and Fast Girls. **Smooch, 2005. ISBN 9780843953985.** J S

High school sophomore Natalie Page has always been viewed as one of the guys, until she makes the Mapleville High variety cross-county track team and is noticed by the popular boys' team captain, Zach Fulton. Unfortunately Natalie has her heart set on her studious math tutor, Matt.

Keywords: crushes; dating; sports

Who Needs Boys? **Smooch, 2005. ISBN 9780843953978.** J S

When fifteen-year-old Allie Morrison's father cancels her trip to spend the summer vacation with him in Los Angeles because his fiancée is pregnant, Allie figures working at her Latin teacher's farmstand with her best friends will be a great way to meet cute older boys.

Keywords: dating; family; friendship; work

Deutsch, Stacia, and Rhody Cohon.

In the Stars. **Simon Pulse, 2007. ISBN 9781416948759.** J S

Eight weeks before Sylvie Townsend's high school graduation, it appears that her best friend, Cherise Gregory's, prediction that love is heading her way is coming true when Sylvie notices Adam, a new boy at school.

Keywords: family; friendship; school; work

Dokey, Cameron.

How Not to Spend Your Senior Year. **Simon Pulse, 2004. ISBN 9780689867033.** S

After moving with her father, Chase, over twenty times, Josephine "Jo" O'Connor quickly adjusts to her new life in Seattle, Washington, by making friends with Elaine Golden and catching the eye of popular Alex Crawford. Just as it seems that Alex is going to ask Jo to the prom, Chase informs Jo that they have to fake their deaths because he is in the Witness Protection Program; after this Jo returns to Beacon High as Claire Calloway.

Keywords: family; friendship; moving; prom; school

Ferraro, Tina.

How to Hook a Hottie. Delacorte Press, 2008. ISBN 9780385904445. **J** **S**

After Brandon, the most popular senior, asks out seventeen-year-old Kate DelVecchio, she starts a matchmaking service with her six-point plan to catch a hottie, with the goal of raising $5,000 by graduation.

Keywords: dating; family; school

Friedman, Aimee.

A Novel Idea. Simon Pulse, 2006. ISBN 978416907855. **J** **S**

High school junior Norah Bloom starts a book club at a local bookstore in Park Slope, Brooklyn, to have an extracurricular activity on her college applications and improve her love life.

Keywords: crushes; school

Guarente, G. P.

Hook, Line & Sinker. Razorbill, 2005. ISBN 9781595140111. **M** **J**

After each broken heart, fifteen-year-old Fiona Delmar buys a fish at Pet Planet, names it after her former crush, and puts the fish in her tank of clueless boys. On the bright side, all of her trips to Pet Planet bring her closer to Jonas, the cute boy who works in the fish department.

Keywords: acting; crushes; family

Hapka, Catherine.

Love on Cue. Simon Pulse, 2009. ISBN 97801416968573. **M** **J**

Off-stage Maggie Tannery is a shy high school student, but onstage she truly shines. So she is naturally excited to find out that her crush Derek will also be trying out for their school's spring production of *Romeo and Juliet*. When Maggie discovers it will be a musical, she turns to cute Nico Vasquez for voice lessons.

Keywords: acting; body image; crushes; school

Something Borrowed. Simon Pulse, 2008. ISBN 9781416954415. **J** **S**

When her boyfriend breaks up with her two weeks before her sister's wedding, seventeen-year-old Ava Hamilton borrows her best friend's boyfriend Jason as a date and unexpectedly ends up falling for him.

Keywords: dating; friendship; wedding

Harrison, Emma.

Tourist Trap. Avon Books, 2006. ISBN 9780060847357. **S**

On Lake Logan in upstate New York the summer before starting college, horse-back-riding enthusiast Cassandra Grace gives riding lessons on her parent's farm to save enough money to enter an upcoming horse-jumping competition. Then she gets distracted by Jared Kent.

Keywords: friendship

Hawthorne, Rachel.

The Boyfriend League. HarperTeen, 2007. ISBN 9780061138379. **J S**

> Dani and her best friend Bird convince their parents to host a Ragland Rattler College baseball player for the summer so they can meet cute baseball players. Bird quickly gets a boyfriend, while Dani falls for Jason, the one boy who is strictly off limits.
>
> **Keywords:** crushes; sports

Snowed In. HarperTeen, p2008, c2008. ISBN 9780061138362. **J S**

> Seventeen-year-old Ashleigh Sneaux adjusts to the climate and small town life when she moves with her divorced mother from Texas to snowy Michigan to run a bed and breakfast. After flirting with Chase and Josh Winter, Ashleigh starts secretly dating Josh, until his longtime girlfriend, Natalie, finds out.
>
> **Keywords:** dating; friendship; kissing; moving

Thrill Ride. Avon Books, 2006. ISBN 9780060839543. **J S**

> To get far away from the arguments about her sister Sarah's upcoming wedding, Megan Holloway leaves her new boyfriend Nick and takes a job at an amusement park the summer before her senior year; there she develops a crush on her roommate's brother Parker.
>
> **Keywords:** dating; family; work

James, Sabrina.

[North Ridge High School]. **J S**

> The following titles, although not formally a series, deal with the same characters and are listed in chronological order.

Secret Santa. Scholastic, 2007. ISBN 9780439026956.

> North Ridge High School students hope to impress their crushes when they participate in a schoolwide "Secret Santa" project before the upcoming Christmas Dance.
>
> **Keywords:** crushes; dances; kissing; school

Be Mine. Point, 2009. ISBN 9780545097390.

> Jennifer has to find a boyfriend quick after she tells Claudia that she plans on winning North Ridge High's most romantic couple contest at the Valentine's Dance.
>
> **Keywords:** dances; dating; friendship; school

Krulik, Nancy E.

Puppy Love. Simon Pulse, 2008. ISBN 9781416961529. **J S**

> In New York City, dog-walker Alana Marks is dating Sammy, but she finds herself confiding in and complaining to Connor, until she realizes that Connor is the son of one of her customers.
>
> **Keywords:** break-ups; dating; kissing; work

Lyles, Whitney.

Party Games. **Simon Pulse, 2008. ISBN 9781416959137.** **J** **S**

> Recently fifteen-year-old Sara Sullivan has been the assistant in her mother's successful event planning company, and now she is in charge of her first account. Unfortunately for Sara, the sweet-sixteen party she has to plan is for the demanding, self-centered socialite Dakota London, who seems interested in Sara's guitar-playing crush, Ian.
>
> **Keywords:** crushes; family; sweet-sixteen party; work

McCarthy, Erin.

Heiress for Hire. **Berkley Sensation, p2007, c2006. ISBN 9780425214848.** **A**

> When twenty-six-year-old Amanda Delmar's wealthy father cuts her off financially, she convinces Danny Tucker, a sweet Ohio farmer, to hire her to take care of his eight-year-old daughter, Piper.
>
> **Keywords:** family; humor; work

McClymer, Kelly.

Getting to Third Date. **Simon Pulse, 2006. ISBN 9781416914792.** **J** **S**

> College freshman Katelyn Spears gives straightforward romantic advice in the *Campus Times* "Mother Hubbard" column. When the readers discover that Mother Hubbard has never had a third date, eighteen-year-old Katelyn agrees to look in her little pink book for three potential candidates, even though she has an enormous crush on Tyler, the newspaper's editor.
>
> **Keywords:** college; crushes; dating

Ostow, Micol.

Crush Du Jour. **Simon Pulse, 2007. ISBN 9781416950271.** **J** **S**

> Sixteen-year-old Laine Harper decides to keep an active schedule rather than focus on boys, until she signs up to co-teach a cooking class at the local community center with Seth McFadden, a cute senior. Their relationship begins to heat up while Laine waitresses at Hype, Seth's family restaurant, until Laine's restaurant critic mother writes a scathing review.
>
> **Keywords:** crushes; family

30 Guys in 30 Days. **Simon Pulse, 2005. ISBN 9781416902782.** **J** **S**

> Newly single college freshman Claudia Clarkson has been out of the dating game so long that she does not know how to flirt with the many cute boys on campus, especially the newspaper's arts editor, Gabe Flynn. Therefore her new roommate, Charlie Norton, suggests that Claudia talk to a different guy every day for thirty days to practice.
>
> **Keywords:** college; crushes; friendship

Palmer, Robin.

Geek Charming. Speak, 2009. ISBN 9780142411223. **J** **S**

After geeky Josh rescues Dylan's very expensive handbag from a mall fountain, she reluctantly agrees to star in his documentary about the popular crowd at Castle Heights High School. The two strike up a surprising friendship.

Keywords: break-ups; cliques; college applications; dating; friendship; school

Ponti, Jamie.

Sea of Love. Simon Pulse, 2008. ISBN 9781416967910. **J** **S**

During her senior year of high school, Darby is miserable when her father moves the family from New York City to Coconut Beach, Florida, so they can own and manage the Seabreeze Hotel. But then Zach Miller, a local boy who works in the hotel part-time, notices her. Unfortunately for Darby, her New York City boyfriend shows up at the hotel in time for the annual Valentine's Day Cupid Ball.

Keywords: dating; moving; work

Rallison, Janette.

How to Take the Ex out of Ex-boyfriend. Putnam, 2007. ISBN 9780399246173. **J** **S**

Sixteen-year-old Giovanni and her popular boyfriend Jesse become rivals and temporarily break up when they become the campaign managers for opposing student council presidential candidates.

Keywords: break-ups; dating; school

It's a Mall World After All. Walker, 2006. ISBN 9780802788535. **J** **S**

In between her part-time job at the mall and her National Honor Society activities, Charlotte is determined to prove that her best friend's boyfriend is cheating.

Keywords: dating; friendship; work

[Samantha and Chelsea]. **J** **S**

The following titles, although not formally a series, deal with the same characters and are listed in chronological order.

All's Fair in Love, War, and High School. Walker Books, 2005. ISBN 978 0802777256.

Samantha Taylor knows her 810 SAT score will not get her into a good college, so this cheerleader decides to run for student-body president, to demonstrate her leadership potential.

Keywords: cheerleading; humor; school

Revenge of the Cheerleaders. Walker, 2007. ISBN 9780802789990.

Seventeen-year-old Chelsea is a popular cheerleader who decides to get back at her younger sister's rocker boyfriend, Rick, after his new

CD, *Cheerleaders in Action*, makes fun of Chelsea and her friends. A companion to *All's Fair in Love, War, and High School*.

Keywords: cheerleading; cliques; dating; school; sisters

Roberts, Laura Peyton.

The Queen of Second Place. **Laurel-Leaf Books, 2006, c2005. ISBN 9780440238713.** **J** **S**

Tired of always coming in second to her archrival Sterling Carter, fifteen-year-old Cassie Howard enters a competition with popular Sterling to see who will become The Snow Queen and will win the heart of the new transfer student, Kevin Matthews.

Keywords: crushes; dances; school

Ruditis, P. J.

Love, Hollywood Style. **Simon Pulse, 2008. ISBN 9781416951384.** **J** **S**

Inspired by her summer job as a movie studio tour guide, college freshman Tracy Vance borrows ideas from her favorite romantic comedy movies to get the attention of her crush, Connor.

Keywords: crushes; work

Toliver, Wendy.

Miss Match. **Simon Pulse, 2009. ISBN 9781416964131.** **J** **S**

Under the pseudonym Miss Match, sixteen-year-old Sasha Finnegan uses her talents to run a successful online matchmaking service for high school students. Then her crush, Derek Urban, asks Miss Match to set him up with Sasha's popular sister Maddie for the upcoming homecoming dance.

Keywords: dating; sisters

Vail, Rachel.

If We Kiss. **HarperTrophy, p2006, c2005. ISBN 9780060569167.** **J** **S**

Charlie has her first kiss with Kevin outside school one morning. But before Charlie has a chance to tell her best friend Tess about her feelings for Kevin, she spies the pair of them kissing, too.

Keywords: dating; family; first kiss; friendship; kissing

Walker, Melissa.

Lovestruck Summer. **HarperTeen, 2009. ISBN 9780061715860.** **J** **S**

Recent high school graduate and indie music fanatic Priscilla "Quinn" Parker moves in with her sorority president cousin Penny for the summer so she can intern at Amalgam Records in Austin, Texas, and find the perfect boyfriend. She doesn't expect country-loving jock Russ to capture her heart.

Keywords: family; internship; music

Weisberger, Lauren.

Everyone Worth Knowing. **Simon & Schuster, 2005. ISBN 9780743262293.** **A**

Bette Robinson has spent the past five years since college working long hours in a boring investment bank and reading romance novels at night. She suddenly quits her job and lands a position in one of the hottest PR companies in Manhattan.

Keywords: dating; family; sexual content; work

Weyn, Suzanne.

South Beach Sizzle. **Simon Pulse, 2005. ISBN 9781416900115.** 🅂

Recent high school graduates Lula Cruz and her best friend Jeff leave New York City to work in South Beach, Florida, for the summer, where Lula enters a local band concert and falls for Enrique, her band's biggest competition.

Keywords: friendship; music

Wood, Maryrose.

Sex Kittens and Horn Dawgs Fall in Love. **Delacorte Press, 2006. ISBN 9780385902960.** 🅹 🅂

Fourteen-year-old Felicia and her best friends Jess and Kat call the girls at their alternative Manhattan high school sex kittens, and the boys are called horn dawgs. When Felicia falls for Matthew, a horn dawg who is seriously interested in science, she asks Matthew to help her research love's X-factor for the upcoming science fair.

Keywords: crushes; friendship; school

Inspirational/Christian

With themes of compassion and forgiveness, faith is woven throughout these stories of young women. The heroines may have the same struggles and weaknesses as their classmates, but their choices are influenced by their faith and values.

Billingsley, ReShonda Tate.

The Good Girlz. 🅹 🅂

For different reasons, Camille, Angel, Jasmine, and Alexis join the Good Girlz, a community service group sponsored by the Zion Hill Missionary Baptist Church in Houston, founded by the pastor's wife. Miss Rachel Adams is a patient leader who provides spiritual guidance. Over time the members of Good Girlz grow to depend on each other as they share their secrets, struggles, and desires. Each book in the series is a story based on one of the Ten Commandments.

Keywords: African American; friendship; Hispanic American

Nothing But Drama. Pocket Books, 2006. ISBN 9781416525608.

In alternating chapters, each girl reveals that in the beginning she was skeptical about the Good Girlz. Tough Alexis is persuaded by Miss Rachel to join the group, while wealthy Alexis signs up just to complete a community service requirement, Camille is court-ordered to join Good

Girlz for hiding her jailbird boyfriend from the police, and Angel is there because she is hiding her pregnancy from her mother. The theme is "honor thy parents."

Keywords: dating; family; pregnancy

Blessings in Disguise. Pocket Books, 2007. ISBN 9781416525615.

Tired of being overworked and underappreciated by her large family, fifteen-year-old Jasmine seeks out the father she never knew. To impress Donovan, her first real boyfriend, Jasmine goes against what she knows is right, takes stolen clothing from the other members of the Good Girlz, and is arrested.

Keywords: dances; dating; family; kissing

With Friends Like These. Pocket Books, 2007. ISBN 9781416525622.

Friends become rivals as the four high school juniors compete to be the hostess of *Teen Talks*, a new teen TV talk show. The theme is "thou shall not bear false witness."

Keywords: dating; family

Getting Even. Pocket Books, 2008. ISBN 9781416558736.

When Alexis and Jasmine discover that they are both dating Anthony Vickers, they plot to get back at the two-timing football player.

Keywords: dating

Fair-weather Friends. Pocket Books, 2008. ISBN 9781416558767.

After watching their fabulous step show performance, Camille convinces Jasmine and Angel to pledge the new exclusive high school sorority. When Angel does not get into Theta Ladies because she is Hispanic, Jasmine and Camille have to decide if they want to be a part of a racist group.

Keywords: school

Mackall, Dandi Daley.

Faithgirlz! Blog On. M

Gracie Doe, Annie Lind, Jazz Fletcher, and Storm Novelo are young teenage girls from different backgrounds who become friends and connect with God after Gracie hires them to help with her blog Web site.

Grace Notes. Zonderkidz, 2006. ISBN 9780310710936.

As an outsider at Big Lake High School, sophomore Gracie Doe prefers to write about her classmates in her anonymous blog, until a new girl discovers her secret identity and Grace learns how to connect with someone else.

Keywords: family; friendship; religion; school

Love, Annie. Zonderkidz, 2006. ISBN 9780310710943.

Annie Lind, who gives relationship advice as Professor Love for the Web site, neglects her friends when her dream date asks her to the Homecoming Dance.

Keywords: dances; dating; friendship

Just Jazz. Zonderkidz, 2006. ISBN 9780310710950.

When her parents tell Jasmine "Jazz" Fletcher that she has to start selling her art or stop working in a studio, she hopes winning the citywide art contest will prove that being an artist is her true calling.

Keywords: family; friendship; religion; self-acceptance

Storm Rising. Zonderkidz, 2006. ISBN 9780310710967.

Used to being the center of attention with her bright clothes and makeup, high school freshman Storm Novelo keeps a secret from everyone expect Annie, Jazz, and Grace: she really is a genius. Finally she learns to accept who she really is.

Keywords: family; friendship; religion; self-acceptance

Grace Under Pressure. Zonderkidz, 2007. ISBN 9780310712633.

Grace asks for God's help when she feels the burden of completing her school newspaper assignment, writing her blog, and difficulties at home with her mother.

Keywords: family, religion, school

Upsetting Annie. Zonderkidz, 2007. ISBN 9780310712640.

Annie becomes jealous when her pretty cousin Shawna returns from Paris to live with her and quickly becomes the center of attention

Keywords: cheerleading; family; jealousy; school

Jazz Off-key. Zonderkidz, 2007. ISBN 9780310712657.

Jazz's excitement about her one-woman art show at the Big Lake Spring Fling turns into uncontrollable rage when her younger sister, Kendra, ruins the paintings she was going to showcase.

Keywords: family; religion

Storm Warning. Zonderkidz, 2007. ISBN 9780310712664.

Determined to make her father proud and perhaps snap him out of his depression, Storm joins the Big Lake High School Quiz Bowl team, even though the other members strive to make her lose.

Keywords: family; friendship; school

Moore, Stephanie Perry.

Work What You Got. **Kensington, 2009. ISBN 9780758225429.** S

College sophomore Hayden relies on her Christian faith to guide her as she pledges Beta Gamma Pi sorority, participates in dangerous hazing events, and follows her dating creed.

Keywords: African American; dating; sororities

I didn't want to be a child, and I didn't want to be a woman, and sometimes I just didn't know how to be in between.

—Lauren Myracle, *Eleven*

Chapter 2

Gossip Chick Lit

Ever wondered what the lives of the chosen ones are really like? Well, I'm going to tell you, because I'm one of them.

—Cecily von Ziegesar, *Gossip Girl*

Despite being classified as chick lit, "gossip lit"—also known as privileged lit— has very little in common with traditional girl-next-door humor. While readers of humorous chick lit will get a few laughs with their romance, readers of gossip lit get a steamy plot and revealing exposés that fulfill their own Hollywood fantasies. Most gossip lit provides a window into the world of the wealthy, whether it be models, beautiful socialites, heiresses, superstars, or otherwise sophisticated people whose photos appear in *The New York Times* style section or are featured in *Teen Vogue*. Part of the enjoyment of gossip chick lit is being a voyeur to a glamorous lifestyle that is a fantasy otherwise only witnessed on teen dramas. The setting for this subgenre is typically New York City, Los Angeles, or the elite boarding schools of New England.

Although growing up as a beautiful, wealthy girl who travels to exciting places, wears trendy clothes, and dates hot guys is an unattainable fantasy, readers can relate to the other heroine often present in gossip lit. She is a normal yet attractive girl-next-door type, thrust into the world of the elite by winning a scholarship, landing a glamorous internship, or accepting a nanny position with a rich and powerful family. Known as "assistant lit," the premise of this category is an exposé that reveals the secrets of the elite world.

The cover designs for gossip chick lit are also strikingly different. Like the novels themselves, the fashion-conscious designs are suggestive; instead of cartoons, polished photographs of models grace the covers. Typically the photos only show parts of girls' bodies. On the cover of *Au Pairs* is a photo of three white girls in skimpy bikinis, and the original *Gossip Girl* cover is a photo of three girls in trendy clothes who are clearly the "it" girls at the party. When we do see girls' faces, they are the faces of flawless models, as found on the cover of *The Clique*. Without using words, the covers tell us that these girls are beautiful, and we know we want to be one of them.

To amplify the importance of fashion as well as embracing consumer culture, the newest trend in gossip lit covers is a pattern reminiscent of designers' logos, such as Louis Vuitton and Coach. In fact, gossip lit can be very educational for aspiring fashionistas. Many books read like a guide to which designers are hot and which lip gloss will give the right look.

Successful series books with an ensemble cast dominate privileged lit. The biggest hit so far has been Cecily von Ziegesar's <u>Gossip Girl</u>. Like the characters in the series, von Ziegesar is an insider who grew up in the world of the chosen few. She reportedly based the series on her own experiences in a private school on the Upper East Side.

Although the <u>Gossip Girl</u> series was written for teens, twenty-somethings have been seen reading these salacious books centered on the lives of wealthy New York City teens. The series has a reputation for being racy, yet like most reputations, it is exaggerated. Yes, most of the characters smoke cigarettes and drink alcohol and yes, a few characters smoke marijuana, but most only talk about who is doing drugs rather than partaking in it themselves. The books also have a reputation for being smutty. In the first few novels several characters are virgins contemplating when is the right time, and "hooking up" usually means kissing in the corner at a party. As the series progresses, so does the sexual activity of the characters.

However, despite the series' popularity, librarians should be careful about which of these must-haves they decide to add to a middle school or children's department. Some parents and critics have expressed concern that the casual sex, drug use, and emphasis on physical rather than inner beauty found in some gossip chick lit makes it too racy for their tweens.

Chapter Organization

Taking into account the popularity of the gossip lit subgenre, the following bibliography is a selected list of titles that represent what is currently in print; it is not intended to be inclusive. Titles in this chapter are divided into categories that share a similar theme or quality, such as young women working in the fashion industry. All series books are arranged in chronological order. This includes prequels that may have been published after the original series was complete.

Boarding School

Often in a quiet, posh New England neighborhood an outsider, possibly a transfer or scholarship student, hobnobs with the beautiful offspring of the rich and alumni. Once the outsider understands that boarding school students have their own rules and code to follow, she is accepted by her peers.

Archer, Lily.

The Poison Apples. **Feiwel and Friends, 2007. ISBN 9780312367626.** ◼J ◼S

After being sent away to Putnam Mount McKinsey, an elite boarding school in rural Massachusetts, fifteen-year-olds Molly Miller, Alice Bingley-Beckerman, and Reena Paruchuri form The Poison Apples Club, a society of mistreated stepdaughters, have a mission to take revenge on their evil stepmothers.

Keywords: boarding school; East Indian American; family; friendship

Brian, Kate.

Private. [S]

Reed Brennan's dreams come true when she receives a partial scholarship to one of the top-ranked schools in the country. She happily leaves behind her prescription-drug-addicted mom in suburban Pennsylvania for the ivy walls at Easton Academy, where the school code is "Tradition. Honor. Excellence." On her first day at Easton, Reed notices the Billings Girls, named after their exclusive dormitory; Noelle Lange, Ariana Osgood, Kiran Hayes, and Taylor Bell are the most popular girls, and Reed will do anything to be included in this clique. Reed quickly realizes that the drama of getting into Billings is just the beginning.

Keywords: dating

Last Christmas: Private Prequel. Simon Pulse, 2008. ISBN 9781416913696.

Before Reed Brennan ever set foot on campus, Ariana Osgood was a popular, overachieving junior with a perfect boyfriend and a few well-kept secrets. Then a Christmas vacation blizzards traps her on campus with bad boy Thomas Pearson, and Ariana begins her downward spiral.

Private. Simon Pulse, 2006. ISBN 9781416918738.

Once she leaves her depressing home life, Reed Brennan is determined to make a new beginning for herself as a sophomore at Easton Academy. Reed quickly captures the attention of cocky Thomas Pearson and ethereal Ariana Osgood. After a challenging initiation process, Reed is transformed from "new girl" to "Billings Girl."

Keywords: cliques; family; friendship

Invitation Only. Simon Pulse, 2006. ISBN 9781416918745.

After Reed's boyfriend, Thomas, mysteriously disappears from campus, her only hope is that he will show up at Legacy, an ultra-exclusive party for private school students in New York City. Meanwhile, Reed is being blackmailed by her roommate into finding evidence against her friends.

Keywords: friendship; mystery

Untouchable. Simon Pulse, 2006. ISBN 9781416918752.

The police question everyone at Easton Academy when popular Thomas Pearson is found dead on campus. Reed is torn about her feelings for Josh Hollis, and mourning Thomas, when Josh is arrested for murder.

Keywords: friendship; murder; mystery

Confessions. Simon Pulse, 2007. ISBN 9781416918769.

Once Reed realizes the truth, she is determined to prove Josh's innocence by convincing a witness to speak to the police. Once all charges against Josh have been dropped, Reed discovers that one of the Billings Girls committed the crime.

Keywords: mystery

Inner Circle. Simon Pulse, 2007. ISBN 9781416950417.

> Despite the headmaster's mandate, the current Billings leader, Cheyenne Martin, organizes the traditional initiation rituals for Constance, Missy, Lorna, Kiki, Astrid, and Sabine. Throughout the semester Reed clashes with Cheyenne about the new girls and her boyfriend, Josh.

> **Keywords:** friendship

Legacy. Simon Pulse, 2008. ISBN 9781416950424.

> After Cheyenne Martin's funeral, Noelle Lange returns, and Reed's first task as the new president of Billings Hall is get Easton Academy the coveted invitation to Legacy. At Legacy, Reed and Josh break up after Reed hooks up with Noelle's longtime boyfriend Dash.

> **Keywords:** break-ups; death; friendship

Ambition. Simon Pulse, 2008. ISBN 9781416958826.

> Despite being upset about her recent break-up and new suspicions about Cheyenne's suicide, Reed convinces the new headmaster that she can raise $5 million to save Billings Hall by organizing a glamorous fund-raiser in New York City.

> **Keywords:** break-ups; friendship; mystery

Revelation. Simon Pulse, 2008. ISBN 9781416958833.

> After a video of Reed kissing Noelle's boyfriend Dash is spread around campus, Reed returns from Thanksgiving vacation to discover that she has unanimously been kicked out Billings and now has to reside in a crummy single in Pemberly, next to Ivy Slade, a girl who is dating Reed's ex and who possibly killed Cheyenne.

> **Keywords:** friendship; mystery

Paradise Lost. Simon Pulse, 2009. ISBN 9781416958840.

> Now that Cheyenne's murderer has been revealed, Reed accepts Noelle's invitation to join her and several Easton Academy students on an exclusive Caribbean cruise. During the vacation Reed attracts the most sought-after guy, Upton Giles.

> **Keywords:** friendship; sexual content; vacation

Suspicion. Simon Pulse, 2009. ISBN 9781416958857.

> During her vacation at Saint Barths, Reed's life is threatened by one of Upton's secret lovers.

> **Keywords:** dating; kissing; mystery; vacation

Privilege. S

In this companion to Kate Brian's <u>Private</u> series, Ariana Osgood is expelled from Easton Academy and sent to the Brenda T. Trumbull Correctional Facility for Women for murdering her ex-boyfriend, Thomas Pearson. Determined to return to her former life, Ariana escapes the facility and takes on the identity of Briana Leigh Covington, a Dallas socialite.

Privilege. Simon Pulse, 2008. ISBN 9781416967590.

Ariana Osgood has been plotting her escape from the Brenda T. Trumbull Correctional Facility for Women for the past two years, and now her time has come after a fake suicide attempt. Ariana successfully runs away from the facility and moves in with her cellmate's former best friend, sixteen-year-old Briana Leigh Covington, with a plan to steal her money and get revenge.

Keywords: death; friendship, murder

Beautiful Disaster. Simon & Schuster BYFR, 2009. ISBN 9781416967606.

After killing Briana Leigh Covington, Ariana assumes her identity, dyes her hair, and enrolls as a junior at the elite Atherton-Pryce boarding school, where she is invited to join the most coveted dorm in campus.

Keywords: cliques; crushes

Brown, Hobson.

The Upper Class. s

Like many boarding schools in New England, Wellington is a home away from home for the children of the powerful and social elite. Wellington students are expected to maintain the time-honored traditions that come with good breeding and class.

Keywords: dating

The Upper Class. HarperTeen, 2007. ISBN 9780060850821.

Roommates Laine Hunt and Nikki Olivetti are both transfer students at Wellington boarding school in Greenwich, Connecticut. Although the in crowd immediately accept Laine, and Nikki finds a boyfriend, both girls feel that they do not belong.

Keywords: family; friendship

Miss Educated. HarperTeen, 2007. ISBN 9780060850838.

Determined to successfully complete his second semester at Wellington and not be sent to military school, Chase Dobbs tries to avoid getting in trouble when he is assigned to be lab partners with eccentric Parker Cole. The unlikely pair immediately bond after they make a surprising discovery, just as Laine Hunt makes an unexpected return.

Keywords: death; school; sexual content

Off Campus. HarperTeen, 2008. ISBN 9780060850845.

Before heading back to school for a second year at Wellington, Nikki Olivetti spends a week with her college-bound boyfriend and meets new transfer student Delia Breton. Nikki and Delia quickly hit it off, as rumors fly on campus about Delia's wild past.

Keywords: friendship; sexual content

Crash Test. HarperTeen, 2008. ISBN 9780060850852.

> While Laine listens to her therapist and tries new things like spending time with Noah, Parker's new friend Jamie Drake introduces her to prescription drugs.
>
> **Keywords:** acting; drug addiction; friendship; sexual content

Gramont, Nina de.

Gossip of the Starlings. **Algonquin Books of Chapel Hill, 2008. ISBN 978-1565125650. A**

> In 1984, after being caught in bed with her boyfriend, John Paul, Catherine Morrow is sent to the Ester Percy School for Girls in New England, where she befriends the troubled senator's daughter, Skye Butterfield.
>
> **Keywords:** dating; death; family; friendship; sexual content

Lawrence, Sara.

Those Girls. **S**

> At Stagmont, England's most exclusive boarding school for girls, seventeen-year-old Jinx Slater and her close friends in Tanner House enjoy sneaking out, partying, and older boys.
>
> **Keywords:** friendship

Those Girls. Razorbill, 2007. ISBN 9781595141699.

> When glamorous Stella Fox joins the girls at Stagmont two weeks into the term, Liberty Latiffe falls under her spell, despite her best friend Jinx Slater's warnings. Liberty ends up displeasing her strict Muslim father.
>
> **Keywords:** dating; family; school; sexual content

Crush Worthy. Razorbill, 2008. ISBN 9781595141736.

> After a fun New Year's Eve party, Jinx is left trying to interpret Jamie's mixed messages, while also uncovering a plan to take over the school that involves beautiful Russian triplets and their bodyguard.
>
> **Keywords:** break-ups; crushes; family; mystery

Lockhart, E.

🏅 *The Disreputable History of Frankie Landau-Banks.* **Hyperion, 2008. ISBN 9780786838189. J S**

> Frances "Frankie" Landau-Banks's transformation over the summer into a real beauty attracts the attention of Matthew Livingston, the most popular senior at Alabaster Prep boarding school. When Frankie discovers that like her father, Matthew is a member of the Loyal Order of the Basset Hounds, she tries to infiltrate the all-male secret society.
>
> **Keywords:** dating; humor
>
> **Awards:** BBYA 2009

Peterfreund, Diana.

Ivy League. 🅐

Like every previous literary magazine editor, Amy Haskel expects to be selected to join Quill & Ink, one of the many secret societies at Eli University. However, Amy is surprised when she is asked to join Rose & Grave, one of the oldest and most elite secret societies in the country. Historically a male-only society, Rose & Grave has invited several bright young women to enter its secret chambers. This change of tradition does not sit well with several members, who adamantly disagree with their nominations.

Keywords: college

Secret Society Girl. Delacorte Press, 2006. ISBN 9780385340021.

When Amy Haskel agrees to join Rose & Grave, she participates in a series of bizarre initiation rituals and falls for a fellow member, George Prescott.

Keywords: crushes; friendship

Under the Rose. Delta, 2007. ISBN 9780385340038.

The current students in the Rose & Grave society receive an anonymous warning letter, and Amy "Bugaboo" Haskel decides to find out who is leaking the society's secrets.

Keywords: dating; friendship; sexual content

Rites of Spring (Break). Delta Trade Paperbacks, 2008. ISBN 9780385341936.

After surviving a series of pranks and personal attacks from a rival society, Amy looks forward to spending spring break with her fellow diggers on Cavador Key, their private island in Florida. But then she falls off the ferry and nearly drowns.

Keywords: dating; friendship; mystery

Tap & Gown. Delta, 2009. ISBN 9780385341943.

During her last semester at Eli University Amy must write her senior thesis, satisfy one more science credit, and most important, select her replacement in Rose & Grave.

Keywords: dating; graduation

Schneider, Robyn.

Better Than Yesterday. Delacorte Press, 2007. ISBN 9780385733458. 🆂

In alternating chapters, Skylar Banks and Charley Morton tell the story of the summer before their senior year, when they risked their academic future by leaving Hilliard Preparatory School in search of their missing friend, Blake Dorsey, in New York City.

Keywords: family; friendship; mystery

Sittenfeld, Curtis.

Prep. **Random House, 2005. ISBN 9780812972351.** **A**

Lee Fiora enters Ault boarding school with dreams of being one of the beautiful in the catalog and ends up being a quiet observer with a secret lover.

Keywords: dating; first love; friendship; jealousy; sexual content

von Ziegesar, Cecily (created by).

The It Girl. **S**

In the first spin-off series inspired by Cecily von Ziegesar's <u>Gossip Girl</u>, Jenny Humphrey is determined to become a sophisticated city girl when she transfers to an exclusive boarding school in upstate New York. Fortunately for Jenny, a bed is now vacant in the room of popular students Callie Vernon and Brett Messerchmidt's, because Waverly Academy's it girl, Tinsley Carmichael, was expelled last spring. It was a mystery to Brett and Callie why Tinsley was the only one who got expelled when the the three of them got caught taking drugs last spring. Now, to the surprise of everyone, Tinsley has returned, ready reclaim her place as the most sought-after girl at Waverly by hosting wild parties and dating all the desirable boys.

Keywords: friendship

The It Girl. Little, Brown, 2005. ISBN 9780316011853.

Before the semester begins, Jenny moves into the most coveted dorm room and obtains several admirers, including Callie's boyfriend, Easy Walsh, while rumors spread about her past in New York City. While Callie tries to connect with her boyfriend, Jenny's other roommate, Brett, is sneaking around with Mr. Dalton, the new history teacher.

Keywords: crushes; dating; sexual content

Notorious. Little, Brown, 2006. ISBN 9780316011860.

Now back in her old dorm room, Tinsley Carmichael shakes things up at Waverly by going after Brett's crush, Mr. Dalton, and starting Café Society, a girls-only secret society that includes sneaking out to party in a Boston hotel. After breaking up with Callie, Easy looks forward to starting a relationship with her roommate, Jenny.

Keywords: break-ups; dating

Reckless. Little, Brown, 2006. ISBN 9780316011877.

When Tinsley's roof party lands Dumbarton dormitory under house arrest for one week, the boys sneak into the dorm on Saturday night for a wild party, where Tinsley hooks up with a freshman, Easy kisses both Jenny and Callie, and secrets are revealed.

Keywords: dating; kissing; parties

Unforgettable. Little, Brown, 2007. ISBN 9780316113489.

As WOW, the Women of Waverly Club, are bonding, new and reunited couples' secret relationships are exposed at a barn party that goes ablaze.

Keywords: dating; kissing; lesbian

Lucky. Poppy/Little, Brown, 2007. ISBN 9780316113472.

As Dean Marymount investigates who started the fire at Miller Farm, Tinsley and Callie try to shift the blame from themselves onto Jenny and her new crush, Julian.

Keywords: crushes; dating

Tempted. Little, Brown, 2008. ISBN 9780316025089.

Two weeks after almost getting expelled from Waverly Academy, Jenny hopes to discover her secret admirer at the Halloween masquerade ball and to prove that she is the current it girl. Jenny wins best costume. Meanwhile, hurt by Easy's rejection, Callie enters what she thinks is a spa but in reality is a rehab boot camp; she calls Tinsley for help.

Keywords: break-ups; dances; dating; drinking; kissing

Infamous. Little, Brown, 2008. ISBN 9780316025072.

After becoming friends while rescuing Callie in Maine, Jenny and Tinsley decide that the three of them should spend Thanksgiving break in New York City to rest, relax, and party with some cute new boys.

Keywords: break-ups; crushes; dating; family; kissing

Adored. Poppy, 2009. ISBN 9780316025096.

Now that Easy has been expelled, Callie starts dating Brett's secret crush, Sebastian Valenti. Meanwhile, Tinsley is obsessed about Julian's virginity, and Jenny is being filmed by a crew of underclassmen.

Keywords: dating; kissing

Nannies and Au Pairs

While working as a nanny or au pair, a pretty teenage girl discovers the world of the super rich, makes new friends, and sets her sights on a cute boy. Similar to the stories in the boarding school section, often the protagonists is an outsider whom teen readers can relate to. In this case, though, the heroine's only access to the world of privilege and glamour is as an employee.

Ashton, Victoria.

Confessions of a Teen Nanny. M J

When best friends Liz and Adrienne accept nanny positions in the same building on Fifth Avenue, they are immersed in the world of the elite New York society, which includes debutantes, charity balls, and $800 shoes.

Keywords: dating; friendship; work

Confessions of a Teen Nanny. HarperCollins, 2005. ISBN 9780060775247.

Adrienne considers herself lucky when she becomes the newest nanny for a wealthy family—the money is great, and although eight-year-old Emma is a prodigy, she is easy to take care of. Adrienne has also made friends with Emma's beautiful halfsister Cameron. Then she learns that Cameron is out to steal Adrienne's boyfriend.

Rich Girls. HarperCollins, 2006. ISBN 9780060731809.

Although Adrienne hates Cameron for stealing her boyfriend, she agrees to help her prepare for the debutante ball at the Plaza. Meanwhile, Liz is confused by Parker's hot and cold treatment—does he want her or not?

Juicy Secrets. HarperCollins, 2006. ISBN 9780060731854.

In between all the nanny work and school, the girls still have time for love. Now over Brian, Adrienne takes a chance with Graydon, regardless of his reputation as a player. After Parker's father is charged with embezzlement, Liz is determined to prove that they can still have a great time, without spending money.

de la Cruz, Melissa.

The Au Pairs. **s**

Each summer on the Perrys' large South Hampton estate, three au pairs share an attic bedroom in the servants' quarters as well as responsibility for the children. The au pairs, Eliza Thompson, Mara Waters, and Jacqui Velasco, look forward to the time when the children are asleep so they can concentrate on their complicated romances and getting into the coolest parties. Surprisingly, the three young women develop a strong friendship that continues even after they stop working together.

Keywords: dating; friendship; sexual content; work

❦ *The Au Pairs.* Simon & Schuster, 2004. ISBN 9780689870668.

Eliza Thompson, Mara Waters, and Jacqui Velasco are three girls from different backgrounds who come together for shopping, partying, and occasional work as au pairs for a wealthy family in South Hampton and instantly become paparazzi favorites.

Awards: Quick Picks 2005

Skinny-Dipping. Simon & Schuster, 2005. ISBN 9781416903826.

The second summer is all about break-ups, hook-ups, and making up for the au pairs, especially because the Perrys have hired Phillippe Dufourg to replace Eliza while she works in the Hamptons' newest night club.

Sun-Kissed. Simon & Schuster, 2006. ISBN 9781416917465.

During the last summer before college, Eliza is designing clothes and Mara is writing for *Hamptons* magazine, while Jacqui is trying to keep the Perrys marriage together with the help of her three new boyfriends.

Crazy Hot. Simon & Schuster, 2007. ISBN 9781416939610.

In the final installment of the series, Mara, Eliza, and Jacqui realize what they want. Mara writes a humorous blog and wins back her true love; Eliza and Jacqui find success as a designer and model team that includes a twenty-page spread in *Vogue.*

Keywords: fashion; modeling

Mayer, Melody.

The Nannies. 🅂

When they leave their homes and become nannies to wealthy families, three very different girls become close friends. Kiley McCann entered the television contest, *Platinum Nanny,* with the hope of moving out of Wisconsin and becoming the live-in nanny for a rock star's three kids. When the show is canceled, Kiley accepts this job as a way to live in California. Lydia Chandler grew up in California but has spent the past eight years in the Amazon with her humanitarian parents. Then her Aunt Kat asks Lydia to return and take care of her two cousins. The final nanny, Esme Castaneda, grew up in the mean streets of Echo Park, a place where gangs run the neighborhood. The three nannies come together to help each other with ongoing work and romantic dilemmas.

Keywords: dating; friendship; Hispanic American; work

🏵 *The Nannies.* Delacorte Press, 2005. ISBN 9780385732833.

Kiley, Esme, and Lydia become fast friends when they each accept a live-in nanny position in Beverly Hills, California. After a few days of real babysitting, the girls settle into a routine of meeting at the country club during the day and dancing all night.

Awards: Quick Picks 2006

Friends with Benefits. Delacorte Press, 2006. ISBN 9780385903011.

The nannies use their connections to get into the hottest events and start a nanny placement company while they try to navigate their new romances.

Have to Have It. Delacorte Press, 2006. ISBN 9780385733519.

While Lydia is learning to drive and sticking to her aunt's rules, Esme looks after the twins during the Goldhagen's Jamaican vacation. All the while Kiley is trying to find a new nanny position after her boss is arrested and the three kids are placed under state protection.

Keywords: sexual content

Tainted Love. Delacorte Press, 2007. ISBN 9780385903677.

The fun in the sun is temporarily over as the three nannies are consumed with worry and regret. Esme is worried that her boyfriend is seeing someone else and that a new nanny will take her place, Kylie is having panic attacks, and Lydia regrets cheating on her boyfriend.

Keywords: sexual content

All Night Long. Delacorte Press, 2008. ISBN 9780385905060.

As the newest seniors at Bel Air High, Kiley, Esme, and Lydia rely on their friendship. Kiley testifies in her employer's trial; Esme fears that another nanny is trying to take over her life, including her boyfriend Jonathan; and Lydia tries to get Billy back after cheating on him.

Keywords: school; sexual content

Bad to the Bone. Delacorte Press, 2009. ISBN 9780385735186.

> While Lydia has a lot of free time on her hands, Kiley is running around doing extra errands for her boss; Esme is worried that her parents will be deported after an immigration raid.

Keywords: family

McLaughlin, Emma, and Nicola Kraus.

The Nanny Diaries. St. Martin's Paperbacks, p2005, c2002. ISBN 9780312948047. **A**

New York University senior Nanny accepts a part-time childcare position for a wealthy Park Avenue family to pay for her small apartment. She finds she is expected to complete many tasks outside of her job description while essentially raising four-year-old Grayer.

Keywords: affairs; dating; movie tie-in; work

Reisfeld, Randi, and H. B. Gilmour.

Oh Baby! Scholastic, 2005. ISBN 9780439677059. **J** **S**

> After graduating from Shafton High, best friends Abby and Jaime leave boring Ohio for a few months to work as nannies in New York City and California.

Keywords: dating; friendship; work

Debutantes and Glamour Girls

Stories about beautiful young women who have grown up in a world of privilege, attend elite prep schools, live in luxurious homes, and have access to fashionable nightspots. In many of the series books the characters' flawless appearance seems effortless, but they work hard to maintain their position as queen bees, even including backstabbing their best friends.

Brian, Kate.

🌶 *The Princess and the Pauper*. Simon & Schuster, 2003. ISBN 9780689870422. **M** **J**

> On her goodwill tour in California, Carina, the princess of Vineland, pays her look-a-like, Julia, $10,000 to attend a ball so she can hang out backstage with a rock star. Scandal breaks out when photos of Julia and handsome Markus are taken outside the ball.

Keywords: dating; family; humor; kissing
Awards: Quick Picks 2004

de la Cruz, Melissa.

The Ashleys. **M** **J**

> Known simply as the Ashleys, Ashley Spencer, Ashley "Lili" Li, and Ashley "A.A." Alioto are the most popular seventh graders at Miss Gamble's Preparatory School for Girls in San Francisco. As the leader of the tight-knit clique, Ashley

Spencer decides who gets a SOA, the Seal of Approval. Former scholarship student Lauren Page has been bullied by the Ashleys since kindergarten, and now that her father has made a lot of money with a popular Web site, Lauren hopes to infiltrate the group.

Keywords: cliques; friendship

There's a New Name in School. Aladdin Mix, 2008. ISBN 978141469066.

Recently rich and newly accessorized by a professional stylist, Lauren Page is determined to join the Ashleys, the most popular clique in seventh grade, with the intention of knocking them off their pedestal.

Keywords: dances; family; school

Jealous? Aladdin Mix, 2008. ISBN 9781416934073.

Right before Lauren invites the Ashleys to participate in the new reality show *PreTeen Queen*, ashleyrank.com debuts on the Web, giving each seventh-grade girl in Miss Gramble's school a rating based on style, social presence, smile, and smarts. Lili's competitive side comes out, and she is determined to be number one, while A.A. is jealous that Ashley is dating her close friend, Tri Fitzpatrick.

Keywords: crushes; dating; school

Birthday Vicious. Aladdin Mix, 2008. ISBN 9781416934080.

As if dating two boys were not enough, Lauren gives her old friend Sadie a much-needed makeover. Ashley plans an elaborate sweet-thirteen party, Lili sneaks away on a camping trip, and A.A. is fighting with her friend and crush, Tri.

Keywords: family; parties

Lip Gloss Jungle. Aladdin Mix, 2008. ISBN 9781416934097.

The Ashleys are in crisis mode when they are challenged by the S. Society to see who will come up with the winning Congé proposal and be the most popular clique at Miss Gramble's.

Keywords: family; jealousy; kissing

Dean, Zoey.

Privileged. Warner Books, 2007. ISBN 9780446548434. **S**

Recent Yale graduate Megan Smith relocates to Palm Springs to tutor twin heiresses Rose and Sage Baker. She plans to pay off her student loans and write an exposé that will launch her writing career. Originally published as *How to Teach Filthy Rich Girls.*

Keywords: family; friendship; TV tie-in; work

The A-List. **S**

Anna Percy is a classic beauty with poise and grace; however, she is looking for a little excitement and perhaps a sexy boyfriend, so when her mom suggests she spend the last half of her senior year in Los Angeles with her dad,

Anna decides that this is the change she is looking for. On the flight to California Anna meets Ben Birnbaum, the handsome Princeton student. It is through Ben that Anna meets the daughters of three of the most powerful men in the movie and music biz: Samantha Sharpe, Cammie Sheppard, and Dee Young. The three girls quickly become her closest friends and sworn enemies. Although Anna has many boyfriends in California, she never forgets about her first love, Ben.

Keywords: dating; friendship

The A-List. Little, Brown, 2003. ISBN 9780316734356.

Anna Percy moves from Manhattan to sunny LA to live with her father and complete a six-month internship before attending Yale in the fall. She quickly makes waves at Beverly Hills High School when she snags the most desirable boy on the West Coast, Ben Birnbaum.

Keywords: family; first love; school; sexual content
Awards: Quick Picks 2004

Girls on Film. Little, Brown, 2004. ISBN 9780316734752.

It has been less than a week since Anna's move to LA, and already her life has become very complicated. First Ben is aggressively trying to win her back after he deserted her on New Year's Eve, then her big sister Susan gets kicked out of rehab, moves into the Beverly Hills Hotel, and befriends Anna's nemesis, Cammie. To her surprise, Anna finds solace working with Sam on a short screenplay for class.

Keywords: break-ups, family, school

Blonde Ambition. Little, Brown, 2004. ISBN 9780316734745.

As Anna discovers California guys, Ben becomes jealous and possessive when he spies Anna flirting with Danny, a young TV writer, and Django, her dad's cute assistant. Meanwhile, now that Cammie has her mind set on Anna's ex, Adam, she sets out to destroy Anna by ruining her reputation and consequently is fired from her internship on a new teen TV show.

Keywords: break-ups; family; internship; school
Awards: Quick Picks 2006

Tall Cool One. Little, Brown, 2004. ISBN 9780316735087.

As Cammie's and Adam's relationship is heating up, Anna decides to get away from boys by helping her dad check out an exclusive resort in Mexico. To escape her stepmother's baby plans, Sam decides to join Anna in Mexico and returns home with a sexy new guy.

Keywords: sexual content; vacation

Back in Black. Little, Brown, 2005. ISBN 9780316010924.

The A-list forgo the senior trip to Washington, D.C., for the casinos in Las Vegas. Once in Sin City, Cammie enters an amateur showgirl contest, Sam pines for Eduardo, Anna invites Ben to meet her, and secrets are revealed under hypnosis.

Keywords: vacation

Some Like It Hot. Little, Brown, 2006. ISBN 9780316010931.

Anna, Cammie, Sam, and Dee all prepare for an over-the-top Hollywood-style prom, with a stylist, couture dresses, handsome dates, and a party on a movie set replica of the Colisseum of Rome.

Keywords: prom; school

American Beauty. Little, Brown, 2006. ISBN 9780316010948.

As everyone is looking forward to graduation and the biggest pre-graduation party, Anna is concerned that Ben is hiding something, Sam tries to win back Eduardo, and Cammie continues to investigate her mother's death.

Keywords: family; graduation; mystery

Heart of Glass. Little, Brown, 2007. ISBN 9780316010962.

To complete their community service after they are arrested for trespassing, archenemies Anna and Cammie help organize a charity fashion show for at-risk teens. Sam spends the summer reading scripts for her dad's production company and discovers that her young stepmother is cheating on him.

Keywords: affairs; community service; family; fashion; work

Beautiful Stranger. Little, Brown, 2007. ISBN 9780316113526.

In New York City, Sam surprises her fiancé Eduardo, who is working at the United Nations; broken-hearted Anna starts dating her childhood friend Logan Cresswell; and back in California, Cammie invests in Ben's new nightclub, Bye Bye Love.

Keywords: break-ups; kissing

California Dreaming. Little, Brown, 2008. ISBN 9780316113533.

In the final book in the original <u>A-List</u> series, Anna questions her future at Yale and writes about her recent experiences in a screenplay, Cammie realizes she belongs with Adam, and Sam breaks off her engagement and uses her father's influence to direct Anna's screenplay for a major studio.

Keywords: break-ups; college; family

The A-List: Hollywood Royalty. ⑤

The next A-list generation stars Hollywood elite who are accustomed to the paparazzi, such as popular Kidz Network actress Amelie Adams-Sparks, Hollywood heartthrob Hunter Sparks, and Myla Everhart, the oldest adopted daughter of Hollywood's hottest couple, as well as her longtime boyfriend Ash Gilmour. Also included in the series are newcomers to the Hollywood scene Josephine "Jojo" Milford and Jacob "Jake" Porter-Goldsmith.

Hollywood Royalty. Little, Brown, 2009. ISBN 9780316031813.

A lot has changed over the summer. While filming a movie, Amelie tries to show her crush, Hunter, that she is more grown up than her fairy princess character; Myla and Ash break up; Jojo moves to Hollywood to live with her very famous biological parents; and Jake hopes his new body and longer hair will be enough to date Amelie.

Keywords: acting; break-ups; crushes; dating; family; kissing

Sunset Boulevard. Little, Brown, 2009. ISBN 0316031820.

When the movie *Class Angel* is filmed at Beverly Hills High, celebrity actress Amelie Adam discovers what real high school is like, Jake Porter-Goldsmith lets his lead role go to his head, and JoJo goes from being popular to a social outcast again. Meanwhile Myla can't get over her recent break-up with Ash, even though he is now dating the British singer Daisy.

Keywords: acting; break-ups; dating; family; friendship

Godbersen, Anna.

The Luxe. **S**

At the turn of the twentieth century, scandal, gossip, and secrets spread among and about the young members of New York's high society.

Keywords: family; friendship; historical fiction

The Luxe. HarperCollins, 2007. ISBN 9780061345661.

In 1899, eighteen-year-old Elizabeth Adora Holland and her friends enjoy a luxurious lifestyle as members of Manhattan's upper class. When Elizabeth is forced to accept wealthy twenty-year-old Henry Schoonmaker's marriage proposal even though he is in love with her younger sister Diana and has had an affair with her best friend Penelope Hayes, she takes drastic measures to be with the one she loves. Meanwhile, her former maid Lina Broud plots her rise in society.

Keywords: kissing; love

Rumors. HarperCollins, 2008. ISBN 9780061345692.

In the last month of the nineteenth century, all of Manhattan's high society is speculating about Elizabeth's mysterious death, except for her sister Diana and friend Penelope, who know that Elizabeth is living in California with her true love, Will. Now that her engagement to Henry Schoonmaker is broken, both Diana and Penelope are determined to marry the eligible bachelor.

Keywords: death; love; sexual content; wedding

Envy. HarperCollins, 2009. ISBN 9780061345722.

After blackmailing Henry into marriage, Penelope tries to keep Henry away from Diana by paying her brother Grayson to pursue Diana during a vacation at the Palm Beach Hotel. Meanwhile, Elizabeth is back in New York mourning the death of Will, and Lina's benefactor, Carey Lewis Longhorn, dies.

Keywords: death; love; sexual content

Goldberg, Amanda, and Ruthanna Khalighi Hopper.

Celebutantes. St. Martin's Press, 2008. ISBN 9780312362294. **A**

After another bad break-up with an actor, twenty-six-year-old fashion-obsessed Lola Santisi decides to give her life some direction by using her connections as the daughter of an Academy Award–winning Hollywood director to convince an A-list celebrity to wear couture gowns designed by her best friend, Julian Tennant, to the Oscars.

Keywords: acting; break-ups; dating; family; fashion; friendship; humor; sexual content; work

Harrison, Lisi.

The Clique. **M** **J**

Massie Block, Dylan Marvil, Kristen Gregory, and Alicia Rivera are the undisputed members of the pretty committee. As the most popular seventh graders at the Octavian Country Day School for Girls in Westchester County, New York, they have as many admirers as they have enemies, who would gladly knock them off their pedestal. Massie Block is enjoying her role as the leader of the most popular clique in school, when Claire Lyons's family moves into her family's guesthouse and she is forced to be friendly with a girl who wears Keds! Over time Claire is officially accepted into the clique and is invited to Massie's exclusive Friday night sleepovers.

Keywords: cliques; friendship

The Clique. Poppy, p2008, c2004. ISBN 9780316040839.

Claire so desperately wants to be friends with the popular group that she devises a plan to sneak into Massie's bedroom and have instant messaging conversations with other members of the clique. Through these messages the tight group is temporarily broken up, and Claire looks like the new girl to be friends with.

Keywords: school
Awards: Quick Picks 2005

Best Friends for Never. Little, Brown, 2004. ISBN 9780316701310.

To prove that she is still number one, Massie Block throws a Halloween boy-girl party on her family's estate. The clique's revealing costumes force the school board to adopt a uniform policy. The girls each try to create the winning design in the new uniform contest.

Keywords: parties; school

Revenge of the Wannabes. Little, Brown, 2005. ISBN 9780316701334.

After stealing first prize in the uniform contest, Alicia breaks away from Massie and starts her own clique. However, Massie sets things straight when she steals the spotlight at the *Teen People* photo shoot.

Keywords: school

Invasion of the Boy Snatchers. Little, Brown, 2005. ISBN 9780316701341.

Tensions rise in the clique after Claire moves into Massie's bedroom and Alicia's Spanish cousin, Nina, tries to steal their boyfriends with a Spanish soccer spell. At the Valentine's Day Dance, Claire, Kristen, Dylan, and Alicia have a contest to see who will kiss a boy first.

Keywords: dances; kissing

The Pretty Committee Strikes Back. Little, Brown, 2006. ISBN 9780316115001.

The girls of Octavian Country Day School are ready to impress the cute Briarwood Boys during their three-day survival trip on Lake Placid, after they take Massie's Underground Clinic for Kissing Boys. After a public argument, Massie has her first kiss with Derrington, while Claire tries to win Cam back after kissing Josh Hotz, Alicia's latest crush.

Keywords: break-ups; crushes; kissing

Dial L for Loser. Little, Brown, 2006. ISBN 9780316115049.

The pretty committee is bored after being expelled from school. Then they are invited to audition for a teen movie. In Hollywood Claire wins the main role, and her boyfriend, Cam, is jealous of her romantic scenes with the leading man. Massie and Alicia make everyone else in Westchester jealous with their assignment as set correspondents for the *Daily Grind* and their photos in *US Weekly*.

Keywords: acting; dating

It's Not Easy Being Mean. Little, Brown, 2007. ISBN 9780316115056.

Hidden under the mattress of a Westchester boy is the key to a secret room at Octavian Country Day School. Massie and the pretty committee are determined to find the key and become the next alphas, the most popular clique in school.

Keywords: mystery

Sealed with a Diss. Little, Brown, 2007. ISBN 9780316115063.

To ensure that the secret room at Octavian Country Day School will be theirs next year, the pretty committee has to snag a cute date for Skye Hamilton's costume party, and Massie has to convince her old crush, Chris, to escort the hostess. As the day of the party approaches, Claire tries to find out if her boyfriend, Cam, is dating another girl from his summer camp.

Keywords: crushes; dating; parties; school

The Clique Summer Collection: Massie. Little, Brown, 2008. ISBN 9780316027519.

After being kicked out of the prestigious Galwaugh Farms Sleepaway Riding Camp, Massie's plans to shop and tan near her Southampton estate are nixed when her parents insist that she get a job to learn a lesson about responsibility. After much thought, Massie gets a job as a sales representative for Be Pretty cosmetics and quickly becomes the company's best salesperson.

Keywords: camp; family; humor; work

The Clique Summer Collection: Dylan. Little, Brown, 2008. ISBN 9780316035651.

> In Hawaii for the Aloha Tennis Open with her TV-host mom, Dylan pretends to be a tennis nut in order to impress the resort owners' son, John Thomas "J.T." Daley. When Dylan records the temperamental tennis star Svetlana Slootskyia losing her temper, Dylan blackmails her for private tennis lessons.

> **Keywords:** crushes; humor; sports; vacation

The Clique Summer Collection: Alicia. Little, Brown, 2008. ISBN 9780316027533.

> During her summer in Spain Alicia is determined on becoming a Spanish alpha, by spending time with her fashionable twin cousins Isobel and Celia and being cast in a pop star's music video, but she ends up working in a hotel with her other cousin, Nina.

> **Keywords:** family, humor, work, vacation

The Clique Summer Collection: Kristen. Little, Brown, 2008. ISBN 978-0316027526.

> After taking an extra-credit summer class for gifted students in Westchester, Kristen gets a job tutor-sitting for wanna-be Massie Ripple Baxter and falls for her surfer older brother, Dune. Kristen and the Witty Committee concoct a plan to lure Dune away from the ninth-grade alpha, Skye Hamilton.

> **Keywords:** crushes; humor

The Clique Summer Collection: Claire. Little, Brown, 2008. ISBN 978-0316027502.

> After living the past year in Westchester, Claire has reunited with her old best friends in Florida. As Claire tries to prove that she has not changed by helping them prepare for the Kissimmee teen beauty pageant, Massie shows up and decides that she wants to compete as well.

> **Keywords:** humor; vacation

Bratfest at Tiffany's. Poppy, 2008. ISBN 9780316006804.

> At the start of eighth grade, Massie is so fearful that the pretty committee will lose their alpha status once the Briarwood Boys invade Octavian Country Day School that she has Alicia, Dylan, Claire, and Kristen pledge a boyfast. When Alicia cannot resist her crush, Josh Holtz, she is temporarily kicked out of the clique.

> **Keywords:** crushes; school

P.S. I Loathe You. 2009. Poppy, 2009. ISBN 97803160068011.

> When the pretty committee put their crushes before their friendship, the popular clique might permanently break up.

> **Keywords:** crushes; dating; school

Boys R Us. Little, Brown, 2009. ISBN 9780316006828.

> Now that the pretty committee has broken up for good, the former members have to decide which side they are on as Massie and Alicia

both form new cliques. Meanwhile the boys are heading back to Briarwood Academy.

Keywords: crushes; dating; school

Hollings, Anastasia.

Beautiful World. HarperTeen, 2009. ISBN 9780061435324. **S**

As the daughter of an untenured boarding school professor, seventeen-year-old Ann "Amelia" Warner desire to be part of the elite world is so strong that she lies and manipulates the gullible heiress Courtney Moore into buying her things and inviting Amelia to stay in her New York City apartment.

Keywords: friendship

Jackson, Lucy.

Posh. St. Martin's Press, 2007. ISBN 9780312363895. **A**

Sweet Julianne Coopersmith doesn't mind that her mom drives a cab while her friends at Griffin School live in elaborative penthouses in Manhattan. Julianne's real concerns are that her bipolar boyfriend cannot stay on his medications and her best friend, Morgan, is mourning the resent loss of her mom.

Keywords: death; family; friendship

Linker, Julie.

Crowned. Simon Pulse, 2008. ISBN 9781416960522. **J S**

Presley Ashbury loves the pageant world, especially the much-needed scholarship money for college. The competition gets dirty when Presley competes against wealthy Megan Leighton in the Miss Teen State beauty pageant.

Keywords: beauty pageants; school

Disenchanted Princess. Simon Pulse, 2007. ISBN 9781416934721. **J S**

Spoiled Beverly Hills teen West Caroline Deschanel goes into culture shock when she is forced to relocate to Possum Grape, Arkansas, and live with her estranged Aunt Sherri while her Hollywood agent father is in prison for embezzlement.

Keywords: family; moving; school

Mechling, Lauren, and Laura Moser.

10th Grade Social Climber. **S**

After her parent's divorce, fifteen-year-old Mimi Schulman moves from Texas to New York City to live with her dad and attend the exclusive Baldwin School.

The Rise and Fall of a 10th Grade Social Climber. Houghton Mifflin, 2005. ISBN 9780618555192.

Mimi Schulman was about to win her bet with a childhood friend that she could become a member of the popular clique at Baldwin High, until part of her diary is posted on the Internet.

Keywords: clique; diary; friendship; school

All Q, No A: More Tales of a 10th Grade Social Climber. Graphia/Houghton Mifflin, 2006. ISBN 9780618663781.

> Upon her return from the Dominican Republic, where she did humanitarian work with her friends, Mimi is determined to write a fantastic article for the school newspaper about Serge Ziff, a Baldwin parent who donated a million dollars. She uncovers Ziff's illegal activities and publishes an exposé in the *New York Tribune.*
>
> **Keywords:** community service; friendship; mystery

Foreign Exposure: The Social Climber Abroad. Houghton Mifflin, 2007. ISBN 9780618663798.

> Mimi was supposed to spend the entire summer with her mother in Germany, but she runs away to stay with Lily and some family friends in London. As an intern for *A-Ha* magazine, Mimi soon spends most of her time in London trying to uncover celebrity gossip.
>
> **Keywords:** family; friendship; internship; travel, work

Millner, Denene, and Mitzi Miller

Hotlanta. S

After their mother married the wealthy car dealer Altimus Duke, African American twin sisters Sydney and Lauren have grown up in the exclusive Atlanta neighborhood of Buckhead.

Keywords: African American; family; sisters

Awards: Quick Picks 2009

Hotlanta. Point, 2008. ISBN 9780545003087.

> When their father is released from prison, overachiever Sydney pays him a visit, while party girl Lauren focuses on her new boyfriend from the wrong side of town. When someone is murdered, the Duke sisters uncover the truth about their stepfather.
>
> **Keywords:** break-ups; dances; dating; murder; mystery; school

If Only You Knew. Point, 2008. ISBN 9780545003094.

> Although Sydney and Lauren should be focusing on their upcoming party, they go against their parents' wishes and sneak around trying to uncover who really killed Lauren's boyfriend's brother. When they discover the truth about their parents, the Duke sisters get really scared.
>
> **Keywords:** break-ups; dating; mystery; parties

What Goes Around. Point, 2009. ISBN 9780545003100.

> Lauren is worried that she may lose her spot as the captain of the dance team because of all the drama around her stepfather being under federal investigation for tax fraud. Meanwhile, Sydney is trying begin a relationship with Jason, but Marcus, keeps getting in the way.
>
> **Keywords:** dating

Minter, J.

The Insider Girl. J S

Patch and Feb Flood's younger sister, high school freshman Flan Flood, takes center stage in this new series inspired by J. Minter's The Insiders series. When Flan attends public school, she quickly discovers that keeping a low-key persona is nearly impossible, because her best friend is the actress Sara-Beth Benny. Almost immediately Flan's old crew of local celebrities and socialites bond with her new public school friends.

Keywords: friendship

Inside Girl. Bloomsbury, 2007. ISBN 9781599900865.

Sick of being known as Patch Flood's younger sister, Flan decides to break out on her own and attend public school. She tries to keep her old social life a secret from her new friends and potential boyfriend.

Keywords: school

The Sweetest Thing. Bloomsbury, 2007. ISBN 9781599900872.

While her sister Feb is suddenly acting like a strict parent, Flan's friends Judith and Meredith are competing to get the popular football player Adam McGregor to notice them. After days of flirting, Adam kisses Flan in front of her sweet boyfriend, Bennett, at Sara-Beth's Halloween party.

Keywords: dating; kissing; sisters

Some Kind of Wonderful. Bloomsbury, 2008. ISBN 9781599901657.

During Thanksgiving break, Flan invites Judith and Meredith to join her family on the island of Nevis in the Caribbean, expecting fun in the sun, but the trip turns into the never-ending vacation from hell when Judith wants to study and Meredith runs off with Flan's old nemesis, Kennedy. Things do turn around when Flan reconnects with her old friend Camille.

Keywords: break-ups; vacation

All That Glitters. Bloomsbury, 2008. ISBN 9781599902579.

After reuniting with her former best friend Camille, Flan decides to return to the exclusive private schools on the Upper East Side and attend Thoney Prep, with the plan of being popular. But first she has to knock down the ruling queen bee, Kennedy Pearson, who is determined to keep her position.

Keywords: school

Perfect Match. Bloomsbury, 2009. ISBN 9781599903354.

When Flan's friends go on a boy boycott, Flan plays matchmaker. She is committed to picking out perfect dates and dresses for the upcoming Valentine's Day Dance so she can enjoy the most romantic holiday with her new boyfriend Alex.

Keywords: dances; dating; school

Lucky Break. Bloomsbury, 2009. ISBN 9781599903569.

After her devastating break-up with Alex, Flan cancels her planned spring break trip to Paris and travels around the world, meeting her family and best friend Sara-Beth, while trying to get over Alex.

Keywords: break-ups; travel

Noël, Alyson.

Art Geeks and Prom Queens. **St. Martin's Griffin, 2005. ISBN 9780312336363.** 🅂

After she moves to Southern California with her former model mom and famous lawyer dad, Rio James is happy when she quickly makes friends with a few AP art students. But then the head cheerleader and queen bee, Kristi, invites Rio to join the popular crowd.

Keywords: cliques; dating; family; friendship; moving; school

Pascal, Francine.

The Ruling Class. **Simon & Schuster, 2004. ISBN 9780689873324.** 🅹 🅂

Sick of being tormented by the ruling class, newcomer Twyla Gay hooks up with other outcasts to seek revenge and take back the school.

Keywords: cliques; crushes; friendship; school

Sykes, Plum.

Bergdorf Blondes. **Hyperion, 2004. ISBN 9781401351960.** 🅰

The heroine known only as Moi happily traded damp England for the party-girl life with the Park Avenue Princesses. When Moi discovers the special glow of engagement ring happiness, she halfheartedly goes along with her best friend and Bergdorf heiress in a hunt for a prospective husband.

Keywords: dating; friendship; humor

The Debutante Divorcée. **Miramax Books/Hyperion, 2006. ISBN 9781401352448.** 🅰

Newlywed Sylvie Mortimer becomes entrenched with the New York City high society set when she befriends the glamorous divorcée Lauren Blount after Sylvie's husband, Hunter, has to attend a business meeting during their honeymoon. Sylvie is happily busy with her new life, which includes working for a hot young designer, redecorating her apartment, and attending fancy parties, until Sophia D'Arlan, a notorious husband stealer, appears to be after Hunter.

Keywords: friendship; humor; marriage; sexual content; vacations; work

von Ziegesar, Cecily.

Gossip Girl. 🅂

The characters in <u>Gossip Girl</u> are born into an exclusive world of privilege, where the only rule is to keep all indiscretions a secret. The teens realize early on that as long as they keep up proper appearances in public, their parents are not concerned about drugs, alcohol, and sex. In addition to inheriting great looks and homes all over the country, the girls have access to the hottest parties and credit cards, so they can have anything they desire. Between every few chapters is a posting from gossipgirl.net that summarizes the stories, lists sightings, gives advice on fashion and romance, and replies to e-mail questions. Who is the gossip girl, creator of gossipgirl.net? It is definitely an insider who spreads rumors and perpetuates gossip.

Keywords: friendship; TV tie-in

It Had to Be You: The Gossip Girl Prequel. Little, Brown, 2007. ISBN 9780316017688.

> Things really heat up during their junior year as Vanessa Abrams meets Dan Humphrey at a party and Serena van der Woodsen and her best friend Blair Waldorf tell their good friend Nate Archibald that they love him.

> **Keywords:** first love; school; sexual content

🎗 *Gossip Girl: A Novel.* Little, Brown, p2007, c2002. ISBN 9780316024563.

> Blair Waldorf is determined to stay queen bee at Constance Billard School, despite gorgeous Serena van der Woodsen's unexpected return from boarding school at midterm. While Serena adjusts to her new outsider status by making friends with artsy Vanessa and Dan, his younger sister Jenny tries to fit in with the elite at the Kiss on the Lips party.

> **Keywords:** dating; kissing; parties; school
> **Awards:** Quick Picks 2003

🎗 *You Know You Love Me.* Little, Brown, 2002. ISBN 9780316911481.

> Blair Waldorf's world is falling apart. It is bad enough that her mother is marrying the wealthy, but tacky, Cyrus Solomon Rose and she will have a vegan, dreadlock-wearing stepbrother, but now Blair realizes that she will not get early admission from her number one pick after she bombed her Yale interview. And worse, her leading man, Nate, has dumped her for Jenny. Perhaps making amends with Serena will heal her bruised heart. At the very least, they can party together.

> **Keywords:** break-ups; college applications; dating; family; school
> **Awards:** Quick Picks 2003

All I Want Is Everything. Little, Brown, 2003. ISBN 9780316912129.

> Between college applications and midterms, the beautiful elite decide to spend a few days at a private resort on the Island of St. Bart's before they bring in the New Year with a wild party. Before the clock strikes midnight, Serena is serenaded by a hot rock star, Jenny learns Nate is still in love with Blair, and it is anger, not love that breaks Dan's writer's block.

> **Keywords:** break-ups; dating; family; kissing; vacations

Because I'm Worth It. Little, Brown, 2003. ISBN 9780316909686.

> Everyone is talking about designers and models as Serena, Vanessa, and Dan are each discovered during New York City's Fashion Week. However, fame

comes at a price, and their secure romances are neglected. Meanwhile, Nate and Blair attend therapy to cope with their addictions and eating disorders.

Keywords: break-ups; dating; drug addiction; fashion; modeling; sexual content

I Like It Like That. Little, Brown, 2004. ISBN 9780316735186.

Spring break in an exclusive ski resort provides the perfect escape for hooking up and partying. The unfortunate few who have to stay in New York City make the best of it by making unexpected discoveries. After some private eye work, Jenny finds out the truth about her boyfriend Leo, as Vanessa and Dan realize they still love each other.

Keywords: dating; first love; sexual content; vacation

You're the One I Want. Little, Brown, 2004. ISBN 9780316735162.

Now that college acceptance letters are in the mail, the time has come to visit the campuses to decide which Ivy League school to attend. Serena takes a break from modeling and finds true love on each of her college tours; Blair discovers her hidden talent while coaching her mom in the delivery room.

Keywords: college; dating; sexual content

Nobody Does It Better. Little, Brown, 2005. ISBN 9780316735124.

When Dan's poetry is discovered, he becomes the lead singer of New York's hottest band, and Jenny becomes their number-one groupie, as she hopes her bad-girl behavior will land her in boarding school. As Blair still waits to hear back from Yale, she moves into Vanessa's hip Brooklyn apartment, and the girls-only senior spa weekend in the Hamptons turns into a wild party.

Keywords: boarding school; college; moving; music; sexual content

Nothing Can Keep Us Together. Little, Brown, 2005. ISBN 9780316735094.

Blair and Dan each have been selected to be the senior speaker at graduation; however, Vanessa and Serena miss Blair's speech by arriving fashionably late. After the ceremony, all the prep school seniors go to the Yale club to celebrate. Although not a senior, Jenny is commemorating her acceptance into Waverly boarding school. Nate is the only one not celebrating, because his diploma is pending after he stole prescription drugs from his coach.

Keywords: boarding school; graduation; parties

Only in Your Dreams. Little, Brown, 2006. ISBN 9780316011822.

New York City is all abuzz about the major film being made at Barney's, featuring Serena and one of the cutest Hollywood actors. After fleeing England when she realized that her boyfriend was more interested in his cousin Camilla, Blair also gets a job on the set, as a fashion assistant. Vanessa becomes a nanny after she is fired due to her experimental camera work. Meanwhile, Dan and Nate stay away from the Hollywood scene and fall for unlikely girls.

Keywords: break-ups; dating; fashion; work

Would I Lie to You. Little, Brown, 2006. ISBN 9780316011839.

A lot can happen the summer before college, especially in the Hamptons. Now official fashion icons, Blair and Serena move into a famous fashion designer's guesthouse. Nate tries to earn his diploma by working for his coach. Back in New York City, Dan's dream job at The Strand bookstore leads to questions about his sexuality.

Keywords: dating; fashion; gay; sexual content; work

Don't You Forget About Me. Little, Brown, 2007. ISBN 9780316011846.

In the conclusion of the original series, true love comes together when Dan realizes that he is not gay but in love with Vanessa, and Nate finally breaks the Serena and Blair love triangle so they can all remain friends.

Keywords: dating; sexual content

von Ziegesar, Cecily (created by).

Gossip Girl—The Carlyles. ⑤

The Upper East Side has a new family to love, loathe, and be jealous of when the Carlyle triplets, Avery, Owen, and Baby, move from Nantucket into Blair Waldorf's luxurious penthouse.

Keywords: family; friendship

The Carlyles. Little, Brown, 2008. ISBN 9780316020640.

When the Carlyle triplets move to Manhattan, Avery is determined to win over the popular clique, despite a run-in with Jacqueline "Jack" Laurent, the reigning queen of Constance Billard School for Girls. Baby wants to get kicked out of school so she can reunite with her boyfriend in Nantucket, and Owen realizes the girl of his dreams from the summer, Kelsey Talmadge, has been dating his new friend and captain of the St. Jude's School for Boys swimming team, Rhys Sterling, since elementary school.

Keywords: break-ups; dating; drinking; school; sexual content

You Just Can't Get Enough. Written by Annabelle Vestry. Little, Brown, 2008. ISBN 9780316020657.

No longer homesick for Nantucket, the Carlyle triplets have settled in. Baby is dating J.P. and is permitted to stay at Constance Billard School for Girls, Avery is set up on a blind date for the St. Jude's swim team date auction fund-raiser, and Owen tries to squash his feelings for Kelsey.

Keywords: break-ups; dating; kissing; school

Take a Chance on Me. Written by Annabelle Vestry. Little, Brown, 2009. ISBN 9780316020664.

As the face of the Cashman Lofts campaign and living in a penthouse with J.P., Jack is back on top, but something does not feel right, and she turns to Avery for friendship. Meanwhile, the swim team falls apart after Owen steals Kelsey from Rhys, Baby's return from Spain leads to twenty hours of therapy, and Avery has an internship at *Metropolitan* magazine.

Keywords: dating; internship; kissing

Love the One You're With. Written by Annabelle Vestry. Little, Brown, 2009. ISBN 9780316020671.

> During Thanksgiving break vacation in the Bahamas, Avery and Rhys admit their feelings, Baby hooks up with her future sister's boyfriend, Jack realizes who she really wants to be with, and the triplets watch their mother get married.

> **Keywords:** kissing; vacation

Wasserstein, Wendy.

Elements of Style. **Knopf, 2006. ISBN 9781400042319.** 🅰

Chronicles the lives and love affairs of Manhattan's elite class as they search for meaning in their lives post 9/11, including Francesa Weissman, the upper East Side's favorite pediatrician; Samantha Acton, a well-bred classic beauty; and Judy Tremont, a gossipy social climber.

Keywords: affairs; dating; death; marriage; work

Fashion Jobs

This section features fashion editors, upcoming models, wanna-be fashion designers, and interns at fashion magazines in New York City. For many of the heroines, this is the first taste of the glamorous world that they so long to be a part of.

Barham, Lisa.

The Fashion-Forward Adventures of Imogene. Ⓜ 🄹 🅂

Self-proclaimed trendsetter Imogene has a gift for fashion and style. In fact, the wealthy girls who attend Greenwich County Academy in Connecticut look forward to reading Imogene's "Daily Obsession" in the school newspaper to learn what will be the next big thing. Unfortunately for Imogene, her family is old money rich but cash poor, so she has to find resourceful ways to get the newest designs.

Keywords: fashion

A Girl Like Moi. Simon Pulse, 2006. ISBN 9781416914433.

> After Imogene maxes out her American Express credit card, her mother not only cancels her upcoming trip to Paris, but she also arranges for Imogene to work for the summer as an intern. Imogene makes the best of a bad situation by landing an internship in New York City writing for a fashion forecasting company, where she meets a very cute Italian boy.

> **Keywords:** internship

Project Paris. Simon Pulse, 2007. ISBN 978416914440.

> Seventeen-year-old Imogene and her best friend Evie finally get to Paris to shop, sightsee, and intern in the fashion industry, when the models go on strike and Couture Week is canceled. As the designers

and socialites plan a mass exodus from Paris, Imogene discovers Monsieur X, a designer who will surely bring back the fashionistas.

Keywords: friendship; internship; travel

Accidentally Fabulous. Simon Pulse, 2008. ISBN 9781416914457.

During their spring break, Imogene and Evie are in Los Angeles to attend a fashion fantasy camp, when Imogene gets discovered and Evie is temporarily left behind.

Keywords: friendship; travel

Bushnell, Candace.

Lipstick Jungle. Hyperion, 2007. ISBN 9780786893966. 🄰

Chronicles the high-powered careers and love affairs of *Bonfire* magazine's editor-in-chief, Nico O'Neilly, fashion designer Victory Ford, and president of *Paradour Pictures* Wendy Healy, three of the most successful and glamorous women in New York.

Keywords: affairs; dating; marriage; sexual content; TV tie-in; work

Cabot, Meg.

Airhead. 🄹 🅂

When a plasma television falls on sixteen-year-old Emerson "Em" Watts at a Stark mega store, Em wakes up weeks later in a hospital to discover that she had a secret whole body transplant operation with the teen supermodel Nikki Howard. Em is then forced by the Stark executives to forget her old life and assume the identity of Nikki, which means photo shoots and runway shows.

Keywords: crushes; family; humor; science fiction

Airhead. Point, 2008. ISBN 9780545040525.

Em, who prefers playing video games with her best friend and crush Christopher to shopping, agrees to take her celebrity-obsessed younger sister Frieda to the opening of a Stark mega store to hear Gabriel Luna play. She is involved in a freak accident that leaves her permanently changed.

Being Nikki. Point, 2009. ISBN 9780545040563.

Em, along with her true love Christopher and Nikki's older brother, try to find out what really happened to Nikki and her mother after the operation.

Keywords: kissing; modeling; mystery; school

Clarke, Nicole.

Flirt. 🄼 🄹

Melanie Henderson, Charlotte Gabel, Alexa Veron, Genevieve Bishop, Olivia Bourne-Cecil, and Kiyoko Katsuda come from around the world to New York City as the first set of interns at *Flirt*, the hippest magazine for teens. For the duration of this chance-of-a-lifetime internship, each girl will work in a department that showcases her talents and interests. During the eight-week internship the girls live in a spacious loft apartment with an artistic house advisor, Emma Lyric, and her cute son, Nick. The colorful covers and larger layout size are designed to make the series look like a trendy fashion magazine. A few volumes include sample pages of *Flirt* magazine highlighting articles written by the interns. The next set of interns—Asha, Elizabeth, Georgia, Mikki, Nova, Naliah, and Sivya—are introduced in book number nine.

Keywords: friendship; internship

Write Here, Write Now. Grosset & Dunlap, 2006. ISBN 9780448442631.

Sixteen-year-old Melanie leaves Berkeley, California, with hopes of being the editorial intern for *Flirt* magazine. Her dreams are soon in jeopardy when she arrives late and underdressed and makes a bad first impression on the editor-in-chief, Josephine Bishop.

Close Up and Personal. Grosset & Dunlap, 2006. ISBN 9780448442648.

Once Alexa adjusts to the differences between laid-back Buenos Aires and the fast pace of New York City, she hopes to make a splash as *Flirt*'s photography intern by taking candid photos of people in Central Park while riding a horse.

High Fashion. Grosset & Dunlap, 2006. ISBN 9780448441221.

Olivia may have become *Flirt*'s fashion intern because her wealthy parents are old friends of Josephine Bishop; nevertheless, she intends to prove to everyone that she is up to the task when she presents her ideas and original accessory designs for the upcoming fall issue. When several photos of Olivia appear in the gossip columns, her parents cut her off until she can remember to act like a proper member of London's high society, including breaking up with her cute boyfriend, Eli.

Keywords: dating; family; fashion

Spin City. Grosset & Dunlap, 2006. ISBN 9780448441238.

As the entertainment intern for *Flirt*, Kiyoko Katsuda initially has a hard time keeping up with the frenzied pace, until she learns how to get organized and discovers that her true passion is composing music for anime films.

Keywords: Asian American; music

Issues. Grosset & Dunlap, 2006. ISBN 9780448443942.

As the interns are getting ready to say good-bye to New York City and all their new friends, Josephine Baker invites the girls to stay on for another semester at *Flirt*, which includes finding time in their busy schedule for school.

Keywords: school

VIPs. Grosset & Dunlap, 2006. ISBN 9780448443959.

The interns have to work together if they are going to survive school and their next assignment. As one of the sponsors of New York City's fashion week, *Flirt* has sent its interns to work behind the scenes assisting famous designers and models, including Kiyoko's sister, Miko.

Keywords: fashion; school; sisters

French Twist. Grosset & Dunlap, 2007. ISBN 9780448444635.

Although Alexa prefers to be behind the camera, she hits the streets of Paris with Kiyoko, meeting with modeling agencies and going on photo shoots. Kiyoko becomes jealous, until she makes an unexpected discovery of her own. Meanwhile, back in New York City, Melanie busily works on selling her jewelry, and Liv edits her school's new 'zine.

Keywords: modeling

London Calling. Grosset & Dunlap, 2007. ISBN 9780448444642.

Olivia brings Melanie along on her two-week trip back home, where her family are members of London's high society. Olivia's prim and proper parents' attempts to keep Melanie's bohemian style hidden backfire when the English boy they planned for their daughter notices her.

Keywords: dating; family; travel

Copycat. Grosset & Dunlap, 2007. ISBN 9780448445618.

Out with the old and in with the new at *Flirt*, as seven interns try to settle in and get their story ideas published. The competition really begins after former child star Georgia Cooper discovers that the new features intern, Elizabeth Cheekwood, has writer's block and is resorting to plagiarism.

Model Behavior. Grosset & Dunlap, 2007. ISBN 9780448445625.

When *Flirt* sponsors a reality show to discover the next supermodel, interns Asha Patel and Nova Burke have to take care of some demanding models.

Keywords: modeling

Daswani, Kavita.

Indie Girl. **Simon Pulse, 2007. ISBN 9781416948926. J S**

After not getting a summer internship at the magazine *Celebrity Style*, sixteen-year-old Indria "Indie" Konkipuddi goes against her Indian American parent's wishes and agrees to baby-sit the editor, Aaralyn Taylor's, toddler. Indie gets closer to her dream of becoming a fashion reporter when she discovers information that could help save the struggling magazine.

Keywords: crushes; East Indian American; family; humor; work

Salaam, Paris. **Plume, 2006. ISBN 9780452287464. A**

Beautiful Tanaya Shah leaves Mumbai, India, to meet Tariq, the man her traditional Muslim family wants her to marry. When her engagement is broken, Tanaya decides to stay in Paris, against her family's wishes, and becomes a successful runway model.

Keywords: East Indian; family; modeling; work

Davis, Dee.

A Match Made on Madison. St. Martin's Griffin, 2007. ISBN 9780312357849. **A**

To prove once and for all who is the best matchmaker in Manhattan, Vanessa Carlson challenges her former mentor, friend, and sometime rival, Althea Sevalas, to convince the elusive bachelor, Mark Grayson, to become a client and get him to the altar first.

Keywords: dating; friendship; marriage; wedding; work

Downing, Erin.

Dancing Queen. Simon Pulse, 2006. ISBN 9781416925101. **J** **S**

When seventeen-year-old Olivia "Liv" Phillips leaves Ann Arbor, Michigan, for a summer internship for Music Mix Europe in London, she lands a great assignment as coordinator for the hottest TV show, starts dating a fashionable pop star, and has a chance to become a music mix VJ.

Keywords: dating; friendship; internship; music; romantic comedy

Gregory, Deborah.

Catwalk. Delacorte Press, 2008. ISBN 9780385904551. **J** **S**

Fashion International High School junior Pasmina Purrstein is one of the house leaders in the annual fashion show competition known as the catwalk. Pasmina may become the next "it" girl because this year the catwalk is being recorded on the TeenStyle Network for a new reality show.

Keywords: fashion; friendship; school

Hayden.

A Matter of Attitude. Kimani TRU, 2008. ISBN 9780373830893. **S**

Fashionable fifteen-year-old Angela Jenkins is so desperate to become a designer that she agrees to pay Shayla Mercer to make sure that Angela is elected Kressler High's director of the holiday fashion show.

Keywords: African American; family; fashion; friendship; school; work

Hogan, Mary.

[Susanna]. **J** **S**

Enthusiastic fifteen-year-old Susanna Barringer cannot wait until college to begin her future career as a celebrity journalist, so she is determined to make her internship meaningful.

Keywords: internship

Susanna Sees Stars. Delacorte Press, 2007, c2006. ISBN 9780385905022.

Fifteen-year-old Susanna Barringer pursues her dream of becoming a celebrity reporter by applying for intern positions at all the New York–based magazines. Although her summer internship at *Scene*, a premiere celebrity gossip magazine, has more to do with running errands than writing stories, Susanna is determined to find the biggest scoop to prove herself.

Keywords: friendship

Susanna Hits Hollywood. Delacorte Press, 2007. ISBN 9780385905039.

When a *Scene* magazine intern and teen celebrity journalist heads to sunny California to report on the Academy Awards, she loses her press pass while exploring Hollywood and must find a way to get behind the velvet ropes.

Keywords: humor

Susanna Covers the Catwalk. Delacorte Press, 2008. 9780385905046.

After months of studying style and reading *Vogue*, Susanna is ready for her second reporting assignment for *Scene* magazine. Susanna has a press pass to cover New York City's fashion week, but it will be up to her to get backstage to meet the hottest designers and models.

Keywords: crushes; fashion; humor

Karasyov, Carrie.

Wolves in Chic Clothing. Broadway Books, 2005. ISBN 9780767917803. **A**

Stylish Julia Pearce's dreams that her sales position at Pelham's Department Store will open a door to jewelry design temporarily comes true when she becomes the assistant to heiress Lell Pelham. Julia is thrust into the glamorous world of social-ites, designer clothes, and charity galas, until Lell's playboy husband, Will Banks, decides to make a play for Julia and Lell finds out.

Keywords: affairs; friendship; gay; marriage; sexual content; work

Karasyov, Carrie, and Jill Kargman.

Summer Intern. HarperTeen, 2007. ISBN 9780061153761. **J S**

Bright Kira Parker learns how the fashion world operates when she spends the summer as an intern for *Skirt,* the premiere fashion and beauty magazine. She re-alizes that although nepotism will get your foot in the door, hard work does pay off, after the boss's daughter lands the exclusive intern position but Kira gets the job as college editor.

Keywords: fashion; internship

Kemp, Kristen.

Breakfast at Bloomingdale's. Scholastic Press, 2007. ISBN 9780439809870. **J S**

Despite her boyfriend's objections, seventeen-year-old Kat Zappe leaves Ken-tucky for New York City to pursue her and her late grandmother's dreams of cre-ating a fashion line that will be showcased at Bloomingdale's.

Keywords: death; family; fashion

Kerlin, Amanda, and Phil Oh.

Secrets of the Model Dorm. Atria Books, 2007. ISBN 9780743298261. **A**

With her dreams of being on the cover of *Vogue*, eighteen-year-old Heather Johnston moves into a one-bedroom apartment with several other young models. Once in New York City, Heather spends her days going on castings and her nights partying in clubs.

Keywords: modeling; sexual content; work

Kraut, Julie, and Shallon Lester.

Hot Mess: Summer in the City. Delacorte Press, 2008. ISBN 9780385904995. **S**

Newly single seventeen-year-old Emma Freeman trades her normal summer job as a lifeguard in the suburbs for an internship in New York City. Emma and her best friend Rachel move in with a beautiful socialite who parties in the hottest night clubs while Emma works all day for a demanding boss.

Keywords: crushes; dating; friendship; work

Krulik, Nancy.

Ripped at the Seams. Simon Pulse, 2004. ISBN 9780689867712. **S**

Eighteen-year-old Sami Granger moves from the Midwest to New York City with dreams of becoming a famous fashion designer. When Sami is forced to work at a lingerie shop after her designs are stolen, she finds success as a designer of custom nightgowns.

Keywords: dating; family; fashion; work

Malkin, Nina.

Orange Is the New Pink. Scholastic, 2007. ISBN 9780439899659. **S**

Seventeen-year-old Babylon Edison is selected as one of the teens to edit *Orange's* first ever "Readers Run Amok" issue. Along with her fellow editors, Emmalee, Nae-Jo, Paulina, and Tabby, Babylon spends a glorious summer in New York City writing stories, interviewing celebrities, and meeting cute boys.

Keywords: African American; dating; work

Maude, Rachel.

Poseur. **S**

Last year sixteen-year-old Janie Farrish felt like an outsider because she had a scholarship to Winston Prep, an excusive private school in Hollywood Hills. Everything changes in tenth grade when her twin brother Jake starts dating "it" girl Charlotte Beverwil and Janie's proposal for specialty study has her working very closely with Petra Greene, the daughter of a plastic surgeon; Melissa Moon, daughter of a rap producer; and Charlotte Beverwil, daughter of a model and movie producer. The four very different girls combine their interest in fashion and design to create Poseur, a new and fresh fashion line. Includes pencil drawings of the characters in their latest fashions.

Keywords: fashion; friendship

Poseur. Little, Brown, 2008. ISBN 9780316065832.

Janie Farrish's wish that tenth grade will be more exciting comes true when she is assigned to work with Petra Greene, Charlotte Beverwil, and Melissa Moon for specialty study. The four girls take "The Trend Set" class seriously by starting their own fashion label, including a huge launch party at the Prada store on Rodeo Drive.

Keywords: dating; school

The Good, the Fab and the Ugly. Little, Brown, 2008. ISBN 9780316065849.

Inspired by the Halloween season, Petra, Charlotte, Melissa, and Janie each create an exclusive couture bag called the Trick-or-Treater. After arguing over whose design to use, the Poseur bag is spotted by an important designer.

Keywords: crushes; dating; school

Pretty in Pink. Poppy, 2009. ISBN 9780316065856.

Now that their handbag has been noticed by fashion icon Ted Pelligan, Petra, Charlotte, Melissa, and Janie are determined to let Hollywood know they are the next big thing.

Messina, Lynn.

Fashionistas. Red Dress Ink, 2003. ISBN 9780373250257. **A**

Vig Morgan joins her fellow associate editors at *Fashionista* in a plot to get rid of editor-in-chief Jane McNeill, with hopes that the magazine will become more than a shrine to celebrities and trends.

Keywords: fashion; work

Savvy Girl. Harcourt, 2008. ISBN 9780152061616. **S**

During seventeen-year-old Chrissy Gibbons's eight-week stint as a summer intern for *Savvy Magazine,* her friendship with the glamorous fashion editor Jessica could cost Chrissy her chance at writing a winning Savvy girl column, and she may forget her real friends when they need her the most.

Keywords: fashion; friendship; internship; kissing; work

Oliver, Jasim.

Project Fashion Trilogy. **S**

Marina, Sinead, and Frankie are three freshmen at Central School of Fashion in London who share a townhouse owned by Sinead's mom. During their first year at college, the roommates help each other with their fashion and romantic dilemmas.

Keywords: college; fashion

Gucci Girls. Simon Pulse, p2007, c2005. ISBN 9781416935346.

In between taking classes and completing assignments, vintage clothing blogger Marina, jewelry designer Frankie, and fashion designer Sinead get distracted by a few cute British boys who live across the square.

Keywords: dating; family

Armani Angels. Simon Pulse, p2007, c2005. ISBN 9781416938118.

As the winter holiday approaches, Marina's relationship with Rob is still going strong, Frankie's modeling career is flourishing, and Sinead continues her on and off relationship with Travis, while they feel the pressure to complete fashion assignments.

Keywords: dating; modeling

Prada Princesses. Simon Pulse, p2007, c2006. ISBN 9781416938125.

While Frankie forgoes the final fashion show of the year to walk the runway in Paris, Sinead's nude body art photos of herself create a stir, and Marina is inspired to design shoes at the last minute.

Keywords: family; modeling; school

Walker, Melissa.

[Violet on the Runway]. **S**

After seventeen-year-old Violet Greenfield unexpectedly becomes an international runway model for a year, she gives up the limelight for college.

Keywords: modeling

Violet on the Runway. Berkley JAM, 2007. ISBN 9780425217047.

In Chapel Hill, North Carolina, shy and awkward seventeen-year-old Violet Greenfield is discovered by an important modeling agent and flies with her mother to New York City for a makeover and auditions. After immediate success, Violet graduates early from high school and moves to New York City, where she is exposed to the darker side of modeling, including drugs and jealous rivals.

Keywords: body image; friendship; school; work

Violet in Private. Berkley JAM, 2008. ISBN 9780425221822.

While her best friends Roger and Julie start college, Violet returns to the runways of Brazil and France, publicity speaks out against eating disorders, and has an affair with the young designer Paulo, even though she is in love with Roger.

Keywords: body image; break-ups; dating; friendship; travel; work

Violet by Design. Berkley JAM, 2008. ISBN 9780425219409.

Now nineteen, Violet trades her modeling career for a normal college life at Vassar College, where she struggles to fit in, makes friends, and eventually finds her talent during her internship at a teen fashion magazine.

Keywords: college; crushes; friendship; internship

Weisberger, Lauren.

The Devil Wears Prada. **Broadway Books, p2004, c2003. ISBN 9780767914765.** **A**

Recent college grad Andrea Sachs keeps her dream of writing for *The New Yorker* while she is the assistant to the powerful editor-in-chief of *Runway* magazine, Miranda Priestly.

Keywords: dating; fashion; movie tie-in; work

Yampolsky, Karen.

Falling Out of Fashion. **Kensington Books, 2007. ISBN 9780758217004.** **A**

The editor-in-chief of *Jill Magazine,* Jill White, has had tremendous success as an alternative voice in the traditional fashion and beauty magazine field. Now Jill has gone from having her face on the cover of *Time* magazine to battling her new parent company, which is more concerned with selling advertising space than keeping loyal readers.

Keywords: fashion; work

Starlets

The spotlight is on fame seekers and sometimes those thrust unwillingly into the limelight, young actresses, singers, and talent scouts usually living in California. The heroines often try to keep a balance between their celebrity persona and their real-life drama, involving family, friends, and of course, boys.

Benway, Robin.

🎖 *Audrey, Wait!* **Razorbill, 2008. ISBN 9781595141910.** **S**

Audrey Cuttler was an ordinary sixteen-year-old girl who had a crush on her coworker, until her rocker ex-boyfriend's song about their recent break-up became a huge hit. Now Audrey is harassed by the paparazzi, gossip magazines, and overzealous fans.

Keywords: break-ups; crushes; dating; romantic comedy
Awards: BBYA 2009

Calonita, Jen.

Secrets of My Hollywood Life. **M** **J**

Sixteen-year-old Kaitlin Burke is very down to earth, despite the fact that she grew up acting on *Family Affair*, a popular nighttime soap opera. Her manager mother, personal assistant, and best friend help Kaitlin maintain her hectic schedule, which includes a lot of premiers and interviews. Her bad twin on *Family Affair* is Sky Mackenzie, a diva in training who goes out of her way to make sure Kaitlin gets her share of bad press. Throughout the novels Kaitlin reveals her Hollywood secrets, such as that celebrities do not like to watch themselves on the big screen.

Keywords: acting; dating

Secrets of My Hollywood Life. Little, Brown, 2006. ISBN 9780316154420.

Disguised in a boring brown wig and color contacts, teen sensation Kaitlin Burke gets a vacation from the tabloids and her crazy schedule when she becomes Clark Hall's newest sophomore and experiences what it is like to be a normal teen. When her backstabbing costar, Sky Mackenzie, blows her cover, Kaitlin may lose her first real boyfriend.

Keywords: school

Secrets of My Hollywood Life: On Location. Little, Brown, 2007. ISBN 9780316154390.

Kaitlin is so thrilled to be dating Austin Meyers and starring in a new movie with a talented director that she doesn't mind that her ex-boyfriend, Drew Thomas, and her nemesis, Sky Mackenzie, are her costars. However, Kaitlin's excitement fades when the publicity department wants the press to write about how she is dating Drew and Austin gets jealous.

Keywords: work

Secrets of My Hollywood Life: Family Affairs. Little, Brown, 2008. ISBN 9780316117999.

In between getting her driver's permit, taking SAT prep tests, and spending time with her boyfriend, sixteen-year-old Kaitlin Burke joins forces her with her costar, Sky Mackenzie, to take down Alexis Holden, a manipulative diva who is determined to be the biggest young star on *Family Affair.*

Keywords: work

Secrets of My Hollywood Life: Paparazzi Princess. Little, Brown, 2009. ISBN 9780316030649.

With fewer than eight *Family Affairs* episodes left to tape, Kaitlin considers what project to work on next, explores her independence with new friends, and feels hurt that her best friend has a new best friend.

Keywords: family; friendship; kissing; work

Cohn, Rachel.

Pop Princess. Simon & Schuster, 2004. ISBN 9780689852053. **J** **S**

When high school outsider Wonder Blake is offered a record deal with her late sister's manager, she becomes an instant pop star and goes on tour singing her catchy single, "Bubble Gum Pop."

Keywords: dating; family; lesbian; music

Coleman, Rowan.

Ruby Parker Hits the Small Time. HarperTempest, 2005. ISBN 9780060776305. **M** **J**

Ruby Parker's average looks have made her one of the most well-liked actresses on *Kensington Heights,* Britain's most popular soap opera. In the real world, however, Ruby fears being fired, is upset over her parents' break-up, and enlists the meanest girl in school to instruct her on how to kiss.

Keywords: acting; family; friendship

Collins, Yvonne, and Sandy Rideout.

Vivien Leigh Reid. ◼ ◼

When fifteen-year-old Vivien Leigh Reid spends time with her second-rate movie actress mother, their relationship becomes increasingly strained after Leigh discovers she also is a talented actress.

Keywords: acting; family

Introducing Vivien Leigh Reid: Daughter of a Diva. St. Martin's Griffin, 2005. ISBN 9780312338374.

> Fifteen-year-old Leigh reluctantly spends the summer in Ireland with her estranged B-list movie star mother, Annika, and discovers that she too wants to be an actress when she lands a minor role in her mother's movie.
>
> **Keywords:** travel

Now Starring Vivien Leigh Reid: Diva in Training. St. Martin's Griffin, 2006. ISBN 9780312338398.

> When Leigh goes to Los Angeles for the summer to attend an acting class, she wins a role in a popular soap opera and starts acting like her diva mom.

The New and Improved Vivien Leigh Reid: Diva in Control. St. Martin's Griffin, 2007. ISBN 9780312358280.

> Leigh continues her stay in Los Angeles to plan her mother's upcoming wedding to a famous producer and hopes her new role on an action television series will squash her diva reputation.
>
> **Keywords:** wedding

de la Cruz, Melissa.

Cat's Meow. Simon & Schuster. 2001. ISBN 9780743205047. ◼

After celebrating her twenty-fifth birthday for the fourth time, B-list celebrity Cat McAllister goes on a mission to marry a European prince as a way to secure her social status.

Keywords: acting; dating; humor

Dean, Zoey.

Talent. J

As the talented daughters of Hollywood celebrities, eighth graders Mackenzie "Mac" Little-Armstrong, Cordelia "Coco" Kingsley, and Evangelina Becks are the popular girls at Bel-Air Middle School. Emily Mungler completes the group after she relocates from Iowa and moves in with the Little-Armstrong family to pursue acting.

Keywords: friendship

Talent. Razorbill, 2008. ISBN 9781595141781.

> Unlike her gifted family and talented best friends Becks and Coco, twelve-year-old Mackenzie has yet to realize her talent, until she discovers Emily Mungler, an Iowa native using her acting ability to meet the teen heart-throb Davey Woodward. Mac soon realizes that like her Hollywood agent mother, she has an eye for noticing and representing future stars.
>
> **Keywords:** acting; crushes; family

Almost Famous. Razorbill, 2008. ISBN 9781595141897.

> At the beginning of eighth grade, Emily's debut as the cool new girl is overshadowed after her friends' biggest rival at school, Ruby Goldman, wins the social chair election against Mac by passing around a movie exposing their embarrassing secrets.
>
> **Keywords:** crushes; school

Star Power. Razorbill, 2009. ISBN 9781595142009.

> The girls work toward their dream of stardom as Mac produces Coco's debut album, Emily is cast in her first movie with her longtime crush, and Beck models for Quicksilver.
>
> **Keywords:** acting; crushes; modeling

DeVillers, Julia.

How My Private, Personal Journal Became a Bestseller. **Dutton, 2004. ISBN 9780525472834.** M J

> Jamie becomes a best seller and celebrity virtually overnight when her journal is accidentally submitted to her English teacher.
>
> **Keywords:** humor; school TV movie tie-in

Douglas, Lola.

[Morgan Carter]. S

> The following titles, although not formally a series, deal with the same protagonist and are listed in chronological order.

More Confessions of a Hollywood Starlet. Razorbill, 2006. ISBN 9781595140517.

> Morgan Carter has to face new opposition now that her secret identity has been revealed, and she must decide if she should stay in Indiana or move back to Hollywood and leave behind her boyfriend, Eli.
>
> **Keywords:** dating; diary

True Confessions of a Hollywood Starlet. Razorbill, 2005. ISBN 9781595140937.

> The diary entries of Morgan Carter, a fashionable movie star and recovering addict, as she leaves behind the glamour (and the drugs) of Hollywood in exchange for the normalcy of Fort Wayne, Indiana. Disguised as Claudia Miller, Morgan moves in with a family friend, attends the local high school, and comes to terms with her past.
>
> **Keywords:** diary; family; friendship school; self-acceptance

Flinn, Alex.

Diva. HarperTempest, 2006. ISBN 9780060568450. **J** **S**

After breaking free from a physically and emotionally abusive relationship, sixteen-year-old Caitlin McCourt starts to rebuild her self-esteem by attending a performing arts school to pursue her dream of being an opera singer, despite her mother's objections.

Keywords: body image; family

Lockhart, E.

🌵 *Dramarama.* Hyperion, 2007. ISBN 9780786838158. **J** **S**

Best friends Sayde and Demi both have big dreams as they leave Ohio for the Wildewood Academy for Performing Arts Summer Theater Institute. However, tensions rise when Demi is selected for one of the leads and Sayde only gets a bit part, after bombing her audition.

Keywords: acting; dating; friendship; gay; jealousy
Awards: BBYA 2008

Malkin, Nina.

[6X]. **S**

The following titles, although not formally a series, deal with the same characters and are listed in chronological order.

6X: The Uncensored Confessions. Scholastic, 2005. ISBN 9780439724210.

In alternating chapters, the four members of the newly formed pop-rock band 6X chronicle their rise to fame, including learning their instruments and their feelings about the other members of the band.

Keywords: friendship; music

Loud, Fast and Out of Control. Scholastic, 2006. ISBN 9780439724227.

The members of 6X, known as the body, the boss, the boy, and the voice, share their thoughts on dating and the madness of touring.

Keywords: dating; friendship; music

Manning, Sarrah.

🌵 *Guitar Girl.* Speak, p2005, c2003. ISBN 9780142403181. **S**

Inspired by her idol, seventeen-year-old Molly Montgomery forms The Hormones with her two best friends. The band quickly becomes famous after Dean and his friend T join the group.

Keywords: friendship; music; sexual content
Awards: Quick Picks 2005

Margolis, Leslie.

Price of Admission. Simon Pulse, 2007. ISBN 9781416924555. **S**

When Jasmine Green's tell-all screenplay is unexpectedly accepted by her father's movie studio, she tries to keep the indiscretions of her family and friends a secret.

Keywords: family

McLaughlin, Emma, and Nicola Kraus.

The Real Real. HarperTeen, 2009. ISBN 9780061720406. **S**

As one of the few middle-class students in her Long Island neighborhood, high school senior Jesse O'Rourke gladly accepts the $40,000 scholarship when she becomes one of six students selected for *The Real Hampton Beach*, a new reality show. Once the show airs, Jesse becomes an instant celebrity, but at a cost.

Keywords: dating; school

Mendle, Jane.

Better Off Famous? St. Martin's Griffin, 2007. ISBN 9780312369033. **J** **S**

While visiting her great-aunt Alexandra in New York City, sixteen-year-old Annie Hoffman's secret audition at Julliard turns into a starring role on the new teen television show *Country Day*. As Annie becomes a hot TV starlet, she drops her old friends in Alabama to party with celebrities and soon discovers the negative price of fame.

Keywords: acting; friendship

Michaels, Jamie.

Kiss My Book. Delacorte Press, 2007. ISBN 9780385734998. **S**

Fifteen-year-old Ruby Crane is worshipped by her classmates because she has a successful book, a movie deal, and a cute boyfriend, until she is accused of plagiarism.

Keywords: family; school

Reisfeld, Randi.

Starlet. **J** **S**

All the school plays and community theater have paid off for seventeen-year-old Jacey Chandliss. As a winner on *Generation Next: The Search for America's Top Young Actor*, Jacey won a part in a big Hollywood movie. After filming *Four Sisters*, Jacey leaves Michigan and moves into a small house in Beverly Hills, California, with her older cousin Ivy and best friends Desiree and Dash. Now her entourage includes a publicist, a stylist, and an agent. Jacey tries to live up to her reputation as Hollywood's hottest starlet despite a catty blogger who is devoted to spreading negative gossip.

Keywords: acting

Starlet. Hyperion, 2007. ISBN 9781423105015.

After getting fabulous reviews for her role in *Four Sisters*, Jacey Chandliss begins working on her second feature film, while her two-year relationship with Logan weakens because she has to work during prom weekend and she befriends indie actor Matt Canseco.

Keywords: dating; moving

Everyone Who's Anyone. Hyperion, 2007. ISBN 9781423105022.

Although still unsure where she stands with Matt, Jacey's career is on fire. Following her teen choice nomination, she receives an offer from a big studio to star in a series of superhero movies, and also models for two major advertising campaigns.

Keywords: modeling

All Access. Hyperion, 2007. ISBN 9781423105039.

Jacey is promoting her recent movie and being a guest judge on *Generation Next*, when tabloid blog articles accuse her of seeing one of the contestants behind her boyfriend Matt's back. When Matt believes the gossip, the couple breaks up, and Jacey has to confront her estranged father alone.

Keywords: break-ups; dating; sexual content; work

Roter, Jordan.

Girl in Development. **Dutton, 2006. ISBN 9780142408223.** **J** **S**

When Samantha Rose receives an unexpected high school graduation present from her wealthy uncle, she quickly relocates to his large guesthouse with her older cousin Kate and begins an internship at Authentic Pictures, a Hollywood development company.

Keywords: dating; family; internship; moving

Senate, Melissa.

Theodora Twist. **Delacorte Press, 2006. ISBN 9780385903226.** **J** **S**

When they star in a reality show to reinvent Hollywood actress Theodora Twist's party girl reputation, she and boring Emily Fine realize they have a lot more in common than a childhood home.

Keywords: friendship

Shaw, Tucker.

🌠 *Confessions of a Backup Dancer.* **Simon Pulse, 2004. ISBN 9780689870750.** **J** **S**

Seventeen-year-old Kelly Kimball chronicles her journey from the dancing studio to lead backup dancer on the hottest summer tour with the reigning princess of pop.

Keywords: friendship; music; work
Awards: Quick Picks 2005

Sheldon, Dyan.

Confessions of a Teenage Drama Queen. **M** **J**

Fifteen-year-old Mary Elizabeth Cehas has a flare for the dramatic. Seeking attention at her new school in Dellwood, New Jersey, she calls herself Lola, tells larger-than-life stories, and pursues her acting career.

Keywords: friendship; humor

🎗 *Confessions of a Teenage Drama Queen.* Candlewick Press, p2005, c1999. ISBN 9780763628277.

> When Mary Elizabeth Cep moves from New York City to a New Jersey suburb, she changes her name to Lola, dresses dramatically, tells embellished tales, and competes against the most popular girl at Dellwood High for the lead in the school's production of *My Fair Lady*.
>
> **Keywords:** acting; movie tie-in
>
> **Awards:** Quick Picks 2000

My Perfect Life. Candlewick Press, 2002. ISBN 9780763628284.

> Ella Gerard was bored with her perfect life in suburban New Jersey until her eccentric best friend, Lola Cep, tricks Ella into coming out of the shadows and running for student council president against Carla Santini, the most popular girl at school.
>
> **Keywords:** family; school

Confessions of a Hollywood Star. Candlewick Press, 2005. ISBN 9780763630751.

> Days before graduating from Dellwood High School, the budding actress Lola Cep comes up with a few plans to get on the set of the major Hollywood movie being filmed in town, while already bragging to her classmates that she has a walk-on part.
>
> **Keywords:** acting

Shull, Megan.

Amazing Grace. Hyperion, 2005. ISBN 9780786856909. **J S**

> Wanting to get away from the limelight, tennis superstar and spokes model Grace "Ace" Kincaid changes her name to Emily O'Brien, moves into a retired FBI agent's Alaska cabin, and tries to live like a normal fifteen-year-old girl.
>
> **Keywords:** romantic comedy; self-acceptance; sports

Sisman, Robyn.

A Hollywood Ending. Plume, 2008. ISBN 9780452286139. **A**

> Concerned about her career, Oscar winning American actress Paige Carson leaves Hollywood to perform a Shakespearean play in London. After a rough start, Paige adjusts to the unpampered life and begins a romance with her landlord, Ed Hawkshead, a documentary filmmaker.
>
> **Keywords:** acting; moving; romantic comedy; work

Triana, Gaby.

Backstage Pass. HarperTeen, 2005. ISBN 9780060560195. **J S**

> After growing up traveling the world with her rock star dad and manager mom, when they move to Miami, Florida, sixteen-year-old Desert McGraw tries to keep her family's real identity a secret from her new friends and her boyfriend, Liam.
>
> **Keywords:** family; friendship

Van Etten, David.

[Mallory]. M J

The following titles, although not formally a series, deal with the same protagonist and are listed in chronological order.

All That Glitters. Alfred A. Knopf, 2008. ISBN 9780375946783.

As the soap opera she developed gets closer to production, Mallory has to deal with the network demands that the show be more exciting, the lead actor trying to get fired, and her boyfriend, Keith's, increasing jealously and still find time to sleep and get schoolwork done.

Keywords: acting; dating; family; friendship; kissing; work

Likely Story. Alfred A. Knopf, 2008. ISBN 9780375946769.

As the daughter of a soap opera actress, sixteen-year-old Mallory uses her behind- the-scene knowledge of dramas to create *Likely Story*, a daytime soap opera about high school students.

Keywords: dating; family; friendship; work

Williams, Tia.

[It Chicks]. S

It Chicks. Jump at the Sun/Hyperion, 2007. ISBN 9781423104063.

The aspiring dancers, rappers, and actresses who are fortunate to study at The Louis B. Armstrong School of Performing Arts find plenty of drama off the stage.

Keywords: African American; dating; friendship; school

Sixteen Candles. Jump at the Sun/Hyperion, 2008. ISBN 9781423110323.

As a daughter of a famous TV actress, Skye Carmichael expects to be the center of attention as she gets ready to star in an episode of Music Video Network's hottest reality show, *Sixteen Candles*.

Keywords: African American; dating friendship; jealously

Zindel, Lizabeth.

Girl of the Moment. **Viking, 2007. ISBN 9780670062102.** J S

Fifteen-year-old Lily discovers the inner truth of teenage celebrity when she spends the summer as an intern for Hollywood's latest starlet, Sabrina Snow.

Keywords: friendship; internship

I have a confession to make: My life is not nearly as glamorous as it might seem. Or as easy.

—David Van Etten, *All That Glitters*

Chapter 3

International Relations

I've always had this deep-down conviction that I'm not like every-body else, and there's an amazingly exciting new life waiting for me just around the corner.

—Sophie Kinsella, *Can You Keep a Secret?*

Because chick lit originated in England, there are naturally numerous teen chick lit books that fall into the Brit lit subgenre. Almost everything written about Brit lit points out that the characters have a distinct sense of humor compared to their American counterparts. This is definitely true of the quirky British teen girls who describe their dating and friendship dramas with side-splitting timing. What began with the hilarious diary of Georgia Nicholson continues with Sue Limb's Jess Jordan, who once thought stuffing her bra with minestrone soup in plastic bags was a good idea. You can image the outcome when a bag exploded at a party in front of her crush! From there, younger readers gravitate to the <u>Mates, Dates</u> series by Cathy Hopkins, while older readers thoroughly enjoy reading about Becky Bloomwood's comical exploits and misadventures in Sophie Kinsella's <u>Shopaholic</u> series.

Not all international teen chick lit can be classified as traditional romantic comedies. In general, each country has its own style, and although Irish and Australian heroines can also be quite witty, they are often dealing with heavy issues of identity and family problems. In these longer novels, the young women learn how to fight back against life's obstacles to eventually find love and happiness.

The bulk of this chapter is about teen girls who are studying abroad for the semester or are on vacation with family or friends. Reading about thrilling Caribbean cruises, culture shock in Japan, or romantic European vacations can make for a perfect beach read during those lazy days of summer spent by the pool, or can be a great escape to get through those dreary winter nights.

Chapter Organization

This chapter organizes teen chick lit novels that fall into the international and traveling/vacation subgenre. International titles are arranged by the region that the character lives; travel- and vacation-themed books are organized alphabetically by the author's name.

Brit Lit

These are chick lit novels about teen girls who live in England. Besides location the common characteristic in this section is the situational humor and wit of the heroines.

Day, Susie.

*Serafina67: *Urgently Requires Life**. Scholastic Press, 2008. ISBN 9780545073301. **S**
   In her online blog, fifteen-year-old Sarah writes about her dating mishaps, her father's upcoming wedding, and her nine resolutions to achieve happiness.

   Keywords: blogs; body image; dating; drinking; family; humor; school

Dent, Grace.

LBD. **J** **S**

Ronnie, Fleur, and Claudia are best friends and rock music fanatics who call themselves Les Bambinos Dangereuses.

Keywords: friendship

LBD: (It's a Girl Thing). Speak, 2004. ISBN 9780142401828.
   The self-proclaimed Les Bambinos Dangereuses, fourteen-year-olds Ronnie, Fleur, and Claudia, organize a rock concert at Blackwell school featuring the best local bands after their strict parents won't allow them to attend a summer rock concert.

   Keywords: family; humor; music

LBD: Live and Fabulous. Speak, p2006, c2004. ISBN 9780142406625.
   After receiving free tickets from the rock star Spike Saunders, fifteen-year-olds Ronnie, Fleur, and Claudia convince their parents to let them attend the two-day Astlebury music festival, as long as Fleur's older sister is their chaperone.

   Keywords: humor; music

LBD: Friends Forever! Putnam, 2006. ISBN 9780399241895.
   As a way to repair their strained friendship, sixteen-year-olds Ronnie, Fleur, and Claudia each apply for summer jobs at Destiny Bay, an upscale seaside resort. During the summer the three best friends party, waitress, and even enter the Miss Ultimate Demonboard Babe Contest as a way to raise money for Claudia's mom.

   Keywords: dating; family; work

Dhami, Narinder.

Bindi Babes. **M** **J**

Since their mother's death last year, three pretty British East Indian sisters, Geena, Amber, and Jazz, enjoy getting everything they want (like new sneakers and cell phones) from their father, until their interfering Aunt moves in.

Keywords: British East Indian; family; humor; school; sisters

Bindi Babes. Yearling, p2005, c2003. ISBN 9780440420194.

When their meddling aunt moves in from India, Geena, Amber, and Jazz Dillion team up to marry her off. After the matchmaking fails, the sisters break their unspoken agreement not to discuss their mother, and with the help of their aunt, the entire family starts the healing process.

Keywords: death

Bollywood Babes. Random House Children's Books, p2006, c2004. ISBN 9780440420200.

The Dillion sisters, Geena, Amber, and Jazz, track down the former Bollywood star Molly Mahal and invite her to live with them so she can be the guest of honor at their school's Bollywood-themed fund-raiser. When Molly turns into a diva and flirts with their dad and teacher, Mr. Ahora, the sisters try to get rid of her.

Bhangra Babes. Delacorte Press, p2006, c2005. ISBN 9780385903370.

The trilogy concludes with the Indian-British Dillion sisters helping their auntie plan her upcoming to wedding to Mr. Ahora, while simultaneously competing for the new boy Rocky Gill's affections and befriending a new student who has major attitude.

Keywords: crushes; wedding

Hokins, Cathy.

Mates, Dates. Ⓙ

In the heart of London, four teenage girls are a tight group who spend their free time hanging out and talking. Fourteen-year-old Lucy Lovering sometimes feels inadequate when compared to her best friends, Izzie Foster and Nesta Williams, because she is small for her age and has less experience with boys. The group becomes a solid foursome when bookish TJ befriends Lucy. Each book tells one girl's' story.

Keywords: friendship; humor

🎗 *Mates, Dates, and Inflatable Bras.* Simon Pulse, p2003, c2001. ISBN 978-0689855443.

At first Lucy is upset when her best friend Izzie befriends beautiful Nesta, but then the threesome bond over their insecurities. Lucy is finally able to write her essay, "What Makes Me, Me?" after she discovers her talents as a designer, gets a new haircut, and has her first kiss.

Keywords: body image; family; fashion; first kiss; humor
Awards: Quick Picks 2004

🎗 *Mates, Dates, and Cosmic Kisses.* Simon Pulse, p2003, c2001. ISBN 978-0689855450.

Adding to her already long list of questions about God and spirituality, Izzie "why" Foster wonders how boys think when she gets mixed messages from

Marc. When Izzie finally gives up on Marc, she discovers that Ben, the lead singer of a local band, shares her search for cosmic understanding.

Keywords: crushes; music; spirituality

Awards: Quick Picks 2004

Mates, Dates, and Designer Divas. Simon Pulse, p2003, c2001. ISBN 9780689855467.

When Nesta falls for Simon, a wealthy older boy, she learns how to ride a horse and confronts his snobby friend, Cressida. Originally published in Great Britain in 2001 by Piccadilly Press Ltd. as *Mates, Dates, and Portobello Princesses.*

Keywords: crushes

Awards: Quick Picks 2004

Mates, Dates, and Sleepover Secrets. Simon Pulse, p2003, c2002. ISBN 9780689859915.

After her best friend moves to South Africa, Theresa Joanne (TJ) bonds with Lucy and her mates through sleepovers and makeovers and unexpectedly falls for Lucy's older brother, Steve.

Keywords: crushes; family; humor

Mates, Dates, and Sole Survivors. Simon Pulse, p2004, c2002. ISBN 9780689859922.

After spending the first few days of summer vacation wishing she had a boyfriend like her mates, Lucy follows Izzie's advice and writes down the qualities she wants in a boyfriend. When Lucy attends a relaxation camp with her dad, she meets, Daniel, a boy who temporarily helps her forget about Nesta's brother, Tony.

Keywords: crushes; dating; family; friendship

Mates, Dates, and Mad Mistakes. Simon Pulse, p2004, c2003. ISBN 9780689867224.

Now that they are going into year ten, Izzie wants to leave the old Izzie behind by creating a new image that includes new clothes, piercing her belly button, and dating bad boy Josh Harper.

Keywords: body image; crushes; dating

Mates, Dates, and Sequin Smiles. Simon Pulse, p2004, c2003. ISBN 9780689867231.

Nesta thinks her new braces are going to ruin her social life and snogging skills, until she joins an acting class and meets gorgeous Luke. Originally published in Great Britain in 2001 by Piccadilly Press Ltd. as *Mates, Dates, and Pulling Power.*

Keywords: acting; body image; crushes; dating

Mates, Dates, and Tempting Trouble. Simon Pulse, p2005, c2004. ISBN 9780689870620.

During a joint school project, TJ befriends and unexpectedly falls in love with Nesta's new boyfriend, Luke de Biasi. When Nesta' finds out, the mates temporarily spilt up, as Lucy sides with Nesta and Izzie sides with TJ.

Keywords: break-ups; crushes; dating; school

Mates, Dates, and Great Escapes. Simon Pulse, p2005, c2004. ISBN 9780689876950.

The school trip to Florence, Italy, with her mates is the perfect way for Lucy to get over her recent break-up with Tony, especially when she meets a sweet American boy who shows her around the beautiful sites.

Keywords: break-ups; crushes; dating; school; travel

Mates, Dates, and Chocolate Cheats. Simon Pulse, p2006, c2005. ISBN 9780689876967.

As a way to lose the eight pounds she recently gained over the holiday vacation, Izzie tries several fad diets and works out at the gym every day. She ultimately learns how to eat healthier and regains her self-esteem after performing on a new television show for teens.

Keywords: body image

Mates, Dates, and Diamond Destiny. Simon Pulse, p2006, c2005. ISBN 9780689876974.

To impress William Lewis and prove to her mates that she thinks about others, Nesta organizes The Diamond Destiny Dance, a charity event that includes a fashion show with a local celebrity model, which raises a lot of money for hospice and the terminally ill.

Keywords: crushes; fashion

Mates, Dates, and Sizzling Summers. Simon Pulse, 2006. ISBN 9780689876981.

One week before reconnecting with her soulmate, Luke de Biasi, TJ starts dating Ollie Axford, a Casanova son of a rock star; her father is hospitalized after having a stroke. The series concludes with the four girls agreeing that boys will come and go, but they will be best mates forever.

Keywords: dating; family

Kinsella, Sophie.

Can You Keep a Secret? **Dial Press, 2004. ISBN 9780385336819.** A

Twenty-five-year-old marketing assistant Emma Corrigan confesses her deepest secrets to Jack Harper, a fellow air passenger, only to discover later that Jack is the founder of her company.

Keywords: dating; humor; romantic comedy; work

Shopaholic. A

Perpetual shopper Rebecca "Becky" Bloomwood constantly gets in debt, but always finds humorous ways to end up on top.

Keywords: humor

Confessions of a Shopaholic. Dell, p2003, c2001. ISBN 9780440241416.

Financial writer Becky Bloomwood ignores the letters from her bank and credit card companies and does a lot of shopping in the shops and boutiques of London. Becky tries to earn extra money by working at a clothing boutique, making fancy picture frames, and buying lottery tickets; she has a turn of good luck after she appears on the television program *Morning Coffee*.

Keywords: dating; family; friendship; movie tie-in; romantic comedy; work

Shopaholic Takes Manhattan. Dell, 2004, c2002. ISBN 9780440241812.

Becky accompanies her serious boyfriend, Luke Brandon, to New York City in hopes that her screen tests and breakfast meetings will lead to her own television show. When a British tabloid exposes Becky's extravagant shopping habits, she is forced to find a new profession.

Keywords: dating; romantic comedy; travel; work

Shopaholic Ties the Knot. Bantam Dell, p2004, c2003. ISBN 9780440241898.

Becky is truly happy as a personal shopper at Barney's and living with her boyfriend, Luke, in Manhattan, so when Luke proposes, Becky is so thrilled that she somehow agrees to have her mom plan a simple wedding in England, while her cold stepmother-to-be, Eleanor, simultaneously plans an elaborate wedding at The Plaza on the same day.

Keywords: dating; family; romantic comedy; weddings; work

Shopaholic and Sister. Dial Press Trade Paperbacks, 2005. ISBN 9780385336826.

After a ten-month honeymoon around the world, Becky returns to London with the hottest handbag and dreams of surprising her friends and family, only to discover that her best friend, Suze, has a new best friend. Her parents inform Becky that she has a long-lost older sister. Becky fantasizes about bonding with her new sister while shopping, until she finds out that Jess is a frugal environmentalist.

Keywords: family; friendship; marriage; sisters

Shopaholic and Baby. Dial Press, 2007. ISBN 9780385338707.

In England Becky is determined to have the most stylish pregnancy, including a gorgeous nursery, designer pram, and water birth delivery. Things get complicated when Becky's celebrity obstetrician, Venetia Carter, turns out to be Luke's ex-girlfriend.

Keywords: family; marriage; pregnancy

Limb, Sue.

Zoe & Chloe: On the Prowl. Viking, 2008. ISBN 9780670011209. **J** **S**

Best friends Zoe and Chloe try some crazy antics to get dates for the quickly approaching Earthquake Ball, including posting a want ad.

Keywords: dances; dating; friendship; humor; sisters

Girl, 15. **M** **J**

Funny and likable Jess Jordan, along with her mother, gorgeous best friend, and friend turned boyfriend, have plenty of misadventures and misunderstandings.

Keywords: family; friendship; humor

Girl, Barely 15: Flirting for England. Delacorte Press, 2008. ISBN 978-0385735384.

> Fourteen-year-old Jess Jordan's dreams of hanging out with a handsome French boy as part of a student exchange program are squashed when she has to spend two weeks with Edouard, a small and shy boy who barley speaks English. Her best mate, Flora, hooks up with cute Gerard on a disastrous camping trip.
>
> **Keywords:** crushes; school

Girl, 15, Charming But Insane. Laurel-Leaf Books, 2007, c2004. ISBN 978-0440238966.

> Fifteen-year-old Jess Jordan has to deal with her grandmother moving in, her nearly perfect best friend Flora's crush on her childhood friend Fred, and trying to think of something intelligent to say to her crush, Ben Johnson.
>
> **Keywords:** body image; dating

Girl, Nearly 16, Absolute Torture. Laurel-Leaf Books, p2008, c2005. ISBN 9780440238973.

> Jess's summer plans with her friend turned boyfriend Fred are ruined when her mom announces that they will be going on a two-week trip visiting historical sites. The trip concludes with throwing Grandpa's ashes in the sea and calling in on her dad.
>
> **Keywords:** dating; gay

Girl, Going on 17, Pants on Fire. Delacorte Press, 2006. ISBN 9780385902465.

> Right before school begins, things go downhill for Jess. First she breaks up with Fred because he suggests that they keep their relationship a secret so he can keep his loner reputation, then her mom starts to date, and her favorite teacher is replaced by one who immediately dislikes Jess.
>
> **Keywords:** break-ups; dating; school

Mason, Sarah.

Party Girl. Ballantine Books, p2006, c2003. ISBN 9780345469564. **A**

> Party planner Isabel Serranti becomes attracted to Simon Monkwell, her childhood tormenter, while planning a charity ball at his family's country estate.
>
> **Keywords:** dating; family; romantic comedy; work

McKnight, Gillian.

[Alexis and Helene]. **J S**

> The following titles, although not formally a series, deal with the same characters and are listed in chronological order.

To Catch a Prince. Simon Pulse, 2006. ISBN 9780689877346.

> When sixteen-year-old Helene gets an internship at a London museum, her stepsister Alexis joins her. On their transcontinental flight they make a wager to see who could win the heart of Prince William.

They take the competition so seriously that they might wreck their close friendship and the possibility of real romance.

Keywords: dating; family; humor; internship; travel

The Frog Prince. Simon Pulse, 2006. ISBN 9780689877353.

After her mom abandons her, Alexis joins her stepsister, Helene, in Paris with her wealthy father and actress stepmother. The stepsisters' talents are discovered when Alexis interns at Vedette, a fancy fashion design house, and Helene becomes their newest model.

Keywords: dating; family; fashion; humor; modeling; travel

O'Connell, Tyne.

The Calypso Chronicles. 🆓 🆂

As an American and a serious fencer, Calypso Kelly felt like an outsider her first term at Saint Augustine's School for Ladies, where the students are blond, willowy, and have descended from powerful English families. Calypso is finally accepted by most of her classmates when she snags the most sought-after boy at Eades, Prince Frederick, who is a fit fencer and second in line to the British throne.

Keywords: boarding school; dating; friendship; humor; sports

🏵 *Pulling Princes.* Bloomsbury, 2004. ISBN 9781582349572.

During the summer term, fourteen-year-old Calypso Kelly is thrilled to be rooming with her best friend Star and hanging out with Prince Freddy, on and off the fencing mat, until Honey O'Hare sends pictures of the royal couple kissing to the tabloids.

Keywords: kissing

Awards: Quick Picks 2005

Stealing Princes. Bloomsbury, 2005. ISBN 9781582349923.

It goes from bad to worse for Calypso when she has to room with Lady Portia Herrington Brigs and the Honorable Honey O'Hare, while her best friend, Star, seems to drop her for the new girl, Indie. Honey's schemes cause Calypso to falsely accuse Portia of trying to steal Prince Freddy.

Dueling Princes. Bloomsbury, 2006. ISBN 9781582349008.

Now Prince Freddy's official girlfriend, fifteen-year-old Calypso is training hard for the National Fencing competition when her British mother, Sarah, decides to leave her father back in Hollywood and relocate to England.

Keywords: family

Dumping Princes. Bloomsbury, 2006. ISBN 9781582348520.

The entire year eleven at Saint Augustine help Calypso come up with a plan to get Prince Freddie back so she can perform a counter dump, while she also prepares for her first international fencing tournament, in Italy.

Keywords: break-ups

Rennison, Louise.

Confessions of Georgia Nicolson. **J** **S**

Georgia Nicolson is a humorous, self-obsessed teen who writes regularly in her diary about her best friends, weird family, large half-Scottish wildcat Angus, and often embarrassing experiences with boys. To help readers understand Georgia's often made-up language, a glossary is included at the end of each volume. The series is more character driven than plot driven.

Keywords: animals; diary; family; friendship; humor

🎀 *Angus, Thongs, and Full-Frontal Snogging:* **Confessions of Georgia Nicolson.** HarperCollins, 2000. ISBN 9780060288143.

Fourteen-year-old Georgia writes in her diary about kissing lessons, her appearance, her dad relocating to New Zealand, her cat terrorizing the neighbor's pet, her best friend Jas dating, and her crush on the seventeen-year-old musician Robbie.

Keywords: body image; dances; dating; kissing

Awards: BBYA 2001, Quick Picks 2001, Printz-Honor 2001

🎀 *On the Bright Side, I'm Now the Girlfriend of a Sex God: Further Confessions of Georgia Nicolson.* HarperCollins, 2001. ISBN 9780060288136.

Georgia tries to convince her parents that she should stay in England when they move to New Zealand, so she can continue kissing the sex god "S.G." Robbie. When S.G. decides Georgia is too young to date, she tries to make him jealous by dating Dave the Laugh.

Keywords: body image; break-ups; dating; kissing

Awards: Quick Picks 2002

🎀 *Knocked Out by My Nunga-nungas: Further, Further Confessions of Georgia Nicolson.* HarperTempest, p2002, c2001. ISBN 9780066236568.

Fifteen-year-old Georgia looks forward to the end of her boring five-day vacation in Scotland so she can be reunited with her official boyfriend, Robbie. However, Georgia gets confused when she kisses her ex-boyfriend, Dave the Laugh.

Keywords: body image; dating; kissing; vacation

Awards: Quick Picks 2003

Dancing in My Nuddy-pants: Even Further Confessions of Georgia Nicolson. HarperTempest, p2004, c2002. ISBN 9780060097486.

While Robbie, the sex god, is away on tour not even a weekend trip to Paris can distract Georgia from thinking about Dave the Laugh.

Keywords: body image; dating, kissing, sports

Away Laughing on a Fast Camel: Confessions of Georgia Nicolson. HarperTempest, p2006, c2004. ISBN 9780060589363.

For about two months sixteen-year-old Georgia is depressed that Robbie has moved to New Zealand; then she meets Masimo, the half-American, half-Italian new lead singer of the Stiff Dylans.

Keywords: crushes; kissing

Then He Ate My Boy Entrancers: More Mad, Marvy Confessions of Georgia Nicolson. HarperTempest, p2006, c2005. ISBN 9780060589370.

> Although Georgia was determined to bump into Masimo during her trip to the United States, she spends her time in Memphis, Tennessee, sunbathing. Upon her return to England, Georgia is confused about boys because Robbie wrote her a nice letter, Dave wants to be her boyfriend again, and Masimo wants to date Georgia and Lindsay.
>
> **Keywords:** dating; kissing; vacation

Startled by His Furry Shorts. HarperTeen, p2007, c2006. ISBN 9780060853860.

> After giving Masimo an ultimatum to date her exclusively or not at all, Georgia fills her time in rehearsals for *Macbeth* with Dave and thinking about Robbie.
>
> **Keywords:** acting; break-ups; dating; kissing

Love Is a Many Trousered Thing. HarperTeen, 2007. ISBN 9780060853877.

> Now that Robbie is back in England and Masimo wants to be her boyfriend, Georgia spends two weeks lamenting about her two possible boyfriends, right up until her camping trip with Dave and the Ace gang.
>
> **Keywords:** dating; kissing

Stop in the Name of Pants! HarperTeen, 2008. ISBN 9780061459320.

> While her official boyfriend Masimo is in Italy for summer vacation, Georgia takes care of Angus, who was run over by a car. She also can't stop flirting with her mate Dave.
>
> **Keywords:** dating; kissing

Are These My Basoomas I See Before Me? HarperTeen, 2009. ISBN 9780061459351.

> In the final installment of the series, Masimo's break-up with Georgia leads her to finally start a romantic relationship with her friend Dave the Laugh.
>
> **Keywords:** break-ups; kissing

Rushton, Rosie.

The Dashwood Sisters' Secrets of Love. **Hyperion Paperbacks, p2006, c2005. ISBN 9780786851379.** 🇯 🇸

> After their parents' divorce and their father's sudden death, thirteen-year-old Georgie, fifteen-year-old Abby, and sixteen-year-old Ellie are forced to move into a small cottage in Norfolk, where they each become entangled in a romantic exploit. An updated homage to Jane Austen's *Sense and Sensibility*.
>
> **Keywords:** dating; divorce; family; sisters

Sheldon, Dyan.

[Planet Janet]. 🇯 🇸

> The following titles, although not formally a series, deal with the same protagonist and are listed in chronological order.

Planet Janet. Candlewick Press, p2003, c2002. ISBN 9780763620486.

The diary of sixteen-year-old Janet Bandry, who along with her best friend Disha enters a "Dark Phase," which includes wearing only dark clothes, dying her hair black, listening to jazz music, and crushing on Elvin, an aspiring filmmaker, while also dealing with her family's on-going drama.

Keywords: crushes; dating; diary; family; humor

Planet Janet in Orbit. Candlewick, p2005, c2004. ISBN 9780763627553.

Despite the fact that her best friend Disha and her newly divorced mom are in love, Janet starts to leave her "Dark Phase" behind as she gets her first job, celebrates her seventeenth birthday, has disastrous driving lessons, and writes the school newspaper's advice column.

Keywords: diary; divorce; family; friendship; school; work

Tettig, Liz.

My Desperate Love Diary. **Holiday House, 2005. ISBN 9780823420339.** J S

For one year, high school student Kelly Ann writes in a her personnel diary about her looks, her complicated relationship with her cute friend Chris, and her desire to kiss her crush.

Keywords: crushes; dating; diary

Wilson, Jacqueline.

GIRLS Quartet. J

Ellie Allard has two supportive best friends, Nadine and Magda, but she really wants two things, a real boyfriend and to be skinny.

Keywords: friendship

Girls in Love. Dell Laurel-Leaf, 2002. ISBN 9780440229575.

Ninth grader Ellie Allard's goals for her freshman year are to stick to her diet, get glamorous hair, and find a boyfriend like her two best friends Nadine and Magda. After Ellie meets nerdy Dan during her holiday vacation, she pretends that he is her boyfriend back at home.

Keywords: body image; family, humor
Awards: Quick Picks 2003

Girls Under Pressure. Dell Laurel-Leaf, p2003, c1998. ISBN 9780440229582.

After Ellie is called fat during a model search at the mall, she goes on a drastic diet that includes starvation, binging, and purging, until she befriends Zoe, a girl suffering from anorexia.

Keywords: body image; family

Girls Out Late. Dell Laurel-Leaf, p2003, c1999. ISBN 9780440229599.

Chubby Ellie is so head over heals in love with her new artistic boyfriend Russell that she lies to her dad, breaks curfew, and has secret after-school trysts at McDonalds.

Keywords: dating; family

Girls in Tears. Delacorte Press, p2003, c2002. ISBN 9780385901048.

In the final installment, the once tight relationships are strained: Ellie's dad and stepmom are fighting, Nadine and Madga are keeping secrets, and Ellie's boyfriend Russell betrays her twice.

Keywords: break-ups; dating; family

Whytock, Cherry.

The Life of Angelica Cookson Potts. Ⓜ Ⓙ

Fourteen-year-old Angelica "Angel" Cookson Potts is a food lover who sometimes worries that she is too big and busty, especially when she is next to her three beautiful best friends and ex-model mother.

Keywords: body image; crushes; family; food; friendship; humor; recipes

My Cup Runneth Over: The Life of Angelica Cookson Potts. Simon Pulse, 2004. ISBN 9780689865510.

After Angel buys a supportive bra, she is the surprise hit of the school fashion show and receives her first kiss. First published in Great Britain with the title *Angel: Disasters, Diets, and D-cups.*

Keywords: first kiss; school

My Scrumptious Scottish Dumplings: The Life of Angelica Cookson Potts. Simon & Schuster Books for Young Readers, 2004. ISBN 9780689865497.

After a family vacation in Scotland, one of Angel's best friends, Mercedes, moves to the United States, and her eccentric father's one-person protest gets the whole family banned from Harrods department store.

My Saucy Stuffed Ravioli: The Life of Angelica Cookson Potts. Simon & Schuster Books for Young Readers, p2006, c2004. ISBN 9780689865503.

During her vacation in a seaside villa in Italy with her parents, cook, and three best friends, Angel makes a few embarrassing mistakes, including wearing a see-through bikini and suspecting that her mother is having an extramarital affair.

Keywords: vacation

Aussie Gals

Chick lit stories about girls who live in Australia. The common thread found among the novels is a delicate balance between humor and serious issues of self-acceptance, identity, and family.

Abdel-Fattah, Randa.

Does My Head Look Big in This? Orchard Books, p2007, c2005. ISBN 978-0439919470. Ⓙ Ⓢ

At the start of the new semester at her elite prep school, sixteen-year-old Amal Abdel-Hakim decides to wear a hijab, the Muslim head scarf, to show her dedication to the Muslim faith, to the surprise of her supportive family and friends.

Keywords: body image; family; friendship; humor; Muslim Palestinian; religion; school

Ten Things I Hate about Me. Orchard Books, p2009, c2006. ISBN 978-0545050555. **J** **S**

> Since seventh grade, sixteen-year-old Jamilah Towfeek has been dyeing her hair blonde, wearing blue contact lenses, and calling her self Jaime to hide her Lebanese Muslim identity, until she is finally honest with an online friend.
>
> **Keywords:** cliques; family; friendship humor; Lebanese Muslim; religion; school; self-acceptance

Hantz, Sara.

The Second Virginity of Suzy Green. Flux, 2007. ISBN 9780738711393. **S**

> To fit in with the popular crowd at her new school and be more like her deceased sister, seventeen-year-old Suzy Green reforms her party girl ways and joins the virginity club at Saint Peter's.
>
> **Keywords:** dating; family; school; sexuality

Lowry, Brigid.

Things You Either Hate or Love. Holiday House, 2005. ISBN 9780823420049. **J** **S**

> To make money for her favorite band's big May Day concert, fifteen-year-old Georgia Reeves tries babysitting, with disastrous results; has a brief stint at a bakery, and winds up at a local grocery store, where she gets to work with her crush, Hunter.
>
> **Keywords:** body image; family; first kiss; humor; work

Moriarty, Jaclyn.

🎗 *Feeling Sorry for Celia*. St. Martin's Griffin, 2000. ISBN 9780312287368. **S**

> When private school student Elizabeth Clarry is assigned a pen pal from a neighboring public school, Elizabeth confesses her thoughts about running away, her workaholic father, and her unstable best friend Celia, who just ran away to join the circus. Written entirely in notes, etc.
>
> **Keywords:** family; friendship; humor; school; sports
>
> **Awards:** BBYA 2002

Shanahan, Lisa.

The Sweet, Terrible, Glorious Year I Truly, Completely Lost It. Delacorte Press, 2006. ISBN 978385735162. **J** **S**

> Even though public speaking makes fourteen-year-old Gemma Stone want to vomit, she tries out for the high school play with bad boy Raven De Head and agrees to wear a ridiculous outfit for her older sister's wedding.
>
> **Keywords:** acting; dating; family; humor

Sparrow, Rebecca.

The Year Nick McGowan Came to Stay. **Alfred A. Knopf, p2008, c2006. ISBN 9780375945700.** J S

> In 1989 Nick McGowan, the hottest guy in Year 11, moves into seventeen-year-old Rachel Hill's house after he is kicked out of the boarding school, and the unlikely pair form a friendship.

> **Keywords:** friendship; school

Irish Imports

Chick lit novels about young women who hail from Ireland. All the novels in this section are adult novels that will appeal to older high school students.

Ahern, Cecelia.

PS, I Love You. **Hyperion, 2004. ISBN 9781401300906.** A

> Twenty-nine-year-old Holly Kennedy becomes a young widow when her thirty-year-old husband and soul mate Gerry dies from a brain tumor. After months consumed by grief, Holly discovers that Gerry left ten envelopes, one to be opened each month, with instructions that help Holly heal and learn how to live life again.

> **Keywords:** death; family; friendship; marriage; movie tie-in

Rosie Dunne. **Hyperion, 2005. ISBN 9781401300913.** A

> The story of childhood best friends Rosie and Alex, who remain close after Alex moves to Boston while Rosie becomes a teenage mother in Dublin. Told entirely though e-mails, letters, and instant messages.

> **Keywords:** affairs; death; family; friendship; humor; love; marriage; motherhood; work

Keyes, Marian.

Lucy Sullivan Is Getting Married. **Perennial, p2002, c1996. ISBN 9780060090371.** A

> When a fortune-teller predicts a marriage within a year, twenty-six-year-old Lucy Sullivan is surprised, because she has no real love prospects. Then she begins to date Gus, an Irish musician. As Lucy falls in love, she wonders if Gus is the man the fortune-teller was referring to.

> **Keywords:** dating; family; friendship; romantic comedy

Rachel's Holiday. **Perennial, p2002, c1998. ISBN 9780060090388.** A

> After an accidental drug overdose, twenty-seven-year-old Rachael Walsh agrees to enter the Cloisters, a rehab center in Dublin, where she expects to be pampered in a spalike atmosphere with celebrities. What Rachael discovers is that the run-down center requires shared house work and many hours of humiliating group theory.

> **Keywords:** dating; drug addiction; family; sexual content

World Travelers

A lot can happen when you are away from home. This section features traditional romantic comedies and coming-of-age stories about teen girls on vacation or studying abroad for a semester.

Burnham, Niki.

[Valerie Winslow]. **J** **S**

The following titles, although not formally a series, deal with the same protagonist and are listed in chronological order.

🎖 *Royally Jacked.* Simon Pulse, 2004. ISBN 9780689866685.

After her mother announces that she is a lesbian and is moving in with her girlfriend, and her father accepts a position working for the royal family in Schwerinborg, fifteen-year-old Valerie Winslow leaves behind her friends, including her longtime crush David, to live in a real castle; she ends up falling for Prince Georg.

> **Keywords:** crushes; family; friendship; kissing; lesbian; romantic comedy

> **Awards:** Quick Picks 2005

Spin Control. Simon Pulse, 2005. ISBN 9780689866692.

When the press discovers that Valerie is dating Prince Georg, her father sends her back to Virginia for the winter break, where her old crush, David, is still interested in her.

> **Keywords:** dating; family; friendship; kissing; romantic comedy

Cann, Kate.

California Holiday, or, How the World's Worst Summer Job Gave Me a Great New Life. **Avon Books, p2005, c2003. ISBN 9780060561611.** **S**

Desperate to get out of England after completing her final exams, Rowan relocates to Seattle, Washington, to work as a nanny to four-year-old Flossy. Rowan can't stand her job, so she runs away to San Francisco, where she meets cute Landon, who convinces Rowan to work with him at a country club in California.

> **Keywords:** dating; family; humor; travel; work

Grecian Holiday or, How I Turned Down the Best Possible Thing Only to Have the Time of My Life. **Avon Books, 2002. ISBN 9780064473026.** **S**

After Kelly turns down traveling through Europe with her boyfriend Mike and his mates, she accepts her friend Jade's offer to stay in a picturesque farmhouse in Greece. Kelly has a great time with her newfound independence, until Mike and his friends surprisingly show up.

> **Keywords:** break-ups; dating; friendship; humor

Mediterranean Holiday, or, How I Moved to a Tiny Island and Found the Love of My Life. **HarperTeen, 2007. ISBN 9780061152160.** **S**

> Seventeen-year-old Chloe thinks she is in love with beautiful and confident Davina, until they go on a summer holiday to the Mediterranean island of Caminos with Davina's wealthy family. When Chloe meets a cute boy, she sees another side to Davina.
>
> **Keywords:** crushes; dating; family; friendship; humor; travel

Spanish Holiday, or, How I Transformed the Worst Vacation Ever into the Best Summer of My Life. **Avon Books, p2004, c2001. ISBN 9780060561604.** **S**

> The vacation plans of British teen Laura Harvey and her two best friends, Yaz and Ruth, are temporally ruined when Ruth's boyfriend Tom tags along and forces the girls to visit mainly tourist traps. Then they are asked to take care of an authentic villa, and Laura falls for the cute caretaker's son, Juan.
>
> **Keywords:** crushes; dating; friendship; humor; travel

Delaney, Kaz.

My Life as a Snow Bunny. **Smooch, 2003. ISBN 9780843952964.** **J** **S**

> During Christmas break, sixteen-year-old Jo Vincent is not looking forward to leaving sunny California for a snowy Colorado ski resort with her father and his girlfriend. Then she meets Hans, a Swiss skier.
>
> **Keywords:** family; vacation

Elkeles, Simone.

[Amy Nelson]. **J** **S**

> The following titles, although not formally a series, deal with the same protagonist and are listed in chronological order.

How to Ruin a Summer Vacation. Flux, 2006. ISBN 9780738709611.

> Sixteen-year-old Amy Nelson unexpectedly bonds with a family she never knew, falls for an older boy, and learns to love her estranged father during her summer vacation in Israel.
>
> **Keywords:** family; love; religion

How to Ruin My Teenage Life. Flux, 2007. ISBN 9780738710198.

> With her non-boyfriend Avi back in Israel and her recently married mother expecting a baby, Amy focuses her attention on her religious classes, her annoying new neighbor, Nathan, and finding someone special for her workaholic dad.
>
> **Keywords:** family; friendship; kissing

Friedman, Aimee.

[South Beach]. **S**

> Popular and attractive Alexandria "Alexa" St. Laurent becomes reacquainted with her former childhood friend as they have adventures in many glamorous locations.
>
> **Keywords:** friendship

🔖 *South Beach.* Scholastic, 2005. ISBN 9780439706780.

For spring break, sixteen-year-old Alexandria St. Laurent and her childhood best friend, Holly Jacobson, head to South Beach, Florida, where they tan on the beach, dance in nightclubs, enter bikini contest,s and fall for the same guy.

Keywords: crushes; vacation

Awards: Quick Picks 2006

French Kiss. Scholastic, 2006. ISBN 9780439792813.

Holly sneaks away from her track meet in England to join Alexa in Paris after her friend's sudden break-up with Diego. In Paris Holly flirts with Alexa's cute cousin, Pierre, and Alexa falls hard for a young artist.

Keywords: break-ups; dating; sexual content

Hollywood Hills. Scholastic, 2007. ISBN 9780439792820.

A few days before graduation, Alexa and Holly unexpectedly take a trip to Hollywood Hills, California, to attend a celebrity wedding, where they discover what they both have been looking for.

Keywords: love

Harrison, Emma.

The Best Girl. Harper, 2008. ISBN 9780061228247. **S**

Tomboy and Colorado University freshman Farrah Jane Morris is the best "man" for her brother's extravagant wedding at an elite ski resort where her crush, Connor Davy, works.

Keywords: dating; family; first kiss; romantic comedy; wedding

Hawthorne, Rachel.

Caribbean Cruising. Avon Books, 2004. ISBN 9780060565077. **S**

Eighteen-year-old Lindsay Darnell's plans to break out of her shell, flirt with many boys, and lose her virginity in a one-night stand during her ten-day cruise change when she falls in love with her new stepdad's godson, Walter Hunt.

Keywords: dating; family; first love; sexuality

Island Girls (and Boys). Avon, 2005. ISBN 9780060755461. **S**

Recent high school graduate Jennifer's plans for her last summer with her two best friends, Amy and Celeste, at her grandparent's beach house go out the window when Celeste's boyfriend Noah moves in, Amy flirts with every boy she sees, and Jennifer falls for Dylan, who is about to join the army.

Keywords: friendship; romantic comedy; work

Love on the Lifts. Avon Books, 2006. ISBN 9780060815363. **J** **S**

High school senior Kate Kennedy accepts her Aunt Sue's offer to spend winter break in one of her condos in the Snow Angel Valley resort with her two best friends, Allie Anderson and Leah Locke. The girls' plans to meet some cute ski instructors are put on hold when her older brother Sam shows up with his friends, including Kate's crush, Brad.

Keywords: crushes; friendship; romantic comedy

Johnson, Maureen.

Girl at Sea. **HarperTeen, 2007. ISBN 9780060541453.** **S**

Seventeen-year-old Clio Ford is forced to leave behind her summer job at an art store and her crush to work with her estranged father, his archeologist girlfriend, her daughter Elsa, and a young research assistant, Aidan, as they search for a sunken stone tablet in the Mediterranean Sea.

Keywords: family; first kiss; mystery; romance

🌱 *13 Little Blue Envelopes.* **HarperCollins, 2005. ISBN 9780060541415.** **J** **S**

Along with a passport and an ATM card, seventeen-year-old Ginny Blackstone receives from her late Aunt Peg thirteen letters, with instructions to travel around Europe to visit the best museums, meet artists, and discover her hidden paintings.

Keywords: dating; death; family; romance

Awards: BBYA 2006

Maxwell, Katie.

The Emily Series. **S**

Seattle native Emily Williams goes into culture shock when she travels to England, Scotland, and France with her parents. Sixteen-year-old Emily faithfully e-mails her best friend Dru about her misadventures with foreign boys.

Keywords: humor

The Year My Life Went Down the Loo. **Dorchester, 2003. ISBN 9780843952513.**

Through detailed e-mails to her best friend Dru, sixteen-year-old Emily Williams explains how her new life in the English hamlet of Piddlington-on-the-Weld consists of being embarrassed at school for being an outsider, planning the Halloween dance, and on the weekends going to discos with the local playboy, Aidan.

Keywords: dances; dating; family; kissing; school; travel

They Wear What Under Their Kilts? **Smooch, 2004. ISBN 9780843952582.**

To fulfill a work-study requirement, Emily and her quiet friend Holly spend one month at her aunt and uncle's sheep farm in Scotland, where they have a contest to see who can kiss the hot farmworker, Ruaraidh.

Keywords: crushes; kissing; travel; work

What's French for "Ew!"? **Smooch, 2004. ISBN 9780843952971.**

During her spring break vacation in Paris with her boyfriend Devon, Emily celebrates her seventeenth birthday while taking care of "Jack," a pretend baby, for school.

Keywords: dating; vacation

The Taming of the Dru. Smooch, 2004. ISBN 9780843952988.

In her last month in England before moving back home to Seattle, Emily finally decides that Fang is the one for her; unfortunately, he returns from New Zealand with a new girlfriend.

Keywords: crushes; friendship; work

Life, Love, and the Pursuit of Hotties. Smooch, 2005. ISBN 9780843955491.

In the last installment of the series, Emily graduates from high school, prepares for college, listens to her friend Dru's wedding plans, and goes on a cruise with Fang to Alaska.

Keywords: college; dating; friendship; graduation

Morrison, Jessica.

Buenos Aires Broken Hearts Club. GrandCentral, 2007. ISBN 9780446699129. **A**

When twenty-eight-year-old Cassandra "Cassie" Moore loses her job and fiancé on the same day, she books a six-month trip to Argentina, where she writes a blog about her heartbreak and meets local artist Mateo.

Keywords: break-ups; humor; vacation

Noel, Alyson.

Cruel Summer. St. Martin's Griffin, 2008. ISBN 9780312355111. **S**

Seventeen-year-old Colby Cavendish's plans to spend the summer with the popular crowd, including Levi Bonham, change when she is shipped off to Greece with her eccentric Aunt Tally. Things start to change for Colby once she steps out of the Internet café and meets up with the gorgeous islander Yannis.

Keywords: blogs; crushes; divorce; family; self-discovery

Rahlens, Holly-Jane.

Prince William, Maximilian Minsky, and Me. Press, 2005. ISBN 9780763632991. **M** **J**

When bookish thirteen-year-old Nelly Sue Edelmeister discovers that the high school basketball team will be traveling to England, she enlists eccentric Max to help her make the team and possibly meet her crush, Prince William. While practicing her game, this aspiring astronomer is also planning her bat mitzvah and coping with her parents' fighting.

Keywords: crushes; family; German; religion

S.A.S.S. (Students Across the Seven Seas). **J**

Beginning with the completed application for the Students Across the Seven Seas Study Abroad Program, each book centers around a different American girl, whose experiences studying abroad in a foreign country usually include self-discovery and romance. A map of the country is also included.

Keywords: school; travel

Apelqvist, Eva.

Swede Dreams. Speak, 2007. ISBN 9780142407462.

> After dating Jonas, an exchange student at her high school in Wisconsin, sixteen-year-old Calista Swanson thinks the romance will continue during her semester in Sweden. When Jonas does not respond to her e-mails or phone calls, Calista discovers her own strengths while taking in the sites, and unexpectedly finds love.

> **Keywords:** dating; family

Ferris, Aimee.

Girl Overboard. Speak, 2007. ISBN 9780142407998.

> During her semester on a luxury yacht in the Caribbean Sea, seventeen-year-old Marina Grey realizes that her dreams of becoming a marine biologist are more important than her relationship with her longtime boyfriend back home in Vermont, especially when she gets close to Link, an Australian boy who shares her passion.

> **Keywords:** break-ups; dating

Gerber, Linda.

Now and Zen. Speak, 2006. ISBN 9780142406571.

> Sixteen-year-old Noreli Tanaka is frustrated when everyone assumes she is a native during her summer abroad in Tokyo, Japan, until she stays with her great aunt and uncle in Kyoto and learns about her Japanese heritage.

> **Keywords:** crushes; divorce; family

The Finnish Line. Speak, 2007. ISBN 9780142409169.

> As the daughter of an Olympic skier, sixteen-year-old Maureen Clark is determined to prove her talent at the big exhibition competition during her semester abroad in Finland; surprisingly she gets her first boyfriend.

> **Keywords:** family; first kiss; sports

Guthart Strauss, Peggy.

Getting the Boot. Speak, 2005. ISBN 9780142404140.

> When seventeen-year-old Kelly Brandt and her childhood friend Sheela Ramaswamy live in Italy for three months, Kelly loses her former party girl ways, falls in love with an Italian boy, and discovers her artistic talents.

> **Keywords:** dating; friendship

Hapka, Cathy.

Pardon My French. Speak, 2005. ISBN 9780142404591.

> Seventeen-year-old Nicole Larson's parents have signed her up for a semester in France because they feel Nicole is too serious about her longtime boyfriend Nate. Without her controlling best friends and boyfriend, Nicole takes an emotional journey on which she discovers her confident, adventurous side.

> **Keywords:** break-ups; dating; friendship

French Kissmas. Speak, 2008. ISBN 9780142411339.

> For three weeks during her winter recess, Nicole Larson returns to Paris along with other former S.A.S.S. students to film a promotional video, determined not to reunite with Luc, but she has a hard time resisting him in the city of love and romance.

Keywords: friendship

Jellen, Michelle.

Spain or Shine. Speak, 2005. ISBN 9780142403686.

> Sixteen-year-old Elena Holloway balances her time in Spain among classes, writing a play with a classmate, relaxing on the beach with friends and trying to get the courage to flirt back with Miguel, a seventeen-year-old Spanish boy.

Keywords: family; kissing

Liu, Cynthea.

The Great Call of China. Speak, 2009. ISBN 9780142411346.

> Adopted teen Cece is excited to leave Texas for a semester in China to explore her roots and possibly search for her birth parents.

Keywords: family

Nelson, Suzanne.

Heart and Salsa. Speak, 2006. ISBN 9780142406472.

> Sixteen-year-old Caitlin Wilcox was thrilled to get away from her newly remarried mother to build a school for orphaned children in Mexico with her best friend Sabrina, but Sabrina unexpectedly brings along her secret boyfriend, Brian. While in Mexico Caitlin's new boyfriend, Aidan, helps her accept her new stepfather.

Keywords: divorce; friendship; kissing

The Sound of Munich. Speak, 2006. ISBN 9780142405765.

> During the spring semester of her junior year, bohemian Siena Bernstein is studying in Munich, Germany, with a secret mission to complete her late father's Carpe Diem list and still find time to go on a proper date with her German resident advisor, Stefan.

Keywords: dating; family; kissing

Ostow, Micol.

Westminster Abby. Speak, 2005. ISBN 9780142404133.

> Sixteen-year-old Abby Capsaw leaves behind her good girl personality, cheating ex-boyfriend, James, and overprotective parents in Manhattan during her semester abroad in London. Abbey sees the sights with her new punk rock friend Zoe and British boyfriend Ian, until James surprisingly shows up.

Keywords: drinking; family; kissing

Supplee, Suzanne.

When Irish Guys Are Smiling. Speak, 2008. ISBN 9780142410165.

To escape the loss of her mother and her new stepmother's pregnancy, seventeen-year-old Delk Sinclair spends a semester in Ireland reading poetry, making friends, and falling in love with a sweet Irish boy.

Keywords: family; friendship; kissing

Sher, Abby.

Kissing Snowflakes. Scholastic, 2007. ISBN 9780545000109. **J S**

During her winter break vacation in a Vermont Inn with her dad, brother, and new stepmom, fifteen-year-old Samantha has her first kiss with a beautiful ski instructor, but she realizes that the sweet son of the inn owner, Eric, could be her first real boyfriend.

Keywords: crushes; family; romantic comedy; vacation

Sisman, Robyn.

Summer in the City. Plume, p2005, c1998. ISBN 9780452286122. **A**

When British free spirit Suze Wilding participates in her advertising company's job swap with conservative New Yorker Lloyd Rockwell, the two realize that they make a perfect match.

Keywords: break-ups; dating; romantic comedy; travel; work

Weekend in Paris. Plume, 2003. ISBN 9780452284906. **A**

After impulsively quitting her secretarial job, twenty-something Molly Clearwater hops a train to Paris for a wild weekend of partying and romance and discovers the father she never knew.

Keywords: family; humor; sexual content; travel; work

Swoish, Tammy.

Hot Scots, Castles, and Kilts. Delacorte Press, 2008. ISBN 9780385904506. **J S**

The diary entries of sixteen-year-old Sami Ames as she travels to Scotland with her romance writer mother to help renovate her cousins' estate. She also falls for their hot neighbor, ghost hunts, and ends a longstanding rivalry between two clans.

Keywords: diary; family; ghosts; humor; kissing; wedding

Triana, Gaby.

The Temptress Four. HarperTeen, 2008. ISBN 9780060885687. **S**

The day after graduating from high school, four best friends, Fiona, Yoli, Alma, and Killian, go on a Caribbean cruise despite a fortune-teller's prophecy that one would not return.

Keywords: friendship; travel

This is my proper grown-up blog, for REAL friends, for documentarying my proper grown up life, just as I start having one.

—Susie Day, *Serafina 67: *Urgently Requires Life**

Chapter 4

Magical Maidens

A girl can't spend all *her time battling psychic disturbances. She needs a little romance too.*

—Meg Cabot, *Shadowland*

Recently, teen chick lit novels have incorporated elements of the fantasy genre. These light, humorous tales about witches, ghosts, vampires, and magic spells—with a touch of romance—cannot be confused with high fantasies because they retain traditional chick lit conventions and have heroines whom teen readers can relate to. They are set in our modern world, and the protagonist often is a high school student who encounters supernatural elements or becomes a member of the paranormal world while still being interested in friends, fitting in, and dating.

The majority of the teen chick lit stories begin when a normal teenage girl discovers or inherits supernatural powers, which they have varied reactions to. Although the reader may be thinking that being able to perform spells would be awesome, some heroines are resistant. Since fitting in is so important during the teenage years, it is no real surprise that some characters, such as Meg Cabot's Suze Simon, find their psychic powers a burden. Others are all too happy with their gift; in fact, Sarah Mlynowski's Rachael Weinstein is extremely jealous when her younger sister becomes a witch before her own powers kick in. Once they learn how to use their magical powers, some girls have to become agents for good, such as Buffy the Vampire Slayer, while others use their powers to navigate the high school dating and popularity scene.

Chapter Organization

In this chapter, teen chick lit novels that include fantasy and paranormal elements are categorized by similar themes, such as witches, the undead, and time travel.

Magic and Supernatural Powers

All the teen girls in this section use or develop magic powers. While some use magic for their own gain, most of the heroines find that their powers come with a responsibly to protect the innocent and destroy evil in the world. An underlying theme for many of the novels in this section is empowerment.

Barnes, Jennifer Lynn.

[Felicity James]. J S

The following titles, although not formally a series, deal with the same protagonist and are listed in chronological order.

Golden. Delacorte Press, 2006. ISBN 9780385733113.

> After moving to Oklahoma, fifteen-year-old Felicity "Lissy" Shannon James tries to fit in at Emory High School, where there are two kinds of students, the "Goldens" and the "Nons." Soon Lissy uses her magical ability to see people's auras to uncover an evil plan involving the popular math teacher, Mr. Kissler.
>
> Keywords: family; fantasy; mystery; school

Platinum. Delacorte Press, 2007. ISBN 9780385733953.

> After the leader of the "Goldens," attractive Lilah Covington, starts having ghostly visions, she seeks out Lissy and Lexie James, and together the three girls combine their mystical powers to solve the mystery.
>
> Keywords: fantasy; mystery; school

Bernstein, Jonathan.

Hottie. Razorbill, 2009. ISBN 9781595142122. J S

Popular Beverly Hills freshman Alison Cole gains the power to shoot flames from her fingertips after lightning struck a machine during her experimental plastic surgery. Alison then turns to comic book geek David Eels, and the duo become a superhero team ready to battle evil.

Keywords: family; friendship; humor

Cabot, Meg.

The Mediator. J S

Every since Susannah "Suze" Simon was two, she has been able to communicate with the dead and has understood that she is a mediator who has the responsibility to help troubled spirits move to the next world. In the middle of her sophomore year Suze's mother remarries, and they relocate to Northern California. In addition to her new stepfather and three stepbrothers, Suze realizes that she has to share a house with Jessie, an attractive ghost who was murdered in the 1800s. Suze also discovers she is not the only one who sees ghosts, as the school principal at the Junipero Serra Mission Academy, Father Dominic, is also a mediator. While maintaining her tough girl style, Suze successfully helps ghosts pass on and falls in love with Jesse. The series was originally published under the pseudonym Jenny Carroll.

Keywords: death; ghosts; humor

🌴 *Shadowland.* Avon Books, p2005, c2000. ISBN 9780060725112.

> When her mother remarries, sixteen-year-old Susannah Simon moves from New York City to Carmel, California, and quickly discovers two spirits, Jesse, a cute ghost who occupies her new room, and Heather, an angry cheerleader

who recently committed suicide after her boyfriend broke up with her. Ignoring Father Dominic's request, Suze performs an exorcism to get rid of Heather.

Keywords: family; school

Awards: Quick Picks 2002

Ninth Key. Avon Books, p2005, c2001. ISBN 9780060725129.

Suze is trying not to fall in love with Jesse, the ghost living in her room, when an upset ghost asks Suze to deliver an important message. Suze mistakenly believes the message belongs to her new boyfriend's father, Red Beaumont, and when she contacts him, Suze uncovers an unsolved murder.

Keywords: dating; family; friendship; mystery

Awards: Quick Picks 2002

Reunion. Avon Books, p2005, c2001. ISBN 9780060725136.

While Gina, her best friend from New York City, is visiting, Suze has to convince four teenage ghosts who recently died in a car accident not to seek revenge on Michael Meducci, the other driver. Then Suze discovers that Michael planned the accident.

Keywords: friendship; school

Darkest Hour. Avon Books, p2005, c2001. ISBN 9780060725143.

Suze works as a babysitter at the local hotel and resort where one of her charges, eight-year-old Jack Slater, is also a mediator. While Suze helps Jack and avoids his cute older brother, Paul, the ghost of Jesse's ex-fiancée, Maria de Silva, threatens to kill Suze if her family continues to dig in the backyard. After the remains of Jesse's body are discovered, Jesse is exorcised by Jack, and Suze comes up with a plan to bring him back.

Keywords: first love

Haunted. Avon, 2005. ISBN 9780060751647.

Suze finds herself attracted to Paul Slater, a fellow mediator, despite the fact that Paul is campaigning against her for student body vice president and has threatened to send Jesse back to the afterlife. Meanwhile, Jesse has inexplicably been avoiding Suze since their intimate kiss over the summer.

Keywords: kissing; school

Twilight. Avon Books, p2006, c2005. ISBN 9780060724696.

In the final volume of the <u>Mediator</u> series, Suze goes back in time to stop Paul's plans of getting rid of her boyfriend's ghost by preventing Jesse' 150-year-old murder. Suze is able to bring Jesse back to life and the two go to the winter formal.

Keywords: dances; first love; kissing

Clement-Moore, Rosemary.

Maggie Quinn: Girl vs. Evil. §

After receiving "the Sight" as a gift from her grandmother, smart, wisecracking Maggie Quinn uses her supernatural intuition to battle evil creatures as she graduates from high school and attends Bedivere University.

Keywords: humor

Prom Dates from Hell. Delacorte Press, 2007. ISBN 9780385904285.

As the senior prom approaches, wisecracking Avalon High school reporter Maggie Quinn's inherited psychic powers have her suspecting that the mysterious accidents and illnesses that have recently fallen on the popular seniors are connected to the demon in her dreams. With some help from Justin, Maggie is committed to taking down the revenge-seeking demon at the prom.

Keywords: prom; school

Hell Week. Delacorte Press, 2008. ISBN 9780385734141.

Determined to write an impressive exposé that will get her on the staff at the Bedivere University newspaper, college freshman Maggie Quinn pledges Sigma Alpha Xi sorority and discovers that the sisters use magical powers to become successful.

Keywords: college; dating; sexuality

Highway to Hell. Delacorte BFYR, 2009. ISBN 9780385734639.

While on their way to enjoy spring break in south Texas, Maggie and her sorceress friend Lisa discover that *el chupacabra*, a legendary evil creature from Hispanic folklore, appears to be killing livestock and people.

Keywords: college; mystery

Fredericks, Mariah.

In the Cards. Ⓜ Ⓙ

When Mrs. Etta Rosemont dies, she leaves her thirteen-year-old neighbor Anna, a cat, and an old tarot card set. Along with her two best friends Eve and Sydney, Anna practices reading the tarot cards as a way to learn their future.

Keywords: friendship; humor

Love. Atheneum Books for Young Readers, 2007. ISBN 9780689876547.

Eighth grader Anna uses her new tarot cards to find out if she is destined to be with popular Declan Kelso. When the cards show a potential love match, Anna organizes operation freak victory, including a hair and clothing makeover.

Keywords: crushes; dating

Fame. Atheneum Books for Young Readers, 2008. ISBN 9780689876561.

With the help and encouragement of her best friends, Eve consults the tarot cards to see if she will make it as an actress/singer and auditions for their school's production of *Cabaret*.

Keywords: acting; family; school

Life. Atheneum Books for Young Readers, 2008. ISBN 9780689876585.

> Quiet, animal-loving Syd has always avoided getting her tarot card read, until the summer before high school, when she becomes increasingly worried about her father's alcohol addiction.

> **Keywords:** animals; crushes; family

Jay, Stacey.

You Are So Undead to Me. **Razorbill, 2009. ISBN 9781595142252. J S**

> High school sophomore Megan Berry, a zombie settler who helps the undead with their unfinished business, looks forward to going to the upcoming homecoming dance with her boyfriend Ethan, until someone uses black magic to turn the ordinary undead into violent zombies.

> **Keywords:** dances; dating; humor; school

Lockhart, E.

Fly on the Wall: How One Girl Saw Everything. **Delacorte Press, 2006. ISBN 9780385902991. S**

> At the Manhattan School for Arts and Music, where all the students go out of their way to be different, Gretchen Yee is an artificial redhead, comic-book-obsessed junior who has a major crush on one of the "art rats." Gretchen changes her perspective on boys and herself when she is transformed into a fly in the boy's locker room for one week.

> **Keywords:** Asian American; crushes; divorce; family; friendship; school

Martinez Wood, Jamie.

Rogelia's House of Magic. **Delacorte Press, 2008. ISBN 9780385734776. J S**

> In Southern California, fourteen-year-old Marina Peralta, Fernando Fuego, and Xochitl Garcia grow closer while they learn how to control their psychic powers from Xochitl's grandmother, Rogelia Garcia, who is a traditional Mexican healer.

> **Keywords:** crushes; family; friendship; Hispanic American

Myracle, Lauren.

Rhymes with Witches. **Amulet Books, 2005. ISBN 9780810958593. J S**

> After Jane drops her best friend for the most popular clique at school, the bitches, she discovers that dark magic is the secret that makes the group so powerful.

> **Keywords:** cliques; friendship; school

Perez, Marlene.

Dead Is . . . . J S

> In Nightshade, California, seventeen-year-old Daisy Giordano does not let the fact that she is the only one in her family who does not have supernatu-

ral powers (her mother has premonitions, sister Rose can read thoughts, and sister Poppy has the power of telekinesis) stop her from investigating strange events with her boyfriend, Ryan.

Keywords: humor; sisters

🌳 *Dead Is the New Black.* Harcourt, 2008. ISBN 9780152064082.

When Nightshade High cheerleading captain Samantha Devereaux returns from summer vacation sporting the "walking undead" look, and local girls have mysteriously disappeared, Daisy suspects vampires and joins the squad to investigate.

Keywords: cheerleading; crushes; dating; family; mystery; school
Awards: Quick Picks 2009

Dead Is a State of Mind. Graphia, 2009. ISBN 9780152062101.

The Giordano sisters love dilemmas, as Rose is dating a werewolf, Poppy is in love with a ghost, and Daisy is waiting for Ryan to ask her to the prom. Meanwhile, when the gypsy fortune-teller Duke Sherrad's prediction about a popular teacher comes true, Daisy uses her new powers to investigate.

Keywords: dating; family; mystery; prom; school

Dead Is So Last Year. Graphia/Houghton Mifflin Harcourt, 2009. ISBN 9780152062163.

During summer vacation, the Giordano sisters are not the only ones seeing double; it appears that the town has strange doppelgangers, including their missing father. Meanwhile, all the boys on the football team, including Ryan, have grown bigger almost overnight.

Keywords: dating; mystery; work

Radford, Michelle.

[Fiona Blount]. 🇯 🇸

The following titles, although not formally a series, deal with the same protagonist and are listed in chronological order.

Almost Fabulous. HarperTeen, 2008. ISBN 9780061252358.

In London, fourteen-year-old Fiona Blount, who has wanted to remain anonymous at school, discovers that she may have inherited extrasensory powers of mind control from her missing father.

Keywords: crushes; family; friendship; school

Totally Fabulous. HarperTeen, 2009. ISBN 9780061285318.

Fiona's father sends her to New Jersey for a month so she can spend time with his family and attend a boot camp to control her newfound powers.

Keywords: family

Saidens, Amy.

The Secret Life of a Teenage Siren. Simon Pulse, 2007. ISBN 9781416950653. 🇯 🇸

Like the generations of women before her, Roxy is transformed from a band geek into a beautiful siren on her sixteenth birthday. Roxy uses her powers to attract boys by playing a few notes of her flute to catch her longtime crush, Zach.

Keywords: crushes; dating; mythology; romantic comedy

Snow, Carol.

🌱 *Switch*. HarperTeen, 2008. ISBN 9780061452086. **J** **S**

Like her deceased grandmother, during thunderstorms fifteen-year-old Claire Martin temporarily switches into someone else's body for a few hours. When Claire is trapped in beautiful Larissa's body, she starts dating her secret crush, Nate, while her grandmother moves into her body.

Keywords: crushes; family; self-acceptance
Awards: Quick Picks 2009

Swain, Heather.

Me, My Elf & I. Speak, 2009. ISBN 9780142412558.

Fifteen-year-old Zephyr Addler is a tall, gorgeous elf who moves from the forests of Michigan to New York so she can attend Brooklyn Academy of Performing Arts High School. As Zephyr adjusts to life among humans, she makes friends and starts acting.

Keywords: fantasy; friendship; school

Valdes-Rodriguez, Alisa.

Haters. Little, Brown 2006. ISBN 9780316013079. **S**

Sixteen-year-old Pasquala "Paski" Archuleta struggles to fit in at her new school in Orange County, California, while having physic visions about the reigning queen bee, Jessica Nguyen, whom she competes against in the regional mountain bike race.

Keywords: family; Hispanic American; sports

Witches

The stories in this section are about young women who are or become good witches. In some of the novels, the witches have to keep their abilities a secret from their friends and boyfriends, while others have the ability to perform magic openly. Often the funniest scenes are those in which the witch's first tries at her craft and first attempts at charms and potions are disastrous. Many of the novels are often romantic comedies as well.

Blair, Annette.

The Accidental Witch Trilogy. **A**

Melody Seabright, Kira Fitzgerald, and Victoria Cartwright are friends as well as witches, who live in New England. Each volume in the series centers on how one witch finds love.

Keywords: fantasy; romantic comedy

The Kitchen Witch. Berkley, 2004. ISBN 9780425198810.

Reformed bad boy Logan Kilgarven moves back to Salem, Massachusetts, with his four-year-old son, Shane, taking a new job as the local television producer. When Logan needs a babysitter, he reluctantly agrees to get his downstairs neighbor and supposed witch, Melody Seabright, a job at the station in exchange for regular babysitting. Melody manages to turn a secretarial position into hosting her own cooking show.

Keywords: dating; work

My Favorite Witch. Berkley, 2006. ISBN 9780425207239.

Heartbroken over her recent broken engagement to her cheating fiancé, Kira Fitzgerald, a white witch, accepts a job as the coordinator of events for the Pickering Foundation in Newport, Rhode Island. Kira's first responsibility is organizing a charity event with the boss's grandson, former pro hockey player and playboy Jason Pickering Goddard.

Keywords: family; work

The Scot, the Witch and the Wardrobe. Berkley, 2006. ISBN 9780425213469.

After her grandmother's death, Victoria Cartwright denies that she has inherited magical powers in addition to the key to the unopened wardrobe in the attic. When Victoria opens the wardrobe, she discovers an antique carousel unicorn that was created by Scotsman Rory Mackenzie's ancestors. Rory is determined to bring it back to Scotland to restore his family's name.

Keywords: family; friendship

The Triplet Witch Trilogy. **A**

In Salem, Massachusetts, the Cartwright sisters Harmony, Destiny, and Storm are witches who each possess a psychic gift. Harmony reads the past, Destiny reads the future, and Storm reads the present. They use their powers to solve mysteries and find love while working in a vintage clothing shop with their half-sister Vicki.

Keywords: fantasy

Sex and the Psychic Witch. Berkley Sensation, 2007. 9780425216637.

Harmony Cartwright's powers and the Celtic ring hidden in the hem of the vintage gown she purchased at a charity costume sale lead her to Paxton Castle, off the coast of Massachusetts, to assist the heir, King Paxton, with the ghost who is creating havoc in the castle.

Keywords: family; ghosts; sisters

Gone with the Witch. Berkley, 2008. ISBN 9780425221211.

Due to her psychic gift of sensing the present, every time rebellious Storm Cartwright is near antique restorer Aiden McCloud she hears a baby crying. Sure the baby is his and in need, Storm kidnaps Aiden to find the mysterious baby.

Keywords: paranormal romance; sisters

Never Been Witched. Berkley, 2009. ISBN 9780425226490.

While her sisters are in Scotland, Destiny travels to the Paxton Island Lighthouse to do some soul searching and find her psychic soul mate. On the island, Destiny discovers that Morgan, a paranormal debunker, two ghosts, and a guardian angel will be staying with her.

Keywords: paranormal romance; sexual content

Cabot, Meg.

Jinx. **HarperTeen, 2007. ISBN 9780060837648.** **J** **S**

As descendants of a witch, both Jean "Jinx" Honeychurch and her older cousin Tory believe that they are the prophesized next great witch. While Jean tries to hide her magical powers, Tory actively practices black magic.

Keywords: crushes; dating; family; fantasy

Frankel, Valerie.

Hex and the Single Girl. **Avon, 2006. ISBN 9780060785543.** **A**

In Manhattan, Emma Hutch has used her telepathic abilities to become a successful matchmaker. Then a socialite wants to be set up with software billionaire William Dearborn. Unable to use her powers, Emma discovers that William is more interested in her.

Keywords: dating; fantasy; friendship; humor; work

Gould, Emily.

Hex Education. **Razorbill, 2007. ISBN 9781595141187.** **J** **S**

When fourteen-year-old Sophie Stone moves from sunny Los Angeles to gloomy Mythic, Massachusetts, she discovers that she is descended from the town's first coven of witches; along with her three new friends, she must stop an evil witch from destroying the town.

Keywords: fantasy; friendship; school

Klasky, Mindy.

[The Girl's Guide to Witchcraft]. **A**

After library budget cuts force twenty-nine-year-old Jane Madison to live rent-free in a long unused cottage on the library property, she discovers a hidden room of books about witchcraft and also discovers that she comes from a line of witches.

Keywords: fantasy; humor; work

The Girl's Guide to Witchcraft. **Red Dress Ink, 2006. ISBN 9780373896073.**

When Jane reads from a magical book in her new home, she casts a spell that awakens her gay familiar, makes her irresistible to men, and in the end teaches her about the importance of inner confidence.

Keywords: dating; family

Sorcery and the Single Girl. **Red Dress Ink, 2007. ISBN 9780373895632.**

While dating Englishman Graeme Henderson, Jane has to really practice her magic in order to be admitted, unlike her mother and grandmother, into the powerful and elite Washington Coven, or she could lose her magical books, familiar Neko, and warder David Montrose.

Keywords: dating; family; friendship

Magic and the Modern Girl. Red Dress Ink, 2008. ISBN 9780373895779.

Six months after rejecting the exclusive Washington Coven and not using magic, Jane contacts her attractive protector, David Montrose, when she discovers that she may lose her powers permanently.

Keywords: dating; family; friendship

McClymer, Kelly.

[The Salem Witch Tryouts]. M J

As the daughter of a witch mom and a mortal dad, sixteen-year-old Prudence "Pru" Stewart has always had to keep her magical abilities a secret. Then her family moves from Beverly Hills, California, to Salem, Massachusetts, where she practices magic alongside other witches.

Keywords: fantasy; school

The Salem Witch Tryouts. Simon Pulse, 2007. ISBN 9781415699423X.

Now that Pru and her younger brother Tobias can study witchcraft in the open at Agatha's Day School for Witches, Pru has to take remedial magic classes, tries out for the cheerleading team, and flirts with the school bad boy.

Keywords: family; friendship

Competition's a Witch. Simon Pulse, 2007. ISBN 9781428724396.

As a member of the cheerleading team, Pru has to create a routine that will make her teammates winners at the upcoming regional competition and still find time to flirt with her mortal neighbor, Angelo, and study with her tutor, Samuel, so she can test out of remedial magic classes.

Keywords: crushes; family

She's a Witch Girl. Simon Pulse, 2007. ISBN 978416949022.

Pru begins taking regular magic classes and trains with the cheerleaders for the upcoming national competition against her former best friend. Meanwhile it is revealed that her charming neighbor, Angelo, is really a witch who was switched with a mortal at birth.

Keywords: friendship

Mlynowski, Sarah.

Magic in Manhattan. M J S

Rachel Weinstein was a typical fourteen-year-old girl, living in New York City with her divorced mother and younger, more mature sister, Miri, until Miri inherits magical powers and their mom confesses that witchcraft is passed from mother to daughter. With *The Authorized and Absolute Reference Handbook to Astonish Spells, Astounding Potions, and History of Witchcraft Since the Beginning of Time* (A-squared for short) and their mother, the sisters are able to cast spells and even fly.

Keywords: humor; sisters

Bras and Broomsticks. Delacorte Press, 2005. ISBN 9780385731812.

> After Rachel unsuccessfully tries to use supernatural skills, she convinces her younger sister, Miri, to use her new powers and cast a dancing spell so Rachel can perform in the JFK High School fashion show and become popular.

Keywords: crushes; family

Frogs and French Kisses. Delacorte Press, 2006. ISBN 9780385731829.

> Although mom's rule is that Miri cannot perform magic until she finishes her training, Rachel asks Miri to create a love spell to win back popular Raf Kosrausis. Meanwhile one of Miri's spells forces the school to cancel the prom, and Rachel comes to the rescue.

Keywords: crushes; family; prom

Spells and Sleeping Bags. Delacorte Press, 2007. ISBN 9780385733878.

> Now that Rachel's powers have finally kicked in, the two Weinstein sisters are shipped to Camp Wood Lake in the Adirondacks for the summer. Ignoring her mom's rules, Rachel uses her magic, with disastrous results, including zapping away all her clothes.

Keywords: camp; friendship

Parties & Potions. Delacorte Press, 2009. ISBN 9780385736459.

> Teen witch sisters Miri and Rachel meet other members of the magic community and try to keep their identity a secret at school as they undergo training for the witch coming-of-age ceremony, called a Samsorta.

Keywords: dating; family; school

Swendson, Shanna.

Katie Chandler. **A**

Twenty-six-year-old Texan Katie Chandler is surprised to discover that there is an active magical community in New York City that includes witches, elves, and fairies. Due to her immunity to magic, Katie is aggressively recruited by Magic, Spells and Illusion, Inc., and she accepts a position in the verification office because it means she can work closely with the handsome wizard Owen Palmer.

Keywords: fantasy; work

Enchanted, Inc. Ballantine Books, 2005. ISBN 9780345481252.

> Katie moves from Texas to New York City to pursue a career in business and becomes a member of the Magic, Spells and Illusion team due to her special skills as a nonmagical person. When a former employee of MSI starts marketing black magic, Katie comes up with a plan to stop him and catches the eye of the CEO, Merlin.

Once Upon Stilettos. Ballantine Books, 2006. ISBN 9780345481276.

> While Kaitie investigates the identity of the office spy who broke into Owen Palmer's office, she has to keep her visiting parents busy so they won't discover the truth about her job.

Keywords: crushes; family

Damsel Under Stress. Ballantine Books, 2007. ISBN 9780345492920.

> Katie's dreams of kissing shy Owen Palmer come true at an office party, but she has to postpone their first official date until they can stop a former employee and an evil fairy from exposing the truth about MSI and the magical community, while also staying away from Ethelinda, an incompetent fairy godmother.

> **Keywords:** crushes

Don't Hex with Texas. Ballantine Books, 2008. ISBN 9780345492935.

> Katie leaves her love, Owen, behind in New York City and returns home to magic-free Texas, looking for a simpler life. Bored by her job at family store, Katie discovers that someone is conducting unauthorized spells and committing small crimes. When Owen comes to investigate, they reunite to root out the culprit.

> **Keywords:** dating; family

The Undead

Many vampire and ghost romance books have been published in recent years. For one to appeal to teen chick lit readers, it has to almost be a satire, which either has the timing and humor found in traditional chick lit or the fashion and glamour of gossip lit. In this section the heroines are either a member of the undead, dating one, or destined to destroy one.

Acosta, Marta.

Casa Dracula. A

In northern California, aspiring Latina writer Milagro de Los Santos is seduced by and consequently falls in love Dr. Oswald Grant, whose family suffers from "a genetic autosomal recessive disorder," also known as vampirism. After accidentally exchanging blood with Oswald, Milagro moves into his family's ranch so they can monitor her infection. Once the two become a couple, Milagro stays in a cottage on the ranch with Oswald and his eccentric family.

Keywords: family; fantasy; Hispanic American; humor; vampires

Happy Hour at Casa Dracula. Pocket Books, 2006. ISBN 9781416520382.

> At a book party for her ex-boyfriend Sebastian, aspiring writer and recent ivy league graduate Milagro de Los Santos is seduced by Dr. Oswald Grant, a plastic surgeon and charming vampire. After possibly being infected, Milagro moves in with Oswald's family while Sebastain tries to find her so he can take down the vampire family.

> **Keywords:** sexual content

Midnight Brunch. Pocket Books, 2007. ISBN 9781416520399.

> Now that she has recovered from her infection and is living in a cottage on the ranch with Oswald, Milagro has to impress his parents, who insist that she cannot attend a clan-naming ceremony. When Oswald leaves on a

medical mission, two other vampires decide that she will make the perfect human sacrifice.

The Bride of Casa Dracula. Pocket Books, 2008. ISBN 9781416559634.

Now engaged, Milagro's fashionable friend Nancy is acting as the public wedding planner, and the secretive vampire council has assigned Cornelia Ducharme to guide the couple through the ancient vampire marriage ritual. But first Milagro has to sign an oath of loyalty.

Keywords: friendship; wedding

Conrod, Liza.

High School Bites. **Nal Jam Books, 2006. ISBN 9780451217523.** **J** **S**

The great-great-granddaughter of Bram Stoker's Lucy fulfills her destiny and takes down Dracula at the homecoming dance.

Keywords: dances; family; humor; vampires

de la Cruz, Melissa.

Blue Bloods. **S**

In modern-day New York City, the elite are actually reincarnated vampires who have lived in various bodies for centuries. In addition to wealth and power, Blue Bloods are physically attractive, with beautiful skin and trim bodies. However, something is terribly wrong, and young Blue Bloods are being hunted by another race, called Silver Bloods.

Keywords: family; fantasy; vampires

🎭 *Blue Bloods.* Hyperion, 2006. ISBN 9780786838929.

While the popular students at Manhattan's elite Duchesne prep school, including Bliss Llewellyn and twins Mimi and Jack Force, learn about the vampire code that they must follow, fifteen-year-old Schuyler Van Alen, an outsider who lives with her grandmother, is shocked to find out that she is actually a vampire. After young Blue Bloods are murdered the conclave tries to cover it up, while Schuyler is determined to find out the truth.

Keywords: friendship; murder; school
Awards: Quick Picks 2007

🎭 *Masquerade.* Hyperion, 2007. ISBN 9780786838936.

While plans are getting underway for the exclusive gala known as the Four Hundred Year Ball, Schuyler and her best friend Oliver are in Venice, Italy, searching for the one person who may know the truth about the Silver Bloods, her grandfather Lawrence.

Keywords: friendship; travel
Awards: Quick Picks 2008

Revelations. Hyperion, 2008. ISBN 9781423102281.

> Accused of having Silver Blood in her veins, Schuyler is condemned to live with the Force family as she struggles with her feelings for Jack and Oliver. Jealous about Schuyler, Mimi speeds up plans for her bonding ceremony with Jack. Meanwhile, Bliss's horrific predictions of upcoming trouble come true as a battle between the Silver Bloods and Blue Bloods begins in Rio de Janeiro, Brazil.

> **Keywords:** crushes; jealousy

Van Alen Legacy. Hyperion, 2009. ISBN 9781423102267.

> One year after her grandfather's murder, Schuyler and her conduit Oliver are still on the run from the conclave. Meanwhile Mimi and Kinsley are in Rio searching for Bliss's sister, and Lucifer has taken over Bliss.

> **Keywords:** crushes; friendship

Hurley, Tonya.

[Ghostgirl]. **J** **S**

The following titles, although not formally a series, deal with the same protagonist and are listed in chronological order.

Ghostgirl. Little, Brown, p2008. ISBN 9780316113571.

> On the first day of school, Charlotte Usher's plans to transform from invisible nobody to popular cheerleader do not end when she chokes to death on a gummy bear in the Hawthorne High psychics lab. Despite being dead, Charlotte is determined to attend the Fall Ball with her crush, Damen Dylan.

> **Keywords:** crushes; death; friendship; humor; school

Ghostgirl: Homecoming. Little, Brown, 2009. ISBN 9780316113595.

> Before Charlotte can completely cross over, she has to intern at a hotline for troubled teens when her friend from the living world, Scarlet, self-induces a coma so she and Charlotte can find a way to help her snobby sister, Petula.

> **Keywords:** death; friendship; humor; sisters

Johnson, Maureen.

🌳 *Devilish.* **Razorbill, 2006. ISBN 9781595140609.** **S**

> After her best friend Allison sells her soul to Lanalee, the new sophomore at Saint Teresa's Preparatory School for Girls in Providence, Rhode Island, for popularity, high school senior Jane Jarvis joins forces with Owen, a fourteen-year-old demon fighter, to get it back.

> **Keywords:** dances; fantasy; friendship; school
> **Awards:** BBYA 2007

Kenner, Julie.

[Good Ghouls]. **A** **S**

The following titles, although not formally a series, deal with the same characters and are listed in chronological order.

The Good Ghouls' Guide to Getting Even. Ace Books, p2009, c2007. ISBN 9780441017041.

> Along with her best friend Jenny, smart sixteen-year-old Elizabeth "Beth" Frasier seeks revenge against the Waterloo High star quarterback, Stephen Wills, who turned her into a vampire, while avoiding some vampire hunters who want to destroy her.
>
> **Keywords:** fantasy; friendship; humor; school

Good Ghouls Do. Penguin Group, 2009. ISBN 9780441017447.

> Beth, her boyfriend Clayton, best friend Jenny, and friendly vampire hunter Kevin search for the vampire master so she can become human again. Meanwhile, Beth suspects that Clayton is plotting against her.
>
> **Keywords:** dating; fantasy; humor

Kenner, Julie, Johanna Edwards, and Serena Robar.

Fendi, Ferragamo, & Fangs. **Berkley Jam, 2007. ISBN 9780425215395.** S

> Olivia, Veronika, and Sydney each tells her story, of how she was selected by Vamp Modeling, Inc.'s annual modeling search, moved to New York City, and discovered she needed to became a vampire to really succeed in the agency.
>
> **Keywords:** dating; modeling; vampires

Lockwood, Cara.

Bard Academy. J S

> Located off the coast of Maine, Bard Academy is a gothic boarding school for troubled teens, where Miranda Tate and her friends Samir, Blade, and Hana uncover the secret that their teachers are really ghosts of dead writers like Virginia Woolf and Charlotte Brontë. During her stay at Bard, Miranda helps uncover several mysteries and evil plots to destroy their classmates.
>
> **Keywords:** boarding school; fantasy

Wuthering High. MTV Books/Pocket Books, 2006. ISBN 9781416524755.

> After wrecking her dad's BMW and maxing out her mom's credit cards, fifteen-year-old Miranda Tate is sent away to Bard Academy, an exclusive prep school for troubled teens. Once there, Miranda has nightmares about a student who went missing fifteen years ago and discovers one of her teacher's plans to destroy the entire student population.
>
> **Keywords:** friendship; humor; mystery

The Scarlet Letterman. MTV Books/Pocket Books, 2007. ISBN 9781416524908.

> Even though Miranda is dating Ryan Kent, Bard Academy's reigning sexist boy, she can't help thinking about Heathcliff. Meanwhile, there is a Mysterious Hooded Sweatshirt lurking around on campus, and two teachers disappear.
>
> **Keywords:** break-ups; dating; friendship; humor

Moby Clique. Pocket Books/MTV Books, 2008. ISBN 9781416550501.

> After a summer of reading *Moby Dick* and working in her stepmother's fancy boutique, Miranda was actually looking forward to starting her junior year at Bard, until her younger sister Lindsay enrolls in the school, befriends Miranda's nemesis Parker Rodham, and disappears.
>
> **Keywords:** sisters

Lynn, Erin.

🏃 *Demon Envy.* Berkley Jam, 2007. ISBN 9780425217375. **S**

> Sixteen-year-old Kenzie Sutcliffe accidentally opens a portal into another world, and Levi, a water demon appears in her bathroom. Kenzie has to find a way to close the portal soon, because Levi needs to create jealousy and envy in order to survive.
>
> **Keywords:** crushes; fantasy; school
> **Awards:** Quick Picks 2008

Maxwell, Katie.

[Fran Getti]. **J** **S**

> The following titles, although not formally a series, deal with the same protagonist and are listed in chronological order.

Got Fangs? Smooch, 2005. ISBN 9780843953992.

> Although sixteen-year-old Francesca "Fran" Getti wants a normal life, she is stuck traveling through Europe with her witch mother as part of Gothfaire, where she meets the motorcycle vampire Benedikt, who claims she is his beloved and can redeem his soul. She reluctantly uses her talent of touch telepathy to find a thief.
>
> **Keywords:** dating; family; fantasy; humor; kissing; mystery; vampires

Circus of the Darned. Smooch, 2006. ISBN 9780843954005.

> Fran is working at the Faire as an apprentice to Ben's sister Imogen reading palms, when she accidentally lets out Viking warrior ghosts while walking over an ancient burial site wearing a valknut pendant.
>
> **Keywords:** dating; fantasy; friendship; humor; vampires

Pauley, Kimberly.

🏃 *Sucks to Be Me: The All-True Confessions of Mina Hamilton, Teen Vampire (Maybe).* Mirrorstone, 2008. ISBN 9780786950287. **J** **S**

> In California, sixteen-year-old Mina Hamilton attends vampire classes with a couple of cute boys while she decides if she wants to become a vampire like her parents.
>
> **Keywords:** dating; family; friendship; school; vampires
> **Awards:** Quick Picks 2009

Vail, Rachel.

Gorgeous. **HarperTeen 2009. ISBN 9780060890469.** **J** **S**

Sick of being in the shadow of her beautiful older sisters and ignored by her crush, Tyler Moss, ninth grader Allison Avery makes a deal with the devil that she will be gorgeous to seven people, and in exchange he can control her cell phone.

Keywords: crushes; family; fantasy; friendship

Fairy Tale Variations

Fairy tales are traditionally romantic. Add chick lit humor, and there is the perfect stage for a romantic comedy. Also included are stories about teens who encounter modern-day fairy godmothers who try to help but usually do more harm than good.

Kantor, Melissa.

If I Have a Wicked Stepmother, Where's My Prince? **Hyperion, 2005. ISBN 9780786809608.** **S**

After her father remarries, artistic high school sophomore Lucy Norton moves from San Francisco to Long Island to live with her shallow stepmother and spoiled stepsisters. At her new school Lucy's social status skyrockets when Connor Pearson, the cute captain of the basketball team, shows an interest in her.

Keywords: dating; family; humor; kissing; school

Larbalestier, Justine.

How to Ditch Your Fairy. **Bloomsbury, 2008. ISBN 9781599903019.** **J** **S**

In the futuristic city of New Avalon, where almost everyone has an unseen fairy with special powers, fourteen-year-old Charlie wants to get rid of her parking fairy and ends up teaming up with her enemy, Fiorenze, to switch fairies.

Keywords: crushes; fantasy; friendship; magic; school

Meacham, Margaret.

[Morgan Yates]. **M** **J**

The following titles, although not formally a series, deal with the same protagonist and are listed in chronological order.

A Mid-Semester Night's Dream. Holiday House, 2004. ISBN 9780823418152.

When seventh grader Morgan Yates wishes upon a star for Ben Hennigen to like her back, Gretta Fleetwing, an ambitious fairy godmother in training, appears to create a love charm, unfortunately with disastrous results.

Keywords: crushes; fantasy; humor; school

A Fairy's Guide to Understanding Humans. Holiday House, 2007. ISBN 9780823420780.

> After her dad remarries, fourteen-year-old Morgan Yates is not sure she can adjust to her new school and new stepbrother, until Gretta, her fairy god-mother in training, appears again with a plan to help Morgan fit in. Through-out the book are excerpts from Gretta's diary.
>
> **Keywords:** dating; family; fantasy; humor; school

Palmer, Robin.

Cindy Ella. Speak, 2008. ISBN 9780142403921. **M** **J**

> In this modern-day version of the Cinderella story, high school sophomore Cindy Ella is so fed up that everyone, including her twin stepsisters, is obsessed with the upcoming prom, she writes an antiprom editorial in the school newspaper. On the night of the prom her instant messaging friend, brklynboy, reveals he is really her crush, Adam Silver.
>
> **Keywords:** dances; family; first kiss; prom

Rallison, Janette.

My Fair Godmother. Walker, 2009. ISBN 9780802797803. **M** **J**

> When sixteen-year-old Savannah Delano's boyfriend, Hunter, breaks up with her to date her older, more studious sister, Chrysanthemum "Chrissy" Everstar, a not very good fairy godmother in training, accidentally sends her into fairy tale land and the Middle Ages, where she must defeat magical creatures and discovers her prince.
>
> **Keywords:** break-ups; dating; fantasy; humor; magic; romantic comedy; sisters

Mythology Variations

Mythological legends and characters are given a chick lit spin. Except for the Pandora series, the heroines in this section were normal young women whose worlds collide with characters from the ancient world because of destiny or an accident.

Barnes, Jennifer Lynn.

[Bailey Morgan]. **J** **S**

> The following titles, although not formally a series, deal with the same characters and are listed in chronological order.

🌳 *Tattoo.* Delacorte Press, 2007. ISBN 9781428716438.

> Best friends Bailey, Annabelle, Delia, and Zo receive supernatural powers af-ter they apply temporary tattoos on their bodies as cool accessories for the upcoming dance. The girls must use the powers to destroy an evil fairy who has returned to steal souls.
>
> **Keywords:** cliques; crushes; dances; friendship
>
> **Awards:** Quick Picks 2008

Fate. Delacorte Press, 2008. ISBN 9780385735377.

> As her high school graduation approaches, Bailey Morgan must find balance in her life as one of three mythological fates and prevent a devious Irish Sidhe.
>
> **Keywords:** friendship; humor

Cabot, Meg.

Avalon High. **HarperCollins, 2006. ISBN 9780060755874.** J S

> After recently moving to Annapolis, Maryland, high school junior Elaine Harrison learns that some of her classmates at Avalon High are reincarnations of the King Arthur legend and it is her destiny to save the modern-day Arthur.
>
> **Keywords:** dating; family; fantasy; friendship; school

Childs, Tera Lynn.

[Phoebe Castro]. J S

> The following titles, although not formally a series, deal with the same protagonist and are listed in chronological order.

Goddess Boot Camp. Dutton, 2009. ISBN 9780525421344.

> Phoebe's stepfather signs her up for a remedial goddess boot camp program so she can learn how to use her new divine powers.
>
> **Keywords:** dating; family; mystery; school

Oh. My. Gods. Dutton Children's Books, 2008. ISBN 9780525479420.

> When her mother returns home from a trip abroad with a Greek fiancé, high school senior Phoebe Castro abandons her dreams of winning a cross-country scholarship with her two best friends and relocates to Seropoula, a mysterious island in the Aegean Sea where her stepfather is the headmaster at Plato's Academy and all the students are direct descendants from the Greek gods.
>
> **Keywords:** family; school; sports

Goode, Carlone.

Cupidity. **Simon Pulse, 2005. ISBN 9780689872280.** J S

> Cupid, the god of love, comes out of retirement to help bookish Laura Sweeney find her true love before the homecoming dance and accidentally gets hit by his own arrow.
>
> **Keywords:** crushes; dances; family

Hennesy, Carolyn.

Mythic Misadventures: Pandora. M J

After Pandora "Pandy" Atheneus Andromaeche Helena accidentally releases seven evils into the world during show-and-tell at school, she and her best friends Alcie and Iole go on a quest to recover the evils from all over the ancient world.

Keywords: adventure; humor

Pandora Gets Jealous. Bloomsbury Children's Books, 2008. ISBN 9781599901961.

Thirteen-year-old Pandy brings her father Prometheus's secret box to school to impress her classmates. When the box is accidentally opened and seven evils and miseries escape, Zeus demands that Pandy must retrieve them.

Keywords: school

Pandora Gets Vain. Bloomsbury Children's Books, 2008. ISBN 9781599901978.

Now that they have captured jealousy, Pandy and her friends head to Egypt to retrieve vanity, where they join forces with a cute gladiator school dropout named Homer.

Keywords: friendship

Pandora Gets Lazy. Bloomsbury, 2009. ISBN 9781599901985.

On the way to track down laziness, Pandy is separated from her friends and her beloved dog Dido is kidnapped.

Keywords: friendship

Mancusi, Marianne.

A Connecticut Fashionista in King Arthur's Court. **Dorchester Pub., 2005. ISBN 9780505526335.** A

Twenty-nine-year-old fashion editor Kat Jones is transported back in time to King Arthur's Court, where she is locked away in a tower and rescued by handsome Lancelot.

Keywords: romantic comedy

Time Travel

In the following stories characters are transported to a different time, back in time, or to an alternative world. A common theme is that the heroine develops greater understanding about her life because of the time travel experience.

Colgan, Jenny.

The Boy I Loved Before. **St. Martin's Griffin, p2005, c2004. ISBN 9780312331986.** S

After attending her best friend's wedding, thirty-two-year-old Flora Scurrison, dissatisfied with her life, wishes she could go back in time. She awakens the next day as her sixteen-year-old-self. Flora has one month to decide to stay a teenager or return to adulthood. Originally published in Great Britain as *Do You Remember the First Time?*

Keywords: dating; family; friendship; humor; self-acceptance

Deriso, Christine Hurley.

Do-over. **Delacorte Press, 2006. ISBN 9780385903509.** 🅼 🅹

At the end of seventh grade, Elsa is having a difficult time fitting in until her recently deceased mother appears with a magic family heirloom that she can use until her thirteenth birthday. For one month Elsa's locket gives her the power to rewind the last ten seconds of her life.

Keywords: cliques; family; school

Mlynowski, Sarah.

Me vs. Me. **Red Dress Ink, 2006. ISBN 9780373895885.** 🅰

Twenty-four-year-old Gabby Wolf is torn between starting her dream job in New York City and staying in Arizona and marrying her wonderful boy-friend, Cam. When she makes a wish to have both, she starts living two lives, switching back and forth every day.

Keywords: dating; friendship; humor; wedding; work

Papademetriou, Lisa.

The Wizard, the Witch, and Two Girls from Jersey. **Razorbill, 2006. ISBN 9781595140746.** 🅼 🅹

After arguing over a book needed to complete an English assignment, high school sophomores Veronica Lopez and Heather Simms are zapped into the high-fantasy story *Queen of Twilight*, where the characters assume popular Heather is Princess Arabelle, and it is up to bookish Veronica to find a way back to New Jersey.

Keywords: fantasy; school

Potter, Alexandra.

Me and Mr. Darcy. **Ballantine Books, 2007. ISBN 9780345502544.** 🅰

Feeling that she will never date a man that can compare to Jane Austen's Fitzwilliam Darcy, twenty-nine-year-old New York City bookstore manager Emily Albright spends her Christmas holiday as part of a guided tour in England with other Austen fans, and the real Mr. Darcy appears.

Keywords: romantic comedy

Rigler, Laurie Viera.

[Courtney Stone and Jane Mansfield]. 🅰

The following titles, although not formally a series, deal with the same characters and are listed in chronological order.

Confessions of a Jane Austen Addict. Dutton, 2007. ISBN 9780525950400.

After breaking up with her cheating fiancé, Courtney Stone wakes up to discover that she has been transported to nineteenth-century England in the body of thirty-year-old Miss Jane Mansfield, whose life has some surprising similarities to Courtney's.

Keywords: break-ups; friendship; humor

Rude Awakenings of a Jane Austen Addict. Dutton, 2009. ISBN9780525950769.

Jane Mansfield must quickly adjust to twenty-first-century California when she is transported into Courtney Stone's world, including a demanding job, a cheating ex-fiancé, and an attractive friend.

Keywords: humor; love

Selfors, Suzanne.

Saving Juliet. **Walker, 2008. ISBN 9780802797407.** Ⓢ

Although she comes from a long line of actors, seventeen-year-old Mimi Wallingford would rather go to college than be on stage as Juliet at her family's New York theater opposite teen pop star Troy Summers. When Mimi accidentally breaks a vial holding the ancient ashes of Shakespeare's quill, Mimi and Troy are transported to 1594 Verona and decide to save Juliet from her tragic fate.

Keywords: acting; family; humor

> *I've wished for lots of things in my fourteen years . . . a boyfriend,*
> *world peace, cleavage. But none of my wishes have come true. Until now.*
> —Sarah Mlynowski, *Bras and Broomsticks*

Chapter **5**

Spies and Mystery Solvers

And, for the record, we think fashion and forensics go hand in hand, because we're always dressed to kill.

—Antonio Pagiarulo, *The Celebutantes: In the Club*

Chick lit mysteries are relatively new to the market and yet are already breathing new life into the genre with promises of high fashion meeting high crime. These novels do deliver with intimate first-person narratives, glamorous jobs, and romance. The Pretty Little Liars series by Sara Shepard and the Celebutantes series by Antonio Pagiarulo are two popular teen series books that would easily appeal to fans of the Gossip Girl and A-List series, with their gossip chick lit must-haves of plenty of fashion, beautiful people, and designer names, yet they are unique to the chick lit genre because of the suspense and mystery that run throughout.

Girl detectives have a long history that can be traced back to the 1930s classic Nancy Drew. Like Nancy, spirited sleuths in teen chick lit novels stumble upon mysteries, examine and gather clues, and avoid danger while getting in and out of scrapes. Unlike Nancy, these modern heroines have a more comic voice and breezy manner while pursuing a suspect, and sometimes are even rewarded with romance.

Chapter Organization

Teen chick lit mystery novels are divided into three main categories: mysteries, amateur detectives, and spies. Although the amateur detectives have little or no formal training, they are similar to the teen spies in that they solve a mystery and catch a criminal.

Mysteries

Chick lit thrillers with a touch of romance, secrets, and intrigue. In these suspenseful novels the protagonists do not take on the role of detective; rather, they are often the harassed victim.

Holder, Nancy.

Pretty Little Devils. Razorbill, 2006. ISBN 9781595141491. **S**

Hazel Stone's dreams come true when she is accepted into the most popular clique at school, and she starts dating the new football player, Matty. However, Hazel's dream becomes a nightmare when the clique starts receiving scary death treats and classmates are found dead.

Keywords: cliques; crushes; murder; school

Shepard, Sara.

Pretty Little Liars. **S**

There are juicy secrets to be discovered in the exclusive town of Rosewood, Pennsylvania, where everyone lives in stately homes, attends private schools, and gossips at the country club. Right before summer vacation, the five most popular seventh-grade girls were supposed to have a slumber party, when Alison leaves and disappears forever. Although they were all close to Alison "Ali" DiLaurentis, Spencer Hastings, Aria Montgomery, Emily Fields, and Hanna Martin were a little scared of her because she knew something that each girl wanted to keep hidden. It is now three years later, and although the remaining girls have drifted apart, they never forgot about Alison. It seems that Alison also has not forgotten about them.

Keywords: family; friendship

Pretty Little Liars. HarperTempest, 2006. ISBN 9780060887315.

Spencer, Aria, Emily, and Hanna are high school juniors who never forgot about when their friend Alison disappeared in seventh grade. Now the girls are scared and confused, because they are receiving strange text messages, e-mails, and notes that refer to secrets only Alison knew about. Was Alison back from the grave?

Keywords: murder

Flawless. HarperCollins, 2007. ISBN 9780060887339.

"A" knows that for a few girls at Rosewood Day School, everything is falling apart; Hanna's old habit of binging and purging has returned, Spencer is sneaking around with her older sister's ex, Ali's father is cheating again, and Emily is questioning her sexuality. Could "A" be Toby, the one person who knows the terrible secret that the girls have keep for so many years?

Keywords: affairs; lesbian; school

Perfect. HarperTeen, 2007. ISBN 9780060887360.

No longer only teasing and taunting, "A's" threats become real when Emily and Maya's lesbian relationship, as well as Aria's affair with her English teacher, are exposed and Hanna is hit by a car. Meanwhile, Spencer realizes that she has blocked out details of the night that Alison was murdered.

Keywords: lesbian; murder

Unbelievable. HarperTeen, 2008. ISBN 9780060887391.

As Emily, Hannah, Spencer, and Aria realize the truth about their childhood friend Ali, "A" continues to leave text messages, until Hannah awakes from her coma and remembers who "A" is and someone is arrested for Ali's murder.

Keywords: dating; lesbian; murder

Wicked. HarperTeen, 2009. ISBN 9780061566073.

Now that Ian is going on trial for Alison's murder, Emily, Hannah, Spencer, and Aria try not to be haunted by the recent events; but they start receiving taunting text messages again from "A".

Keywords: dating; murder

Killer. HarperTeen, 2009. ISBN 9780061566110.

While Emily, Hanna, and Aria are seeing new boys and Spencer is upset by being left out of her grandmother's will, more secrets are revealed as the foursome are being stalked and harassed by "A."

Keywords: dating; family

Amateur Detectives

Along with her supportive friends, the amateur sleuth uncovers a mystery, gets in real trouble, and in the end proves herself. Although some of the protagonists see themselves as future detectives, others solve crimes because of circumstances.

Cabot, Meg.

Heather Wells Mystery. A

Former pop star Heather Wells has changed more than her dress size since she toured the malls of America singing her hits as the opening act for her boyfriend's boy band Easy Street. After she told the head of Cartwright records that she will only sing her own songs, Heather's record contract was canceled; her mom took off to Argentina with her manager and all her money; and her fiancé, Jordan Cartwright, started dating the pop star Tania Trace. With nowhere to go, Heather moves into Jordan's private investigator brother's brownstone and becomes the assistant residence hall director at New York College for free tuition. She investigates various murders committed at the Fischer Hall.

Keywords: body image; college; crushes; humor; murder

Size 12 Is Not Fat. Avon Trade, 2006. ISBN 9780060525118.

After quiet freshman Elizabeth Kellogg and Roberta Brace are found dead at the bottom of the elevator shaft in Fischer Hall, twenty-eight-year-old Heather Wells begins an investigation to prove that the girls were not elevator surfing but in fact murdered. At the same time, Heather tries to convince her ex-fiancé, Jordan Cartwright, that they are better off apart.

Keywords: friendship; sexual content

Size 14 Is Not Fat Either. Avon Trade, 2006. ISBN 9780060525125.

As her six-month probation at work is almost over, Heather Wells is getting closer to telling Cooper Cartwright her true feelings when her dad shows up, wanting to rebuild their relationship, and the severed head of the perky cheerleader Lindsay Combs is discovered in a pot in the Fischer Hall cafeteria.

Keywords: family

Big Boned. Avon, 2007. ISBN 9780060525132.

Although Heather is in love with Cooper, she begins dating her vegan remedial math professor, Tad Tocco. Then the interim director of "Death Dorm" (Fischer Hall), Dr. Owen Veatch, is shot in his office, and her friend Sarah's crush, Sebastian Blumenthal, is the prime suspect.

Keywords: dating; sexual content

Fielding, Helen.

Olivia Joules and the Overactive Imagination. **Penguin Books, p2005, c2003. ISBN 9780143035367.** ▧

When Olivia Joules, a British freelance journalist with an overactive imagination, meets the handsome Pierre Feramo at a cosmetics event in Miami, she is convinced that he really is an international terrorist.

Keywords: dating; humor; work

Hale, Stephanie.

[Rand Bachrach and Aspen Brooks]. ⬛

The following titles, although not formally a series, deal with the same characters and are listed in chronological order.

Revenge of the Homecoming Queen. Berkley Jam, 2007. ISBN 9780425216156.

Geeky Rand Bachrach and cheerleader Angel Inves being crowned homecoming king and queen is the just the beginning of a strange week for fashionable Aspen Brooks; it includes two members of the homecoming court and her mother disappearing, surviving a near-fatal fatal allergy attack, breaking up with her football player boyfriend; and falling madly in love with Rand.

Keywords: break-ups; dances; dating; family; friendship; lesbian; school; sexual content

Twisted Sisters. Berkley Jam, 2008. ISBN 9780425219508.

While attending state college with her wonderful boyfriend Rand, Aspen pledges Zeta sorority as a way to investigate the disappearance of Harry's niece, Mitzi.

Keywords: college; dating; sororities

Harris, Lynn.

Death by Chick Lit. **Berkley Books, 2007. ISBN 9780425215241.** ▧

After her first novel was largely ignored, thirty-two-year-old freelance writer Lola Somerville is looking for her next book idea when she discovers her friend's body at a book party. When other chick lit authors are found dead, Lola tries to uncover the killer before she becomes the next victim.

Keywords: friendship; marriage; murder; work

Henderson, Lauren.

[Scarlett Wakefield]. **S**

The following titles, although not formally a series, deal with the same protagonist and are listed in chronological order.

Kiss Me Kill Me. Delacorte Press, 2008. ISBN 9780385734875.

At Saint Tabitha's, one of the most exclusive all girl's schools in London, sixteen-year-old Scarlett Wakefield is a trained gymnast who never hung out with the popular crowd. Then Nadia invites Scarlett to a party in her penthouse. At the party Scarlett's first kiss ends in disaster when her long-term crush, Dan McAndrew, immediately dies from anaphylactic shock. Orphaned Scarlett goes to live with her grandmother at Wakefield Hall Collegiate while trying to uncover the mystery behind Dan's death.

Keywords: crushes; first kiss; friendship; school; sports

Kisses and Lies. Delacorte Press, 2009. ISBN 9780385734899.

During a school break Scarlett stays with Dan's family in their ancestral castle in Scotland to look for clues into his death, befriends his twin, and discovers Dan's murderer.

Keywords: crushes; family; friendship; school; sports

Jaffe, Michele.

[Jasmine Callihan]. **S**

The following titles, although not formally a series, deal with the same protagonist and are listed in chronological order.

Bad Kitty. HarperTeen, 2006. ISBN 9780060781095.

During her summer vacation in Las Vegas, seventeen-year-old aspiring police detective Jasmine Callihan and her three friends Polly, Roxy, and Tom investigate a mystery involving a famous actress/model and her son's disappearance.

Keywords: friendship; humor

Kitty Kitty. HarperTeen, 2008. ISBN 9780060781149.

While in Venice, Italy, with her dad, Jasmine's friend Arabella's body is discovered in a canal. When the police rule the death a suicide, Jasmine is determined to solve the mystery and catch the killer.

Keywords: family; friendship; humor; murder, travel

Kehm, Michelle.

Suzi Clue: The Prom Queen Curse. Dutton Children's Books, 2009. ISBN 9780525479536. **J** **S**

In Seattle, Mountain High School freshman and wanna-be detective Suzi Clue nominates herself for prom queen to find out who is trying to sabotage the prom by pulling pranks on the prom-queen court.

Keywords: humor; prom; school

MacLean, Sarah.

The Season. Orchard Books, 2009. ISBN 9780545048866. **J** **S**

In Regency England, seventeen-year-old Lady Alexandra "Alex" Strafford is reluctantly about to make her debut in London society so she can be married off when she decides to investigate the mystery behind Gavin Sewell's father's suspicious death.

Keywords: friendship; historical fiction; murder

Madison, Bennett.

[Lulu Dark]. **J**

The following titles, although not formally a series, deal with the same protagonist and are listed in chronological order.

Lulu Dark Can See Through Walls. Razorbill, 2005. ISBN 9781595141040.

After her favorite Kate Spade knockoff is stolen with her cell phone inside it, high school junior Lulu Dark becomes a girl detective who, along with her best friends Daisy and Charlie, pursues the thief.

Keywords: friendship

Lulu Dark and the Summer of the Fox. Sleuth Razorbill, 2006. ISBN 978-1595140869.

Although Lulu suspects that her C-list actress mom, Isabelle, is involved with the mysterious Fox, who is terrorizing young Hollywood starlets, Lulu and Daisy launch an investigation after her mom and Lulu's new boyfriend Charlie disappear.

Keywords: family; humor

Mason, Sarah.

[The Colshannons]. **A**

The following titles, although not formally a series, deal with the same characters and are listed in chronological order.

Planning Games. Ballantine, p2004, c2002. ISBN 9780345469557.

Newly promoted crime reporter Holly Colshannon is assigned to work side by side with Detective Sergeant James Sabine and ends up falling in love.

Keywords: romantic comedy; work

Society Girls. Ballantine Books, 2004. ISBN 9780345469571.

> Heartbroken and out of work, Clemmie Colshannon returns home to Cornwall, England, and gets involved in her sister Holly's investigation of the society reporter, Emma McKellan, who disappeared a week before her secret wedding.

Keywords: family; wedding

Pagliarulo, Antonio.

The Celebutantes. J S

Sixteen-year-old triplet heiresses Park, Madison, and Lexington "Lex" Hamilton are New York City celebutantes who attend St. Cecilia's Preparatory School, design a fashion line, and occasionally solve murders.

Keywords: sisters

The Celebutantes: On the Avenue. Delacorte Press, 2007. ISBN 9780385734042.

> The paparazzi are everywhere when at a gala the media empire heiresses Lexington, Madison, and Park Hamilton discover the body of the powerful fashion editor, Zahara Bell. These beautiful celebutantes start an investigation to find the murderer and recover the missing Avenue Diamond.

Keywords: dating; fashion; school

The Celebutantes: In the Club. Delacorte Press, 2008. ISBN 9780385734738.

> Before summer vacation, Madison, Park, and Lex are busy promoting their new fashion line Triple Threat and preparing for the opening night of their father's exclusive night club. However, festivities come to a halt around midnight when Damien Kittle, a popular student at St. Cecilia's Preparatory School, is found dead after apparently being bludgeoned by the diet food heiress Concetta Conoli's pink stiletto.

Keywords: dating; fashion; school

The Celebutantes: To the Penthouse. Delacorte Press, 2008. ISBN 9780385734745.

> Madison, Park, and Lex Hamilton are excited to be invited to join the Royal Crown Society of America, an exclusive private club. During the Ambassadors of the Arts luncheon at the Waldorf-Astoria Hotel, the artist Tallulah Kayson's boyfriend Elijah Traymore is pushed to his death, and the triplets' friend Coco McCaid becomes the prime suspect.

Keywords: death; friendship

Potter, Ellen.

Pish Posh. **Philomel Books, 2006. ISBN 9780399239953.** M

> Clara Frankofile is a very wealthy eleven-year-old girl who enjoys observing the celebrity clientele from the corner of her parents' New York restaurant, Pish Posh, until she joins forces with a twelve-year-old jewel thief to solve a mystery.

Keywords: family; friendship

Shaw, Jennifer.

Killer Cruise. Harper Teen, 2008. ISBN 9780061468742. **S**

Popular Ashley Bishop's week-long sweet-sixteen cruise to the Bahamas with her boyfriend, half-sister, and a few friends is filled with mystery after Ashley breaks up with her boyfriend. When Ashley receives threatening letters and has a few suspicious accidents, she searches for the culprit.

Keywords: crushes; dating; sisters

Sturman, Jennifer.

And Then Everything Unraveled. Point, 2009. ISBN 9780545087223. **S**

After her mother's ship disappears in Antarctica, Delia Truesdale is sent to live with her two aunts in New York City. While trying to fit in at her new school, Delia is determined to prove that her mother is still alive.

Keywords: dating; family; school

Spies

These girls do not inherit magic powers, but rather a destiny to protect society because often their parents were also spies. In these action-packed novels, the spies in training receive formal training in martial arts, computer hacking, and surveillance.

Barnes, Jennifer Lynn.

The Squad. **J** **S**

Known as the God Squad, the Bayport High School varsity cheerleaders are not only beautiful and popular, they are undercover government operatives trained in hand-to-hand combat, each with a unique skill such as weaponry and linguistics. For decades the squad has been taking direction from the mysterious "Big Guys" and secretly training in an underground, soundproof enclosure below the school gymnasium. Transfer student Toby Klein learns the secret about the squad when she is asked to join the team, because in addition to being a third-degree black belt, Toby is an experienced computer hacker.

Keywords: cheerleading; family; friendship; humor; kissing; school

Perfect Cover. Laurel-Leaf, 2008. ISBN 9780385734547.

After a six-stage makeover, sixteen-year-old Toby Klein transforms from a tough girl into the newest member of the Bayport High School variety cheerleading squad. For her first mission Toby has to plant a listening device in cute Jack Peyton's father's office.

Killer Spirit. Laurel-Leaf, 2008. ISBN 9780385734554.

As Toby is getting the hang of cheering and spying, the squad's next assignment is to place surveillance devices on a few terrorist-connected individuals while preparing for homecoming, where half the team is nominated for homecoming queen.

Keywords: dances; dating

Carter, Ally.

Gallagher Girls. ⓜ Ⓙ Ⓢ

Run by a former CIA operative, Gallagher Academy for Exceptional Young Women is a top secret spy school for girls in Roseville, Virginia. Sophomore Cammie "The Chameleon" Morgan and her classmates study covert operations and martial arts and speak fourteen languages.

Keywords: boarding school; family

I'd Tell You I Love You, But Then I'd Have to Kill You. Hyperion, 2006. ISBN 9781423100034.

As the headmistress's daughter and a student at Gallagher Academy for Exceptional Young Women, fifteen-year-old Cammie Morgan is training to be a spy. When Cammie meets Josh, a cute townie, at a fair, she keeps the truth about her school a secret, until she is kidnapped.

Keywords: dating

Cross My Heart and Hope to Spy. Hyperion, 2007. ISBN 9781423100058.

While getting over Josh, Cammie and her friends investigate why the east wing is off limits. They quickly discover that Gallagher Academy has temporarily allowed the students from the Blackthorne Institute for Boys to train with them.

Keywords: dating

Don't Judge a Girl by Her Cover. Hyperion, 2009. ISBN 9781423116387.

At the end of her summer break, Cammie visits her roommate, Macey McHenry, in Boston to witness Macey's father accepting the U.S. vice presidential nomination; the two are almost kidnapped. During the fall of her junior year, Cammie's aunt returns to Gallagher Academy to protect Macey on the campaign trail.

Keywords: friendship

Edwards, Johanna.

Love Undercover. Simon Pulse, 2006. ISBN 9781416924654. Ⓙ Ⓢ

Sixteen-year-old Kaitlyn Nichols becomes a junior spy who has to report to her FBI secret agent dad any suspicious activity involving the cute seventeen-year-old, Blaine Donovan, who has moved into her house as part of the Witness Protection Program.

Keywords: crushes; family; romantic comedy

Gerber, Linda C.

Death by . . . Ⓙ Ⓢ

Aphra Behn Connolly had spent most of her teen years on a tropical island with her father, until she discovered that her mother is a underground CIA operative. Alpha sneaks away from her dad and joins her mother in Seattle, where she learns about the Mole, a dangerous former agent with connections inside the agency. Along with her love, Seth Mulo, Alpha is determined to expose the Mole so her family can live in peace.

Keywords: action; family; murder

Death by Bikini. Sleuth, 2008. ISBN 9780142411179.

Ever since Aphra Behn Connolly's mother left four years ago, she has been working on a remote tropical island that her father owns and manages. Seeing as there are rarely teenagers on the island, sixteen-year-old Alpha is unsure how to act when handsome Seth Mulo arrives with his parents, especially since her father is acting very mysterious. When Aphra discovers an aging rock star's girlfriend dead on the beach, she suspects Seth's dad is a murderer.

Keywords: kissing

Death by Latte. Sleuth/Speak, 2008. ISBN 9780142411186.

In Seattle, Washington, Alpha successfully tracks down her undercover CIA operative mother Nathalie, only to be told it is far too dangerous for her to stay. Before Alpha can get back on a plane, Seth Mulo turns up, needing his ring back to save his father; Nathalie's partner is murdered; and Alpha discovers she cannot trust anyone.

Death by Denim. Sleuth/Speak, 2009. ISBN 9780142411193.

Alpha's mom has been giving her survival training in France, but then their secret identities are exposed, and Alpha sneaks away from her mom to track down a criminal mastermind in Italy, where she meets up with her love, Seth.

Keywords: kissing

Greenland, Shannon.

The Specialists. J S

After being arrested for hacking into the government's main computer system, sixteen-year-old orphan Kelly James agrees to become part of a secret government spy agency that trains teenagers. Kelly's identity is changed to girl genius Gigi, and she moves in with the other teenage prodigies.

The Specialists: Model Spy. Speak, 2007. ISBN 9780142408490.

Convinced by her cute RA David, Kelly James tries to uncover top-secret government information and is caught. When she is arrested, Kelly learns that David is part of a secret spy agency that trains teen agents to go undercover. Kelly, aka Gigi, soon goes on her first mission as an undercover model.

Keywords: crushes; first kiss; modeling

The Specialists: Down to the Wire. Speak, 2007. ISBN 9780142409176.

Computer genius Gigi goes on a mission with Frankie, aka Wirenut, a master at breaking into elaborate security systems to track down a stolen neurotoxin.

Keywords: mystery

The Specialists: The Winning Element. Speak, 2008. ISBN 9780142410523

After two successful missions, Gigi leads her first mission to find Eduardo Villanueva, a notorious chemical smuggler who is responsible for her parents' death.

Keywords: family

The Specialists: Native Tongue. Speak, 2008. ISBN 9780142411605.

On her next mission in South America, Gigi works with Parrot, an expert linguist, where they must try to decode the message on an ancient vase and ensure that it does not fall into the wrong hands.

Keywords: mystery

Isaacs, Susan.

Past Perfect. **Pocket Books, 2008 ISBN 9781416572084. A**

After she receives a phone call from a former coworker who then mysteriously disappears, married mother, successful spy novelist, and television series writer Katie Schottland starts an investigation to find out why she was fired from the CIA fifteen years ago.

Keywords: family; humor; work

Spradlin, Michael P.

Spy Goddess. J S

After getting caught driving a stolen car, fifteen-year-old Rachel Buchanan is sent by the juvenile courts to Blackthorn Academy, a private school in Pennsylvania where the unusual headmaster, Mr. Kim, has directed the students to learn code theory, criminology, and Tae Kwon Do so they can one day become spies who can take down criminal masterminds like Simon Blankenship.

Keywords: adventure

Live and Let Shop. Avon Books, p2006, 2005. ISBN 9780060594091.

When headmaster Kim disappears and *The Book of Seraphim* is stolen from a Washington, D.C., gallery, Rachel Buchanan goes on a mission to rescue them and uncovers Simon Blankenship, a madman and ex-spy, who plans to rule the world.

Keywords: mystery; school

To Hawaii, with Love. HarperCollins, 2005. ISBN 9780060594114.

Rachel and three of her spy school classmates sneak out of Blackthorn Academy and fly to Hawaii to find an ancient artifact before Simon Blankenship can. After being kidnapped, Rachel discovers that she has supernatural powers.

Keywords: friendship; school

If you told me at the beginning of sophomore year that I was going to end up a government operative, I would have thought you were crazy, but if you'd told me I was destined to become a cheerleader, I would have had you committed, no questions asked.

—Jennifer Lynn Barnes, *The Squad: Perfect Cover*

Chapter 6

Lad Lit

I DON'T GET GIRLS. I don't mean like get, which is also true, but I mean I really don't get what's up with them. Why can't they just be normal?
— Rachel Vai, *Do-Over*

Lad lit is a literary genre that features humorous books written by men that focus on young male characters. Like their female counterparts, the teens in these books are often going through dating; love, and family dilemmas. These novels are intended for the male readers who are not interested in fantasy or action novels, but rather are looking for romantic comedies and realistic humor.

The lad lit genre is included in this guide because although the novels have been written for men, many would also appeal to teen chick lit enthusiasts. The British publication *The Snog Log* by Michael Coleman is one such book. With its purple cover decorated with kiss imprints, humorous cast of characters, and silly plot, *The Snog Log* has often been compared to Louise Rennison's teen chick lit classic *Angus, Thongs and Full Frontal Snogging*.

If Meg Cabot is the queen of chick lit, then British author Nick Hornby is the reigning king of lad lit. In *Slam*, his recent young adult novel, sixteen-year-old Sam's first real girlfriend realizes that she is pregnant after they break up, and now the young couple has to work together to prepare for and take care of their infant son. Considering this is probably the biggest fear of sexually active adolescent boys, the book could take on a serious tone, but one cannot help but laugh out loud during the entire read because the character is still very funny despite his tough circumstances.

The lad lit genre will also appeal to female readers who enjoy reading about guys' perspectives on dating and girls. For example, *The Insiders* by J. Minter is about young males, but it is created for female readers who want to know what hot guys are thinking about.

Chapter Organization

This chapter features male-centered comic fiction about broad themes of dating, high school, growing up, and family. Although the narrator is always a male, the novels have a similar humor and breezy style found in traditional teen chick lit novels. These books may need to be booktalked to get boys to read them, because sometimes, despite the content, the covers are too girly for male readers.

Self-Acceptance/Self-Discovery

This section highlights amusing coming-of-age novels written from the male point of view. The boys in the novels struggle with the common adolescent problems of girls, friendship, family, and school.

Acito, Marc.

How I Paid for College: A Novel of Sex, Theft, Friendship & Musical Theater. Broadway Books, 2004. ISBN 9780767918411. **A**

In the 1980s, seventeen-year-old Edward Zanni dreams of being a famous actor. When his father refuses to pay for the prestigious acting program at Julliard, Edward and his friends scheme, embezzle, and blackmail to get the money.

Keywords: acting; college; family; friendship; humor; sexuality

Alexie, Sherman.

🏆 *The Absolutely True Diary of a Part-time Indian.* Little, Brown, 2007. ISBN 9780316013680. **S**

Through his humorous diary entries and comic-style illustrations, fifteen-year-old Arnold "Junior" Spirit tells how he decided to be the first Indian on the Spokane Indian Reservation to attend the local public school.

Keywords: dating; diary; family; humor; Native American; puberty; school; sexual content; sports

Awards: BBYA 2008

Allen, M. E.

Gotta Get Some Bish Bash Bosh. Katherine Tegen Books, 2005. ISBN 9780060732011. **J S**

In England, an unnamed fourteen-year-old boy tries to change his image and boost his self-confidence after being dumped by his girlfriend. A British slang glossary is included.

Keywords: break-ups, humor

Behrens, Andy.

Sex Drive. Speak, p2009, c2006. ISBN 9780142412602. **S**

When seventeen-year-old Ian and his two best friends drive from Illinois to South Carolina so he can lose his virginity to a girl he met on the Internet, he learns a few important lessons along the way. Originally published as *All the Way*.

Keywords: friendship; road trip; sexuality

Cross, Cecil R.

First Semester. Kimani TRU, 2007. ISBN 9780373830824. **S**

James "JD" Dawson leaves the hood determined to become a success at the University of Atlanta, but gets caught up in a partying scene, until he is assigned to work with the pretty tutor Katrina Turner and realizes he needs to get his act together.

Keywords: African American; college; friendship

Fergus, Maureen.

Exploits of a Reluctant (But Extremely Goodlooking) Hero. KCP Fiction, 2007. ISBN 9781554530243. **J** **S**

When an unnamed thirteen-year-old, puberty-obsessed boy is forced to keep a tape-recorded diary and volunteer at a local soup kitchen, he unexpectedly takes a stand against the wealthy.

Keywords: family; humor; puberty

Herrick, Steven.

Kissing Annabel. Simon Pulse, 2009. ISBN 9781416982876. **S**

Although his mom died seven years ago, sixteen-year-old Jack has a hard time letting go, until he gets up the nerve to ask out Annabel. Originally published as *Love, Ghosts & Facial Hair* in 1996 and *A Place Like This* in 1998 by the University of Queensland Press.

Keywords: dating; death; family; first love; friendship; novels in verse; puberty; sexual content

Hornby, Nick.

🎗 *Slam.* Putnam's Sons, 2007. ISBN 9780399250484. **S**

In England, sixteen-year-old Sam is a regular kid who lives for skateboarding, until his first serious girlfriend, Alicia, becomes pregnant and decides to keep the baby.

Keywords: dating; family; humor; pregnancy, sexual content

Awards: BBYA 2008

Jenkins, A. M.

Repossessed. HarperTeen, 2007. ISBN 9780060835682. **S**

Rebellious fallen angel Kiriel leaves hell and enters the body of seventeen-year-old Shaun Simpson moments before he steps in front of a speeding cement truck. Kiriel changes Shaun from a slacker, starts dating, and stands up to a school bully.

Keywords: dating; family; fantasy; humor

Awards: BBYA 2008

Leitch, Will.

Catch. Razorbill, 2005. ISBN 9781595140692. **S**

The summer before leaving his small town of Mattoon, Illinois, for state college, Tim Temples works and parties hard and observes his former baseball player brother and dad while thinking about his place in the world.

Keywords: college; dating; family; sports

Nelson, Blake.

Rock Star, Superstar. Viking, 2004. ISBN 9780670059331. **S**

With his musician father's support, high school sophomore Peter drops jazz band to play bass for the Tiny Masters of Today, a rock band that quickly gains a small following in Portland, Oregon. As the band pursues a record contract, Pete's relationship with his first real girlfriend, Margaret, falls apart.

Keywords: dating; family; music; sexual content

Ruby, Laura.

Play Me. HarperTeen, 2008. ISBN 9780061243271. **S**

High school senior Edward "Eddy" Rochester is an aspiring filmmaker. When MTV passes on his movie and he is dumped, Eddy decides to go on an impromptu road trip to see his struggling actress mom in Miami.

Keywords: dating; family; road trip

Selzer, Adam.

How to Get Suspended and Influence People. Laurel-Leaf, 2008. ISBN 9780440421603. **J S**

Bright eighth grader Leon Noside Harris's classmates rally around him after he is suspended for the avant-garde sex education video he made in advanced studies.

Keywords: humor; puberty; school; sexuality

Sones, Sonya.

🎖 *What My Girlfriend Doesn't Know.* Simon & Schuster Books for Young Readers, 2007. ISBN 9780689876028. **J S**

High school freshman Robin Murphy is distraught that his new girlfriend Sophie becomes a social outcast because of him, and only finds solace in the art class he is attending at Harvard College.

Keywords: college; dating; friendship; kissing; novels in verse
Awards: Quick Picks 2008

Uhlig, Richard Allen.

Boy Minus Girl. Knopf, 2008. ISBN 9780375839689. **J S**

In the 1980s, fourteen-year-old Les Ekhardt thinks it will be another boring Kansas summer, until his cool Uncle Ray comes to visit and teaches him about girls and defending himself against the local bully.

Keywords: crushes; family; humor; puberty; sexuality

Vail, Rachel.

Do-Over. HarperTrophy, p2005, c1992. ISBN 9780060587499. **M** **J**

As eighth grader Whitman "Whit" Levy prepares for his role in the upcoming school play, he kisses Sheila, and his parents announce that they are getting a divorce.

Keywords: acting; crushes; divorce; friendship; humor; kissing

Break-ups and Hook-ups

This section highlights amusing stories about tying to get the girl. Some are dating adventures that are not focused on true love; others feature teenage boys who are more interested in finding that someone special rather than getting a little action.

Barnes, Derrick D.

🎖 *The Making of Dr. Truelove.* Simon Pulse, 2006. ISBN 9781416914396. **S**

After sixteen-year-old Diego Montgomery tries to lose his virginity with his girlfriend Roxy, he is so embarrassed by his performance that they break up and Roxy starts dating a popular basketball player. Heartbroken Diego's best friend Julius convinces him to create an Internet sex advice column under the pseudonym Dr. Truelove, with comedic results.

Keywords: break-ups; dating; family; friendship; humor; romantic comedy, sexual content
Awards: Quick Picks 2007

Behrens, Andy.

Beauty and the Bully. Dutton Books, 2008. ISBN 9780525478980. **J** **S**

Duncan Boone is the lead guitarist in a high school rock band but cannot find a way to get his serious crush, do-gooder Carly Garfield, to notice him, until he hires the school bully to beat him up.

Keywords: dating; humor; music

Burgess, Melvin.

Doing It. Henry Holt, p2004, c2003. ISBN 9780805075656. **A**

During one year of high school, three British teens' drama includes Jon being embarrassed that he is interested in chubby Deborah, Ben's affair with his young drama teacher, and Dino successfully pursuing beautiful Jackie, only to be dumped because he cheated.

Keywords: break-ups; dating; friendship; humor; school; sexual content

Cheshire, Simon.

Kissing Vanessa. **Laurel Leaf, 2006. ISBN 9780440238942.** 🇯 🇸

Despite being shy and awkward around girls, fifteen-year-old Kevin Watts is determined to get the beautiful new girl at school, Vanessa, to reciprocate his affections.

Keywords: crushes; humor; school

Coleman, Michael.

The Snog Log. **Marshall Cavendish, p2009, c2001. ISBN 9780761456094.** 🇯 🇸

In England, fourteen-year-old Robbie Brookes and his friends challenge each other to a kissing contest called a snogathon. At the end of the semester, the boy who kisses the most high-ranking girls in the class will receive $100. There is a glossary in the back of the book.

Keywords: dating; family; friendship; humor; kissing; school; work

Davidson, Dana.

🎗 *Played.* **Jump at the Sun/Hyperion, 2005. ISBN 9780786836901.** 🇸

To secure his place in an exclusive fraternity, Ian Striver, one of the biggest players at Cross High School, has three weeks to seduce Kylie Winship, a plain but sweet junior. After Ian wins the challenge, he confesses that he is really in love with Kylie.

Keywords: African American; dating; friendship; school; sexual content
Awards: Quick Picks 2007

Gayle, Mike.

My Legendary Girlfriend. **Broadway Books, p2003, c2002. ISBN 9780767906555.** 🇦

Will Kelly is a twenty-six-year-old English teacher who has wasted the past three years of his life wishing that his ex-girlfriend, Aggi, would come back to him. Things finally change when he meets Kate.

Keywords: break-ups; dating; friendship; work

Green, John.

🎗 *An Abundance of Katherines.* **Dutton Books, 2006. ISBN 9780525476887.** 🇸

Right after graduating from high school and getting dumped by his girlfriend Katherine, former child prodigy Colin Singleton and his best friend Hassan leave Chicago on a road trip and end up in Tennessee, where they meet Lindsey Lee Wells and get a job working for her mother.

Keywords: break-ups; humor; road trip; work
Awards: BBYA 2007; Printz Honor 2008

Katcher, Brian.

Playing with Matches. **Delacorte Press, 2008. ISBN 9780385735445.** **J** **S**

Seventeen-year-old Leon Sanders befriends and starts dating Melody Hennon, a childhood burn victim with severe facial scars, when his long-time crush, Amy Green, finally shows an interest in him.

Keywords: dating; friendship; humor

Miller, Sarah.

Inside the Mind of Gideon Rayburn. **St. Martin's Press, 2006. ISBN 978-0312333751.** **S**

On his first day at Midvale, a Massachusetts prep school, fifteen-year-old Gideon Rayburn makes a bet with his two cool roommates that he will lose his virginity to cute Molly McGarry by Halloween, even though he is very interested in sexy Pilar Benitez-Jones.

Keywords: boarding school; drinking; friendship; humor; sexual content

Minter, J.

The Insiders. **S**

Back in elementary school, Arno, Mickey, David, Jonathan, and Patch promise not to kiss girls whom another one has a crush on. Once the rule is broken, all bets are off, and the new motto becomes "may the best man win." Now juniors at different private schools in New York City, they are sometimes called the insiders by the Lower East Side crowd. They enjoy their life of privilege, which often means not showing up to class and instead focusing on partying, shopping, and girls. Their parents may be an embarrassment, but they are also the main source for their spending habits. The families are connected in a world where everyone knows everyone else's secrets.

Keywords: friendship

🎗 *The Insiders.* Bloomsbury, 2004. ISBN 9781582348957.

Jonathan's cousin Kelli takes over the New York City scene and breaks a few hearts along the way. Meanwhile Arno, Mickey, David, and Jonathan put aside their girl problems to find the fifth member of their group, Patch, who has been missing for more than a week.

Keywords: dating; family
Awards: Quick Picks 2005

Pass it On. Bloomsbury, 2004. ISBN 9781582349541.

Everyone learns that Jonathan's father stole a lot of money from his business clients. As people start to treat Jonathan differently, even dating a new girlfriend, Ruth, and learning about the indiscretions of his friends' parents cannot squash his embarrassment.

Keywords: dating; family

Take It Off. Bloomsbury, 2005. ISBN 9781582349947.

> After vacationing on his stepmother's yacht, Jonathan and his friends spend winter break on an educational cruise around the Mediterranean with many beautiful girls. While Micky and Arno go after the same girl, Jonathan tries to get in touch with Patch's younger sister, Flan. Back in New York City, David discovers his wild side with Jonathan's new stepbrother, Rob.

> **Keywords:** travel

Break Every Rule. Bloomsbury, 2005. ISBN 9781582346670.

> When *New York Magazine* selects Arno as the Hottest Private School Boy, Jonathan is too jealous to join his friends in planning a wild party, which forces Rob to leave the country. Meanwhile, Mickey organizes a nude photo shoot and discovers that his longtime girlfriend is a lesbian.

> **Keywords:** dating; jealousy; lesbian

Hold on Tight. Bloomsbury, 2006. ISBN 9781582347196.

> Mickey's nude photos are such an instant success in the art community that he is invited to give a lecture at two colleges, and the guys join him as they consider which colleges they want to apply to. On their road trip they learn a few lessons in the love department.

> **Keywords:** road trip

Girls We Love. Bloomsbury, 2006. ISBN 9781582347424.

> The last volume in the series is an <u>Insider Girls</u> novel that focuses on the girlfriends of the insiders. In between fabulous sweet-sixteen parties Flan, Sara-Beth, Philippa, and Liesel are able to reunite with their insider boyfriends in time for summer vacation, while Liv leaves New York without Patch.

> **Keywords:** dating

Van de Ruit, John.

[Spud]. J S

The following titles, although not formally a series, deal with the same protagonist and are listed in chronological order.

Spud. Razorbill, 2007. ISBN 9781595141705.

> In 1990, thirteen-year-old John "Spud" Murphy writes humorous diary entries about his exploits as a scholarship student at an elite boarding school in South Africa, which include pranks, sneaking out at night, dating two girls at the same time, farting, having the lead in the school musical and his crazy family.

> **Keywords:** boarding school; dating; diary; family; friendship; humor

Spud—the Madness Continues. Razorbill, 2008. ISBN 9781595141903.

> Now fourteen, Spud's diary entries about his family, friends, and girlfriends continue. This year, as puberty starts, Spud's voice changes, and he is no longer able to sing soprano in the school choir.

> **Keywords:** boarding school; dating; diary; family; friendship; humor; puberty

Wallace, Rich.

Dishes. Viking, 2008. ISBN 9780670011391. **S**

In Ogunquit, Maine, nineteen-year-old Dan works in a gay bar with his estranged father, plays on their softball team, and starts dating a local waitress.

Keywords: dating; family; gay; sports; work

Romantic Comedy

As in the movies, romantic comedies involve charming "boy meets girl" love stories with an amusing plot that almost always concludes with a happy ending.

Barkley, Brad, and Heather Hepler.

Dream Factory. Dutton Books, 2007. ISBN 9780525478027. **S**

In alternating chapters, recent high school graduate Ella and Luke tell how they met and became friends, and try to answer the question, can two people really live happily ever after while working as costumed characters in Disney World?

Keywords: family; work

Bradley, Alex.

🎗 *24 Girls in 7 Days.* Dutton Books, 2005. ISBN 9780525473695. **J** **S**

Seventeen-year-old Jack Grammar's best friends Natalie and Percy post a personal ad in the online school newspaper for Jack after he was rejected by his crush Pamela two weeks before the senior prom. After receiving over 100 responses, Natalie and Percy select twenty-four girls for Jack to take out, in the hope that he will find the right one to take to the prom.

Keywords: dating; friendship; humor; prom

Awards: Quick Picks 2006

Cheshire, Simon.

The Prince and the Snowgirl. Delacorte Press, p2007, c2006. ISBN 9780385903592. **J** **S**

Fifteen-year-old Tom Miller's job as a Prince George of England impersonator at special events impresses most of the girls at Emerson High, except the brilliant and beautiful Louise. When Tom and Louise are both asked to compete in a National Ski competition in Scotland, Tom's plan to win over Louise fails when the real prince shows up at the hotel.

Keywords: humor; sports; work

Friedman, Robin.

The Girlfriend Project. Walker, 2007. ISBN 9780802796240. **J** **S**

Now that he has contact lenses, girls are finally paying attention to high school senior Reed Walter, and he enlists his best friends Ronnie and Lonnie to teach him how to become an expert dater.

Keywords: dating; friendship

Garfinkle, D. L.

Storky: How I Lost My Nickname and Won the Girl. **Putnam, 2005. ISBN 9780399242847.** J S

Freshman Michael "Storky" Pomerantz chronicles in his journal how he went from being a friendless, scrabble-playing nerd with an unattainable crush with a pregnant mom to being a proud big brother and boyfriend to cute Sydney.

Keywords: crushes; diary; divorce; family; humor; kissing

Korman, Gordon.

[Vince Luca]. J S

The following titles, although not formally a series, deal with the same protagonist and are listed in chronological order.

🏆 *Son of the Mob.* Hyperion, 2002. ISBN 9780786807697.

As the son of a New York mob boss, seventeen-year-old Vince Luca could take advantage of his family's connections but has always wanted nothing to do with the business. Then he gets dragged into helping Jimmy the Rat pay off some debts and discovers an undercover agent, all while secretly dating Kendra Brightly, the daughter of the FBI agent who is assigned to take down his dad.

Keywords: dating; family; friendship; humor; kissing; organized crime

Awards: BBYA 2003, Quick Picks 2003

Hollywood Hustle. Hyperion Paperbacks, p2006, c2004. ISBN 9780786809196.

Eighteen-year-old Vince Luca's hopes of leaving his New York crime family behind when he begins college in Southern California with his girlfriend Kendra are shattered when his older brother Tommy and a few of his mob-connected "uncles" move into the dorm room Vince shares with Trey, the kleptomaniac son of a congressman.

Keywords: college; dating; family; humor; organized crime

Scott, Kieran.

Jingle Boy. **Delacorte Press, 2003. ISBN 9780385901383.** M J

Paul Nicholas loved Christmas so much he was looking forward to portraying Santa at the mall, until his girlfriend, Sarah, dumps him for another Santa, his dad is almost electrocuted hanging up the decorations, and his mom gets fired. Paul and his best friend Holly then decide to join the anti-Christmas underground, which includes stealing decorations.

Keywords: holidays; humor

Shaw, Tucker.

Flavor of the Week. **Hyperion, p2005, c2003. ISBN 9780786856985.** J S

In this adaptation of the Cyrano de Bergerac tale, sixteen-year-old Cyril Bartholomew is a talented chef with dreams of attending the American Institute of Culinary Arts and dating his close friend Rose. When his best friend Nick asks for helping wooing Rose, Cyril cooks for him.

Keywords: dating; food; friendship; humor

Action/Adventure

This section showcases novels about teen boys who get into trouble or are trying to solve a mystery before time runs out.

Ehrenhaft, Daniel.

Drawing a Blank, or, How I Tried to Solve a Mystery, End a Feud, and Land the Girl of My Dreams. **HarperCollins, 2006. ISBN 9780060752538.** ⑤

Carlton Dunne IV prefers to create his comic strip than spend time with his fellow Connecticut boarding school classmates. When his father is kidnapped, Carlton goes to the Scottish countryside to rescue him and meets the beautiful Aileen.

Keywords: boarding schools; family; humor; mystery

Marks, Graham.

Missing in Tokyo. **Bloomsbury, 2006. ISBN 9781582349077.** ⑤

Eighteen-year-old Adam Grey travels from his home in England to Tokyo, Japan, in search of his missing sister Charlie, and falls for sexy Aiko.

Keywords: family; sexual content

Wasserman, Robin.

Hacking Harvard. **Simon Pulse, 2007. ISBN 9781416936336.** ⑤ ⑤

Wadsworth high school valedictorian Alexandra Talese tells how three brilliant hackers, Eric, Max, and Schwartz, accepted a bet to subvert the admissions process and get the slacker Clay Porter into Harvard College.

Keywords: college; friendship; humor; kissing; technology

Westerfeld, Scott.

So Yesterday. **Razorbill, 2004. ISBN 9781595140005.** ⑤

Seventeen-year-old Hunter Braque is paid by marketing companies to search his Manhattan neighborhood for the next trend and participate in focus groups. When his boss, Mandy, mysteriously disappears, Hunter and his new girlfriend, Jen, go on a fast-paced adventure to rescue her.

Keywords: dating; humor; kissing; mystery

"You're thinking I'm a hopelessly romantic idiot. And you know what? You're right."

—Sonya Sones, *What My Girlfriend Doesn't Know*

Chapter 7

Lesbian and Gay Lit

I tried to be straight. Isn't that stupid? Me? It was a fun fantasy. But at the end of the day, it was boys that I wanted to kiss. You still have your options, but I knew something—I don't know what—had already defined me. I just had to figure out the definition and be okay with it.

—Rachel Cohn and David Levithan, *Naomi and Ely's No Kiss List*

Although not traditionally thought of as chick lit, almost all the books in this chapter are feel-good novels that have homosexual and heterosexual main characters who date, go to school, and try to find their place in the world, just as female chick lit heroines do.

Since the 1990s, more and more teen novels in which gay and lesbian characters are the central narrative have been published. Recently new forms of this genre, featuring teens grappling with sexual identity or stories that include teens who just happen to be gay, have been presented in a funny, lighthearted tone.

David Levithan's groundbreaking feel-good novel *Boy Meets Boy* (2003) was the first teen novel about acceptance and celebration of homosexual high school relationships written in this humorous style. Set in a high school where gays are accepted and the popular football quarterback is also a cross-dressing homecoming queen, the story is about dating, and the sexual orientation of the main characters makes no difference.

Since *Boy Meets Boy*, a few other funny novels have hit the scene in which sexuality is not presented as a problem and homosexuality is a given. In a few books, a gay teen and his female best friend both have a crush on the same guy; in others students form a gay–straight alliance in their high school.

Chapter Organization

This chapter organizes humorous novels in which gay and lesbian characters are integral to the plot into two main sections. The first section highlights tales about discovering one's sexual identity, and the second includes stories about friendship and dating, where the characters' sexual orientation is not the main issue.

Coming Out and Self-Acceptance

This section features lighthearted coming out narratives, including its impact on friends and family relationships.

Howe, James.

Totally Joe. **Atheneum Books for Young Readers, 2005. ISBN 9780689839573.** 🄹🅂

As a school assignment, thirteen-year-old Joe Bunch writes in his "alphabiography" about coming out to his supportive family and friends, starting a Gay–Straight Alliance group, and heartbreak when Colin ends their relationship because he is not ready to go public.

Keywords: friendship; gay; school

Johnson, Maureen.

The Bermudez Triangle. **17th Street Production, 2004. ISBN 9781595140333.** 🅂

Nina Bermudez, Avery Dekker, and Melanie "Mel" Forest's close friendship dramatically changes during the summer before their senior year of high school in Saratoga Springs, New York, when Mel accepts that she is a lesbian and begins a romantic relationship with Avery, while Nina falls in love with Steve Carson during a summer leadership program at Stanford University.

Keywords: break-ups; dating; family; friendship; kissing; lesbian; school

Kenry, Chris.

Uncle Max. **Kensington Books, 2002. ISBN 9781575668475.** 🄰

After fourteen-year-old Dillon is suspended, his flamboyant ex-con uncle comes to town and teaches him about bullying, shoplifting, rock climbing, and accepting his own sexuality.

Keywords: family; gay; humor

Kluger, Steve.

My Most Excellent Year: A Novel of Love, Mary Poppins, & Fenway Park. **Dial Books, 2008. ISBN 9780803732278.** 🅂

Through diary entries, instant messages, a school assignment, memos, and e-mails, three eleventh graders write about their freshman year, in which baseball fan T.C. falls for Alejandra, Augie realizes he is gay, and Alejandra discovers her passion for acting.

Keywords: acting; family; friendship; gay; Hispanic American; humor; sports

Larochelle, David.

🏆 *Absolutely, Positively Not . . . .* **Arthur A. Levine books, 2005. ISBN 0439591090.** **J** **S**

At first sixteen-year-old Steve DeNarski denies he is gay by hanging out with the jocks and dating every available girl in his school. When he finally accepts that he is gay, his best friend, Rachel, and his dad are supportive, but he finds real solace when he attends a gay and lesbian support group.

Keywords: dances; dating; family; friendship; gay

Awards: BBYA 2006

Myracle, Lauren.

🏆 *Kissing Kate.* **Dutton Books, 2003. ISBN 9780142408698.** **J** **S**

Sixteen-year-old Lissa is confused and lonely when her best friend Kate snubs her after the two share a passionate kiss at a party, until Lissa befriends Ariel and accepts that she is a lesbian.

Keywords: dating; friendship; lesbian; sexuality

Awards: BBYA 2004

Sloan, Brian.

🏆 *A Really Nice Prom Mess.* **Simon & Schuster, 2005. ISBN 9780689874383.** **S**

For Cameron Hayes, an in-the-closet gay at a conservative all-boy high school in Washington, D.C., the disastrous prom begins when his sexy date, Virginia McKinley, threatens to out Cam to his parents. Cam's misadventures continue when he gets in a fight with his football player boyfriend, Shane Wilson; leaves the prom with a bisexual drug dealer; is involved in a police chase; and has a serious revelation that he needs to be honest with his family and friends.

Keywords: dating; gay; kissing; prom

Awards: Quick Picks 2006

Dating and Friendship

This section features novels from the gay and lesbian perspective about dating and friendship in high school. In many of the stories a straight girl and her homosexual best friend try to determine the sexual orientation of a potential crush.

Cohn, Rachel, and David Levithan.

Naomi and Ely's No Kiss List. **Alfred A. Knopf, 2007. ISBN 9780375844409.** **S**

New York University freshmen and childhood friends Naomi and Ely find their close friendship strained when Ely, who is gay, breaks the "no kiss rule" by kissing Naomi's boyfriend, Bruce the second. After Bruce decides to date Ely, Naomi confronts the truth that Ely will never love her the way she loves him.

Keywords: dating; divorce; friendship; gay; kissing

Hall, John.

Is He or Isn't He. **Avon Books, 2006. ISBN 9780060787479.** ⑤

At the beginning of their senior year, longtime best friends Paige and Anthony are both interested in making the cute new boy at Peppington Prep their boyfriend as soon as they figure out whether he is gay or straight.

Keywords: dating; friendship; gay

Levithan, David.

🎖 *Boy Meets Boy.* **Alfred A. Knopf, 2003. ISBN 9780375832994.** ⑤

In a gay-friendly high school where the quarterback is also a drag queen, sophomore Paul has known since kindergarten that he is gay. Paul is blissfully dating the new senior, Noah, until Paul makes a mistake and kisses his ex-boyfriend. Now Paul has to convince Noah to take him back.

Keywords: break-ups; dating; friendship; gay; school
Awards: BBYA 2004, Quick Picks 2004

Manning, Sarah.

Pretty Things. **Speak, p2006, c2005. ISBN 9780142405390.** ⑤

In Northern London, Brie, Charlie, Walker, and Daisy are teenagers in a love rectangle during a summer theater production of Shakespeare's *Taming of the Shrew.* Brie is in love with her gay best friend, Charlie, who is interested in Walker; meanwhile Walker wants to be with Daisy, a lesbian.

Keywords: acting; friendship; gay; lesbian; sexual content

Medina, Nico.

The Straight Road to Kylie. **Simon Pulse, 2007. ISBN 9781416936008.** ⑤

After gossip quickly spreads in Winter Park, Florida, that out-and-proud, seventeen-year-old Jonathan Parish got drunk and had sex with a female friend, rich Laura Schulberg offers Jonathan a trip to London to see his idol, Kylie Minogue, in concert if he will pretend to be her boyfriend for the rest of the school year.

Keywords: dating; drinking; friendship; gay; humor; sexual content

Papademetriou, Lisa, and Chris Tebbetts.

M or F? **Razorbill, 2005. ISBN 9781595140340.** ⑤

In alternating chapters, best friends and brain twins, Marcus Beauregard and Frannie Falconer, explain how they both formed a massive crush on Jeffrey Osborne when they chatted with him online.

Keywords: dating; family; friendship; gay

Sanchez, Alex.

Getting It. Simon & Schuster, 2006. ISBN 9781416908968. **J** **S**

Inspired by the television program *Queer Eye for the Straight Guy*, fifteen-year-old Texan Carlos Amoroso asks Sal, a gay student, to give him a makeover that will get the attention of his crush, Roxy. Sal agrees to assist Carlos under the condition that Carlos help form a Gay–Straight Alliance.

Keywords: crushes; divorce; friendship; gay; kissing

Shaw, Tucker.

The Hookup Artist. HarperCollins, 2005. ISBN 9780060756208. **S**

Lucas is undeniably the matchmaker of Thomas Jefferson High School in Texas. After another heartbreak, both Lucas and his best friend Cate decide to become boy-free, until they both become interested in the new boy, Derek Griffin.

Keywords: crushes; friendship; gay; kissing

St. James, James.

🎖 *Freak Show.* Dutton, 2007. ISBN 9780525477990. **S**

After seventeen-year-old Billy Bloom, a drag queen, transfers to a conservative high school in Florida, he is verbally and physically attacked, until the football hero, Flip Kelly, becomes his friend and demands that his classmates accept Billy. When Billy and Flip get into an argument after their first kiss, Billy decides to run for homecoming queen.

Keywords: friendship; gay; kissing; school
Awards: BBYA 2009, Quick Picks 2008

LIFE LESSON: Just be who you are, okay?

—James Howe, *Totally Joe*

Appendix

Quick Lists

The quick list appendix is a simple compilation of annotated entries designed first to assist librarians with collection development and then as a guide to promote teen chick lit titles. The lists can be re-created for handouts, pamphlets, and displays as well as presented on the library Web site.

Adult Books for Older Teens

This is a list of chick lit novels written for adults that will easily appeal to high school juniors and seniors as well as college students.

Cabot, Meg.

Queen of Babble. **William Morrow, 2006. ISBN 9780060851989.** **A**

After her graduation party, where she learns that she must complete a thesis before officially graduating with a degree in the history of fashion from the University of Michigan, Lizzie Nichols travels to London to stay with her new boyfriend Andy, only to discover that Andy is a liar and a gambler. Then Lizzie joins her best friend Shari in France to help out at a friend's chateau, where Lizzie falls in love with the chateau owner's son, Jean-Luc.

Davis, Dee.

A Match Made on Madison. **St. Martin's Griffin, 2007. ISBN 9780312357849.** **A**

To prove once and for all who is the best matchmaker in Manhattan, Vanessa Carlson bets her former mentor, friend, and sometime rival, Althea Sevalas, that she will be able to convince the elusive bachelor, Mark Grayson, to become a client and get him down the altar first.

Goldberg, Amanda, and Ruthanna Khalighi Hopper.

Celebutantes. **St. Martin's Press, 2008. ISBN 9780312362294.** **A**

After another bad break-up with an actor, twenty-six-year-old fashion-obsessed Lola Santisi decides give her life some direction by using her connections as the daughter of an Academy Award–winning Hollywood director to convince an A-list celebrity to wear her best friend Julian Tennant's couture gowns to the Oscars.

Karasyov, Carrie.

Wolves in Chic Clothing. **Broadway Books, 2005. ISBN 9780767917803.** **A**

Stylish Julia Pearce's dreams that her salesgirl position at Pelham's Department Store will open a door to jewelry design temporarily comes true when she becomes the assistant to heiress Lell Pelham. Julia is thrust into the glamorous world of socialites, designer clothes, and charity galas, until Lell's playboy husband, Will Banks, decides to make a play for Julia and Lell finds out.

Kerlin, Amanda, and Phil Oh.

Secrets of the Model Dorm. **Atria Books, 2007. ISBN 9780743298261.** **A**

With her dreams of being on the cover of *Vogue*, eighteen-year-old Heather Johnston moves into a one-bedroom apartment with several other young models. Once in New York City, Heather spends her days going on castings and her nights partying in clubs.

Kinsella, Sophie.

Confessions of a Shopaholic. **Dell, p2003, c2001. ISBN 9780440241416.** **A**

Financial writer Becky Bloomwood ignores the letters from her bank and credit card companies and does a lot of shopping in the shops and boutiques of London. Becky tries to earn extra money by working at a clothing boutique, making fancy picture frames, and buying lottery tickets, and has a turn of good luck after she appears on the television program *Morning Coffee*.

Mason, Sarah.

Party Girl. **Ballantine Books, p2006, c2003. ISBN 9780345469564.** **A**

Party planner Isabel Serranti becomes attracted to Simon Monkwell, her childhood tormenter, while planning a charity ball at his family's country estate.

McCarthy, Erin.

Heiress for Hire. **Berkley Sensation, p2007, c2006. ISBN 9780425214848.** **A**

When twenty-six-year-old Amanda Delmar's wealthy father cuts her off financially, she convinces Danny Tucker, a sweet Ohio farmer, to hire her to take care of his eight-year-old daughter, Piper.

McLaughlin, Emma, and Nicola Kraus.

The Nanny Diaries. **St. Martin's Paperbacks, p2005, c2002. ISBN 9780312948047.** **A**

New York University senior Nanny accepts a part-time childcare position for a wealthy Park Avenue family to pay for her small apartment and is expected to complete many tasks outside of her job description, while essentially raising four-year-old Grayer.

Messina, Lynn.

Fashionistas. Red Dress Ink, 2003. ISBN 9780373250257. **A**

Vig Morgan joins her fellow associate editors at *Fashionista* in a plot to get rid of the editor-in-chief, Jane McNeill, in the hope that the magazine will become more than a shrine to celebrities and trends.

Mlynowski, Sarah.

Me vs. Me. Red Dress Ink, 2006. ISBN 9780373895885. **A**

Twenty-four-year-old Gabby Wolf is torn between starting her dream job in New York City and staying in Arizona and marrying her wonderful boyfriend Cam. When she makes a wish to have both, she starts living two lives, switching back and forth every day.

Sittenfeld, Curtis.

Prep. Random House, 2005. ISBN 9780812972351. **A**

Lee Fiora enters Ault boarding school with dreams of being one of the beautiful in the catalog and ends up being a quiet observer with a secret lover.

Sykes, Plum.

Bergdorf Blondes. Hyperion, 2004. ISBN 9781401351960. **A**

The heroine known only as Moi happily traded damp England for the party-girl life with the Park Avenue Princesses. When Moi discovers the special glow of engagement ring happiness, she half-heartedly goes along with her best friend and Bergdorf heiress in a hunt for a prospective husband.

Weiner, Jennifer.

Good in Bed. Washington Square Press, 2002. ISBN 9780743418171. **A**

Twenty-eight-year-old reporter Candace Shapiro is publicly humiliated by the article "Loving a Larger Woman," penned by her ex-boyfriend, Bruce Guberman.

Weisberger, Lauren.

Everyone Worth Knowing. Simon & Schuster, 2005. ISBN 9780743262293. **A**

Bette Robinson has spent the past five years since college working long hours in a boring investment bank and reading romance novels at night. Then she suddenly quits her job and lands a position in one of the hottest PR companies in Manhattan.

African American Chick Lit

This list highlights a few teen chick lit novels in which African Americans are the main characters.

Divine, L.

Drama High Series. **S**

Jayd Jackson is a sixteen-year-old, street-savvy Compton native who is one of the few from the hood to be bused into South Bay High, a privileged white school known as Drama High. As a descendant of spiritual healers, Jayd is having more dreams that are prophesies of future events. Her grandmother, Lynne Mae Williams, the neighborhood mystical healer, teaches Jayd about herbs, potions, and charms.

Hayden.

A Matter of Attitude. Kimani TRU, 2008. ISBN 9780373830893. **S**

Fashionable fifteen-year-old Angela Jenkins is so desperate to become a designer that she agrees to pay Shayla Mercer to make sure that Angela is elected Kressler High's director of the holiday fashion show.

McKayhan, Monica.

Indigo Series. **S**

In Atlanta, Indigo Summer and her best friend Jade are feeling the pressures and joys of high school. Popular Indigo discovers she is in love with her next door neighbor Marcus, is on the school dance squad, and is close to her family, while her best friend Jade struggles to accept her parents' divorce.

Millner, Denene, and Mitzi Miller

Hotlanta Series. **S**

Since their mother married the wealthy car dealer Altimus Duke, African American twin sisters Sydney and Lauren have grown up in the exclusive Atlanta neighborhood of Buckhead.

Mo'Nique.

Beacon Hills High. Amistad, 2008. ISBN 9780061121067. **J** **S**

After getting into Millwood High with her three best friends, thirteen-year-old Eboni Michelle Imes is nervous about starting over in Los Angeles, where big girls don't exactly fit in. However, Eboni quickly makes new friends at her prestigious school and even runs for student council president against one of the most popular girls in her class.

Moore, Stephanie Perry.

Work What You Got. Kensington, 2009. ISBN 9780758225429. **S**

College sophomore Hayden relies on her Christian faith to guide her as she pledges Beta Gamma Pi sorority, participates in dangerous hazing events, and follows her dating creed.

Sarkar, Dona.

How to Salsa in a Sari. **Kimani TRU, 2008. ISBN 9780373830886. J S**

Sixteen-year-old Issa Mazumder, a proud African American and Hindu, is upset when her mother announces her engagement to spoiled Cat Morena's father. It is bad enough that Cat is a Latina princess who recently stole her boyfriend Adam, but she has also made it clear that she has little respect for Issa's heritage.

For Reluctant Readers

This list is a selection of teen chick lit novels from every subgenre that will appeal to reluctant readers because of their cover designs, clear writing style, and engaging plots.

Brian, Kate.

Fake Boyfriend. **Simon & Schuster, 2007. ISBN 9781416913672. J S**

Lane Morris and Vivi Swayne enlist Vivi's younger brother, Marshall, to create a MySpace page for the perfect boy as a way to cheer up their best friend, Isabelle Hunter, who caught her boyfriend cheating right before the prom.

Davidson, Dana.

Played. **Jump at the Sun/Hyperion, 2005. ISBN 9780786836901. S**

To secure his place in an exclusive fraternity, Ian Striver, one of the biggest players at Cross High School, has three weeks to seduce Kylie Winship, a plain but sweet junior. After Ian wins the challenge, he confesses that he is really in love with Kylie.

Day, Susie.

*Serafins67:*Urgently Requires Life*.* **Scholastic Press, 2008. ISBN 9780545073301. S**

In her online blog, fifteen-year-old Sarah writes about her dating mishaps, her father's upcoming wedding, and her nine resolutions to achieve happiness.

De La Cruz, Melissa.

The Au Pairs. **Simon & Schuster, 2004. ISBN 9780689870668. S**

Eliza Thompson, Mara Waters, and Jacqui Velasco are three girls from different backgrounds who come together for shopping, partying, and occasional work as au pairs for a wealthy family in South Hampton and instantly become a paparazzi favorite.

Friedman, Aimee.

Breaking Up. **Scholastic, 2007. ISBN 9781428707412. J S**

High school junior Chloe Sacks temporarily has a falling out with her three best friends when Chloe starts dating Adam, a social outcast at the Georgia O'Keeffe School for the Arts.

Hurley, Tonya.

Ghostgirl. Little, Brown, p2008. ISBN 9780316113571. **J** **S**

On the first day of school, Charlotte Usher's plans to transform from invisible nobody to popular cheerleader do not end when she chokes to death on a gummy bear in the Hawthorne High psychics lab. Despite being dead, Charlotte is determined to attend the Fall Ball with her crush, Damen Dylan.

McClymer, Kelly.

The Salem Witch Tryouts. Simon Pulse, 2007. ISBN 9781415699423X. **J** **S**

Now that Pru and her younger brother, Tobias, can study witchcraft in the open at Agatha's Day School for Witches, Pru has to take remedial magic classes, tries out for the cheerleading team, and flirts with the school bad boy.

Myracle, Lauren.

Ttyl. Amulet Books, 2004. ISBN 9780810948211. **S**

In the beginning of tenth grade, longtime best friends Maddie, Angela, and Zoe instant message after school about Maddie's new friendship with popular Jana, Zoe's relationship with her teacher, and Angela's constant boyfriend drama.

Papademetriou, Lisa.

How to Be a Girly Girl in Just Ten Days. Scholastic, 2007. ISBN 9780439890588. **M**

Tomboy Nicolette "Nick" Spicer has never been interested in shopping and makeup, until she bumps into Ben, the new boy at James Garfield Middle School. When it appears that Ben is more interested in a girly girl on her basketball team, Nick decides to get a makeover for an upcoming party.

Rennison, Louise.

Angus, Thongs, and Full-Frontal Snogging: Confessions of Georgia Nicolson. HarperCollins, 2000. ISBN 9780060288143. **J** **S**

Fourteen-year-old Georgia writes in her diary about kissing lessons, her appearance, her dad relocating to New Zealand, her cat terrorizing the neighbor's pet, her best friend Jas dating, and her crush on the seventeen-year-old musician Robbie.

Shaw, Jennifer.

Killer Cruise. Harper Teen, 2008. ISBN 9780061468742. **S**

Popular Ashley Bishop's weeklong sweet-sixteen cruise to the Bahamas with her boyfriend, half-sister, and a few friends is filled with mystery after Ashley breaks up with her boyfriend. When Ashley receives threatening letters and has a few suspicious accidents, she searches for the culprit.

Sones, Sonya.

What My Mother Doesn't Know. **Simon & Schuster Books for Young Readers, 2001. ISBN 9780689841149. J S**

After her passion for kissing Dylan fizzles out, popular fourteen-year-old Sophie Stein realizes that Robin Murphy, the biggest dork in the ninth grade, is actually a sweet, talented artist. During winter break when all her friends are away, Sophie and Robin quickly fall in love.

Chick Lit for Tweens

The following books are sweet chick lit novels written about girls on the cusp of their teenage years. All the novels are clean enough for middle school readers.

Barnholdt, Lauren.

The Secret Identity of Devon Delaney. **Aladdin Mix, 2007. ISBN 9781416935032. M J**

On her summer vacation at her grandmother's house, seventh grader Devon Delaney told her new friend, Lexi Cortland, that she was super popular and dating Jared Bentley, the hottest boy in school. When Lexi unexpectedly relocates to Devon's school, Devon attempts to keep her lies a secret by hanging out with the popular crowd.

Boggess, Eileen.

Mia the Meek. **Bancroft Press, 2006. ISBN 9781890862466. M J**

At the start of her freshman year at Saint Hilary's Catholic High School, Mia Fullerton is determined to shed her former geeky image by being more outgoing. When Mia wins the election for class president her crush, Jake, asks her out.

Caseley, Judith.

The Kissing Diary. **Farrar, Straus & Giroux, 2007. ISBN 9780374363468. M J**

Twelve-year-old Rosie Goldglitt starts writing in the diary her dad gave her about her feelings about her newly divorced mom dating, her sick grandfather, being bullied by popular Mary Katz, and her desire to be kissed by her crush, Robbie Romano.

Day, Karen.

No Cream Puffs. **Wendy Lamb Books, 2008. ISBN 9780375937750. M J**

In the summer of 1980, twelve-year-old Madison joins her Michigan town's boy's baseball league. As the first girl to play on the league, Madison faces some obstacles while she pitches her team to the championships and develops a crush on a teammate.

Dower, Laura.

The Boy Next Door. **Scholastic, 2006. ISBN 9780439929295.** **M**

In alternating chapters, next door neighbors Taryn and Jeff explain how their friendship changed once they started sixth grade.

Goldschmidt, Judy.

The Secret Blog of Raisin Rodriguez. **Razorbill, 2005. ISBN 9781595140180.** **M** **J**

After moving to Philadelphia, twelve-year-old Raisin Rodriguez keeps a private blog to keep in touch with her two best friends. When Raisin forgets to log out at Franklin Academy, her secrets about trying to fit in are revealed to the entire school.

Kimmel, Elizabeth Cody.

Spin the Bottle. **Dial Books for Young Readers, 2008. ISBN 9780803731912.** **M** **J**

At the beginning of seventh grade, best friends Phoebe and Harper temporarily fight and go their separate ways after Phoebe lands a small part in the school musical, obsesses over her first crush, and tries to impress the older members of the drama club.

Littman, Sarah Darer.

Confessions of a Closet Catholic. **Dutton, 2005. ISBN 9780525473657.** **M** **J**

After her family laughs at her idea to go kosher like their grandmother, eleven-year-old Justine Silver continues to explore her spirituality and decides to become a Catholic like her best friend, Mary Catherine McAllister.

McCoy, Mimi.

The Accidental Cheerleader. **Scholastic, 2006. ISBN 9780439890564.** **M**

Shy Sophie and outgoing Kylie's close friendship is tested when both girls try out for the middle school cheerleading team and Sophie makes the squad, while Kylie has to wear the school mascot costume.

Myracle, Lauren.

Eleven. **Dutton Children's Books, 2004. ISBN 9780525471653.** **M**

After Winnie Perry turns eleven, she slowly drifts away from her longtime best friend Amanda and becomes better friends with Dinah, a girl Winnie previously thought was strange.

The Fashion Disaster That Changed My Life. **Dutton, 2005. ISBN 9780525472223.** **M** **J**

Allsion is thrilled and confused when the most popular girl in seventh grade, Rachael Delaney, invites Allison into her inner circle. Allison tries to stay close to her old friends, Megan and Kathy, while she is hanging out with the popular kids, until she discovers how mean Rachael really can be.

Papademetriou, Lisa.

Accidentally Fabulous. **Scholastic, 2008. ISBN 9780545046671.** **M**

> When seventh grader Amy Flowers earns a full scholarship to the super-exclusive Allington Academy, she looks forward to making new friends, but first she has to be accepted by Fiona, who runs The League.

Rupp, Rebecca.

Sarah Simpson's Rules for Living. **Candlewick Press, 2008. ISBN 9780763632205.** **M**

> One year after her father moved to California and remarried, twelve-year-old Sarah Simpson fills a journal with lists and rules about her crazy life, which includes her parents and their significant others as well as her part in the school play.

Sedita, Francesco.

Miss Popularity. **Scholastic, 2007. ISBN 9780439888141.** **M**

> Popular Cassie Knight has to leave her cute summer dresses and her best friends in Texas when her family relocates to Maine. As the newest sixth grader at Oak Grove Prep School, Cassie is not accepted until she organizes a charity fashion show.

Trueit, Trudi Strain.

Julep O'Toole : Confessions of a Middle Child. **Puffin Books, p2007, c2005. ISBN 9780142407981.** **M**

> Eleven-year-old Julep O'Toole often feels like an invisible girl at home because she has a perfect older sister and a mischief-making little brother, Cooper. Perhaps Julep will no longer be invisible at school, now that the most popular girl asked Julep to her Halloween party.

Urban, Linda.

A Crooked Kind of Perfect. **Harcourt, 2007. ISBN 9780152060077.** **M**

> Ten-year-old Zoe Elias dreams of being a piano-playing prodigy who performs at Carnegie Hall, like her idol, Vladimir Horowitz. Instead, every afternoon Zoe practices on the Perfectone D-60, an electric organ, while her semireclusive dad bakes with her friend, Wheeler Diggs.

Hispanic American Chick Lit

This list highlights teen chick lit novels in which the protagonist is a strong Latina.

Alegria, Malin.

Sofi Mendoza's Guide to Getting Lost in Mexico. **Simon & Schuster Books for Young Readers, 2007. ISBN 9780689878114.** **S**

> During the Memorial Day weekend, seventeen-year-old Sofie Mendoza sneaks across the border with her friends to attend a house party in Tijuana, Mexico. Af-

ter the wild party, Sofie is denied reentry into California because her documents are false, and she is temporarily forced to live with her Aunt Luisa while her immigrant parents try to find a legal way to bring Sofie back.

De La Cruz, Melissa.

Fresh Off the Boat. HarperTrophy, p2006, c2005. ISBN 9780060545420. **J** **S**

After immigrating to San Francisco from the Philippines, Vicenza is trying to fit in at her exclusive all-girls' school, where she is on a scholarship. When Vicenza e-mails her friends back home, she lies about how horrible her new life is. Only when she stops denying her new life do her new peers accept her.

Goldschmidt, Judy.

Raisin Rodriguez Series. **M** **J**

After she moves to Philadelphia, Seventh grader Raisin Rodriguez keeps her best friends current on her daily drama through a private blog.

Martinez Wood, Jamie.

Rogelia's House of Magic. Delacorte Press, 2008. ISBN 9780385734776. **J** **S**

In Southern California, fourteen-year-old Marina Peralta, Fernando Fuego, and Xochitil Garcia grow closer while they learn how to control their psychic powers from Xochitil's grandmother, Rogelia Garcia, who is a traditional Mexican healer.

Medina, Nico.

Fat Hoochie Prom Queen. Simon Pulse, 2008. ISBN 9781416936039. **S**

Madge Diaz, a well-liked high school senior bets popular Bridget Benson that she will become this year's prom queen. As the prom gets closer the campaign schemes get ugly, especially when Bridget suggests that Madge is too fat to wear the crown.

Osa, Nancy.

Cuba 15. Delacorte Press, 2003. ISBN 9780385900867. **M** **J** **S**

Despite growing up in a family that pumps with Cuban pride, Violet Paz agrees to have a *quinceañera* as long as she can change certain parts of the traditional ceremony.

Serros, Michele.

Honey Blonde Chica. Simon Pulse, 2006. ISBN 9781416915911. **S**

Every since her former best friend, Dee Dee, came back from Mexico as a glamour girl, fifteen-year-old Evie Gomez is torn between her old easygoing Flojo crew and the fashionable Sangro clique.

Triana, Gaby.

Cubanita. Harper Collins, 2005. 9780060560225. **S**

> After her high school graduation, Isabel Diaz breaks up with her longtime Cuban boyfriend, starts dating an older boy from the day camp where she works, and learns to appreciate her crazy Cuban American family after her mother is diagnosed with breast cancer.

Valdes-Rodriguez, Alisa.

Haters. Little, Brown 2006. ISBN 9780316013079. **S**

> Sixteen-year-old Pasquala "Paski" Archuleta struggles to fit in at her new school in Orange County, California, while having physic visions about the reigning queen bee, Jessica Nguyen, whom she competes against in the regional mountain bike race.

In the Media (TV and Movie Tie-ins)

The following chick lit books have been the inspiration for hit television series, major motion pictures, and made for TV movies.

Ahern, Cecelia.

PS, I Love You. Hyperion, 2004. ISBN 9781401300906. **A**

> Twenty-nine-year-old Holly Kennedy becomes a young widow when her thirty-year-old husband and soul mate Gerry dies from a brain tumor. After months consumed by grief, Holly discovers that Gerry left ten envelopes, one to be opened each month, with instructions that help Holly heal and learn how to live life again.

Brashares, Ann.

Sisterhood of the Traveling Pants Series. **J** **S**

> Right before their first summer apart in fifteen years, best friends Lena Kaligaris, Tibby Rollins, Bridget Vreeland, and Carmen Lowell discover that Carmine's thrift store jeans magically fit and flatter their different bodies.

Bushnell, Candace.

Lipstick Jungle. Hyperion, 2007. ISBN 9780786893966. **A**

> Chronicles the high-powered careers and love affairs of *Bonfire* magazine's editor-in-chief, Nico O'Neilly, fashion designer Victory Ford, and president of Paradour Pictures Wendy Healy, three of the most successful and glamorous women in New York.

Cabot, Meg.

Princess Diaries Volume I. **HarperCollins, 2000. ISBN 9780060292102.** **J** **S**

Avid diary writer Mia Thermopolis is a geeky vegetarian high school freshman living in New York City with her artist mother when she finds out that her father is really the Prince of Genovia, a small principality near the south of France. As the heir to the throne, Mia has to take princess lessons with her grandmother while still being a typical high school student with friends, having a serious crush, and showing ineptitude in math.

Dean, Zoey.

Privileged. **Warner Books, 2007. ISBN 9780446548434.** **S**

Recent Yale graduate Megan Smith relocates to Palm Springs with plans to pay off her student loans and write an exposé that will launch her writing career by tutoring twin heiresses Rose and Sage Baker. Originally published as *How to Teach Filthy Rich Girls*.

DeVillers, Julia.

How My Private, Personal Journal Became a Bestseller. **Dutton, 2004. ISBN 9780525472834.** **M** **J**

Jamie becomes a best seller and celebrity virtually overnight when her journal is accidentally submitted to her English teacher.

Harrison, Lisi.

The Clique. **Poppy, p2008, c2004. ISBN 9780316040839.** **M** **J**

Claire so desperately wants to be friends with the popular group that she devises a plan to sneak into Massie's bedroom and have instant messaging conversations with other members of the clique. Through these messages the tight group is temporarily broken up, and Claire looks like the new girl to be friends with.

Kinsella, Sophie.

Confessions of a Shopaholic. **Dell, p2003, c2001. ISBN 9780440241416.**

Financial writer Becky Bloomwood ignores the letters from her bank and credit card companies and does a lot of shopping in the shops and boutiques of London. Becky tries to earn extra money by working at a clothing boutique, making fancy picture frames, and buying lottery tickets and has a turn of good luck after she appears on the television program *Morning Coffee*.

McLaughlin, Emma, and Nicola Kraus.

The Nanny Diaries. **St. Martin's Paperbacks, p2005, c2002. ISBN 9780312948047.** **A**

New York University senior Nanny accepts a part-time childcare position for a wealthy Park Avenue family to pay for her small apartment and is expected to complete many tasks outside of her job description, while essentially raising four-year-old Grayer.

Sheldon, Dyan.

Confessions of a Teenage Drama Queen. **Candlewick Press, p2005, c1999. ISBN 9780763628277.** **M** **J**

When Mary Elizabeth Cep moves from New York City to a New Jersey suburb, she changes her name to Lola, dresses dramatically, tells embellished tales, and competes against the most popular girl at Dellwood High for the lead in the school's production of *My Fair Lady*.

Von Ziegesar, Cecily.

Gossip Girl Series. **S**

The characters in Gossip Girl are born into an exclusive world of privilege, where the only rule is to keep all indiscretions a secret. The teens realize early on that as long as they keep up proper appearances in public, their parents are not concerned about drugs, alcohol, and sex. In addition to inheriting great looks and homes all over the country, they have access to the hottest parties and credit cards to buy anything they desire.

Weiner, Jennifer.

In Her Shoes. **Atria Books, 2002. ISBN 9780743418195.** **A**

The rift between thirty-year-old attorney Rose Feller and her younger flighty sister Maggie gets bigger when Maggie moves in with Rose, until their estranged grandmother contacts them.

Weisberger, Lauren.

The Devil Wears Prada. **Broadway Books, p2004, c2003. ISBN 9780767914765.** **A**

Recent college grad Andrea Sachs keeps her dream of writing for *The New Yorker* while she is the assistant to the powerful editor-in-chief of *Runway* magazine, Miranda Priestly.

Serious Chick Lit

The titles in this list prove that chick lit is not only about dating and boys. All these novels raise issues that would be ideal for book discussion groups.

Abdel-Fattah, Randa.

Does My Head Look Big in This? **Orchard Books, p2007, c2005. ISBN 9780439919470.** **J** **S**

At the start of the new semester at her elite prep school, sixteen-year-old Amal Abdel-Hakim decides to wear a hijab, the Muslim head scarf, to show her dedication to the Muslim faith, to the surprise of her supportive family and friends.

Ten Things I Hate about Me. **Orchard Books, p2009, c2006. ISBN 9780545050555.** **J** **S**

Since seventh grade, sixteen-year-old Jamilah Towfeek has been dying her hair blonde, wearing blue contact lenses, and calling her self Jaime to hide her Lebanese Muslim identity, until she is finally honest with an online friend.

Elkeles, Simone.

How to Ruin a Summer Vacation. Flux, 2006. ISBN 9780738709611. **J S**

Sixteen-year-old Amy Nelson unexpectedly bonds with a family she never knew, falls for an older boy, and learns to love her estranged father during her summer vacation in Israel.

Johnson, Maureen.

The Bermudez Triangle. 17th Street Production, 2004. ISBN 9781595140333. **S**

Nina Bermudez, Avery Dekker, and Melanie "Mel" Forest's close friendship dramatically changes during the summer before their senior year of high school in Saratoga Springs, New York, when Mel accepts that she is a lesbian and begins a romantic relationship with Avery, while Nina falls in love with Steve Carson during a summer leadership program at Stanford University.

13 Little Blue Envelopes. HarperCollins, 2005. ISBN 9780060541415. **J S**

Along with a passport and an ATM card, seventeen-year-old Ginny Blackstone receives from her late Aunt Peg thirteen letters with instructions to travel around Europe to visit the best museums, meet artists, and discover her hidden paintings.

Mackler, Carolyn.

The Earth, My Butt and Other Big Round Things. Candlewick, 2005. ISBN 9780763619589. **J S**

As a way to cope with her skinny, attractive Manhattan family, fifteen-year-old Virginia Shreves hides her junk food, follows a fat girl code of conduct, and secretly hooks up with Froggy Welsh the Fourth, until Virginia discovers some dark secrets that change how she feels about her perfect family and herself.

Vegan Virgin Valentine. Candlewick Press, 2006. ISBN 9780763621551. **J S**

Mara has been working nonstop to beat her ex-boyfriend for the position of class valediction, and with all her advanced placement classes, she barely has time to socialize. Unexpectedly Mara falls madly in love with Dan and decides to decline a summer program at Johns Hopkins so she can spend more time with him.

Na, An.

The Fold. Putnam, 2008. ISBN 9780399242762. **J S**

During the summer before her senior year of high school, Joyce Kim's Aunt Gomo offers to pay for eyelid surgery to make Joyce look more American, and perhaps as attractive as her older sister, Helen.

Scott, Elizabeth.

Stealing Heaven. HarperTeen, 2008. ISBN 9780061122804. **J S**

Eighteen-year-old Danielle has grown up moving from town to town with her professional thief mother. Then they move to Heaven, a small New England beachfront town, where Danielle gets her first best friend, her first boyfriend, and a chance to settle down.

Shull, Megan.

Amazing Grace. **Hyperion, 2005. ISBN 9780786856909. J S**

Wanting to get away from the limelight, tennis superstar and spokesmodel Grace "Ace" Kincaid changes her name to Emily O'Brien, moves into a retired FBI agent's Alaska cabin, and tries to live like a normal fifteen-year-old girl.

Sittenfeld, Curtis.

Prep. **Random House, 2005. ISBN 9780812972351. A**

Lee Fiora enters Ault boarding school with dreams of being one of the beautiful in the catalog and ends up being a quiet observer with a secret lover.

Bibliography

Acosta, Marta. "Being Labeled "Women's Fiction" May Not Be Such a Bad Thing." *PublishersWeekly.com*, January 3, 2007. http://www.publishersweekly. com/index.asp?layout=articleid=CA6396633

Alderdice, Kit. "Chick Lit for Teens and Tweens." *Publishers Weekly*, November 15, 2004: 24–27.

Baratz-Logsted, Lauren. *This Is Chick-lit*. Dallas, TX: BenBella Books, 2005.

Bosman, Ellen, and John P. Bradford. *Gay, Lesbian, Bisexual, and Transgendered Literature: a Genre Guide*. Westport, CT: Libraries Unlimited, 2008.

Candy Covered Books: Chick Lit & Women's Fiction Book Reviews, May 18, 2009. http://www.candycoveredbooks.com/

Carpan, A. Carolyn. *Rocked by Romance: a Guide to Teen Romance Fiction*. Westport, CT: Libraries Unlimited, 2004.

Cart, Michael, and Christine A. Jenkins. *The Heart Has Its Reasons: Young Adult Literature with Gay/Lesbian/Queer Content, 1969–2004*. Lanham, MD: Scarecrow Press, 2006.

"ChickLitBooks.com. . . Modern, fun & intelligent fiction for women." *Chick Lit Books*, May 18, 2009. http://chicklitbooks.com/whatis.php

Conant, Eve. "Branding for Beginners." *Newsweek*, March 17, 2008, 6.

Danford, Natalie. "The Chick Lit Question." *Publishers Weekly*, October 20, 2003.

Ferriss, Suzanne, and Mallory Young. *Chick Lit: The New Woman's Fiction*. New York: Routledge, 2006.

Finan, Kristin. " 'Chick Lit' for Teen Readers Comes of Age." *Houston Chronicle*, February 9, 2005.

Goodnow, Cecelia. "Teens Buying Books at Faster Rate in Decades." *Seattle Post-Intelligencer*, March 8, 2007.

Herald, Diana Tixier. *Teen Genreflecting: a Guide to Reading Interests*. Connecticut: Libraries Unlimited, 2003.

"Ivy League Chick: Extracurricular Expose." *New York Observer*, July 17, 2006.

Maughan, Shannon. "Gossip Girl's Got Legs." *PublishersWeekly.com*, May 14, 2007.

McCarroll, Christina. "Guy Novels That Guys Don't Seem to Read: 'Lad Lit' Offers a Lens into the Book Industry and Men's Lives—for Better or for Worse." *The Christian Science Monitor*, August 5, 2004.

Mlynowski, Sarah. *See Jane Write: a Girl's Guide to Writing Chick Lit*. Philadelphia: Quirk Books, 2006.

Pattee, Amy. "Considering Popular Fiction and Library Practices of Recommendation: The Literary Status of 'The Clique' and Its Historical Progenitors." *The Library Quarterly* 78, no. 1 (January 2008): 71–98.

"Picking on Chick Lit: Those Breezy Women's Novels Are Catching Some Heat." *Albany Times Union*, August 10, 2003.

Shamlian, Janet. "New Trend in Teen Fiction: Racy Reads." *MSNBC News*, August 15, 2005.

Stasio, Marilyn. "A Girl's Guide to Killing." *New York Times*, August 21, 2005.

"A Timeline of the Chick Lit Genre. (Spotlight)." *The Buffalo News*, April 6, 2008.

Vnuk, Rebecca. "Hip Lit for Hip Chicks." *Library Journal* (July 15, 2005).

Waters, Jen. *You Know They Want Them: The Current Trend of Teen Chick Lit Novels*. The University of British Columbia, School of Library, Archival and Information Studies, December 6, 2004. Available at www.slais.ubc.ca/PEOPLE/students/resumes/J_Waters/YouKnowYouLoveMe.pdf (accessed February 1, 2005).

Yardley, Cathy. *Will Write for Shoes: How to Write a Chick Lit Novel*. New York: Thomas Dunne Books/St. Martin's Press, 2006.

Author/Title Index

Book titles are italic; series titles are underscored.

Subject Index

About the Author

CHRISTINE MELONI has been a librarian for more than eleven years. Recently she has written about trends in young adult literature in *Library Media Connection*, including one of the first articles about teen chick lit. She currently is the library media specialist at John W. Dodd Middle School in Freeport, New York, and an adjunct professor at the Palmer School of Library and Information Science at Long Island University, where she teaches how to use literature in the school media center.